open heart

Praise for *Seven Thousand Ways to Listen*

"A meditative approach to silencing the world's noise. . . . Readers receive tools necessary to slow down and learn to listen in a deep, meaningful way. . . . Nepo provides thorough methods for reaching deeper into the inner self."

—*Kirkus Reviews*

"Thought-provoking exploration of the art of listening. Nepo's background as a poet shines through in his writing, which can be truly beautiful."

—*Booklist*

"A consummate master of telling stories and parables about people's hopes, dreams, yearnings, fears, sorrows and triumphs. . . . Nepo has written a masterwork on the spiritual practice of listening."

—Frederic and Mary Ann Brussat, *Spirituality & Practice*

"Oprah Winfrey has said that the writing of Mark Nepo takes her breath away. She's not alone: his *Book of Awakening* and *Finding Inner Courage* have been word-of-mouth bestsellers in our bookstores and online. *Seven Thousand Ways to Listen,* his latest effort, displays the deep synergy of his poetry and thought. His attentiveness to the natural lyricism of life is conveyed in language that is both memorable and profound. Both autobiographical and philosophical, this marvelous work teaches us to respond to the physical and spiritual challenges of life."

—Barnes & Noble

"This masterpiece on listening comes at a vital time when divisions in America run rampant around politics, race, and religion."

—Debra Moffitt, *BeliefNet*, author of *Awake in the World*

" 'Listening is the doorway to everything that matters,' claims Mark Nepo. In a world where we try to make ourselves known by making noise, that's a revolutionary claim. Revolutionary but true. Read this beautiful book and learn to listen anew—to those closest to you, to strangers, to nature, to your own heart, and to the great silence. Everything that matters is found on the other side of the noise, and this book, written by a master listener, can help us find our way to it."

—Parker J. Palmer, author of *Healing the Heart of Democracy, Let Your Life Speak,* and *A Hidden Wholeness*

"Mark Nepo is . . . an insightful religious thinker and a decidedly credible voice of contemporary spirituality . . . an eloquent spiritual teacher."

—Herbert Mason, Professor of History and Religious Thought, Boston University, and translator of *Gilgamesh: A Verse Narrative*

"If you live the questions, life will move you into the answers. Mark Nepo offers you a map to explore the sacred in your own being."

—Deepak Chopra, author of *Spiritual Solutions*

"Ninety percent of writing is listening. To receive the world and to receive ourselves. In this book Nepo has generously taught us how to listen. Do the reflective exercises he suggests to lead you deeply down the path."

—Natalie Goldberg, author of *The True Secret of Writing* and *Writing Down the Bones*

"Nepo has mastered a unique way of inviting the reader into a meditative state while reading his sublime wisdom about everyday life. I found his work a comfort—and that's a rare find these days."

—Caroline Myss, author of *Entering the Castle* and *Defy Gravity*

"This profound and lyrical book teaches us the lost art of listening. And as we learn to listen, we open to the myriad voices of life and the silent mysteries of the soul and begin to sense the truth of being alive. Mark Nepo's words are always like choice wine for the soul, to be sipped slowly, allowing their flavor into all the secret places of our being. Beneath and between his words we can hear this greatest wonder we call life. This is the real gift of this wonderful book."

—Llewellyn Vaughan-Lee, Sufi teacher and author of *Prayer of the Heart in Christian and Sufi Mysticism*

"Mark Nepo is a Great Soul. His resonant heart—his frank and astonishing voice—befriend us mightily on this mysterious trail."

—Naomi Shihab Nye, author of *You and Yours* and *19 Varieties of Gazelle: Poems of the Middle East*

SEVEN THOUSAND WAYS TO LISTEN

SEVEN THOUSAND WAYS TO LISTEN

Staying Close to What Is Sacred

MARK NEPO

ATRIA PAPERBACK

New York London Toronto Sydney New Delhi

ATRIA
PAPERBACK

An Imprint of Simon & Schuster, Inc.
1230 Avenue of the Americas
New York, NY 10020

First Atria Paperback edition October 2013

ATRIA PAPERBACK and colophon are trademarks of Simon & Schuster, Inc.

Permission information for excerpts from previously published material is on page 277.

For information about special discounts for bulk purchases, please contact Simon & Schuster Special Sales at 1-866-506-1949 or www.business@simonandschuster.com.

Book design by Ellen R. Sasahara

Manufactured in the United States of America

24   23   22   21

The Library of Congress has catalogued the hardcover edition as follows:

Nepo, Mark.
Seven thousand ways to listen : staying close to what is sacred / Mark Nepo.
p. cm.
Includes bibliographical references.
1. Spiritual life. 2. Spirituality. 3. Listening—Religious aspects. I. Title.
BL624.N454 2012
204—dc23
2012012442

ISBN 978-1-4516-7466-8
ISBN 978-1-4516-7468-2 (pbk)
ISBN 978-1-4516-7469-9 (ebook)

[We] will not perish for want of information;
but only for want of appreciation . . . What we lack is not
a will to believe but a will to wonder. . . . Reverence is one
of [our] answers to the presence of mystery . . .

—ABRAHAM HESCHEL

I didn't know when I began this book on listening that my hearing was already breaking down. It's been disorienting and yet freeing. I only know that my need to listen more deeply has been answered with an undoing that has made me listen with my eyes, my heart, my skin. Now I wonder softly: Does a plant listen by breaking ground? Does sand listen by accepting the waves it can never escape? And how do stubborn souls like us listen?

I feel like a painter who, after mastering certain brushes over the years, has come to the end of brushes; who in an effort to get closer to the light has thrown his brushes into the fire, to ignite more light. I am left finally to paint with my hands. I hope there is something helpful here.

—MN

CONTENTS

The Work of Love

TO MY READER

I WAS HAVING LUNCH with Olasope Oyelaran, a linguist from Nigeria. As we talked, he brought languages alive like tropical plants and spoke of them as rooted things that sprout and reach in all directions for the light. He marveled that there are seven thousand living languages on Earth. And these are only the ones we know of. The music of his African voice flowed beneath his overtones of English. Listening to him affirmed the things that come before us and which, thankfully, outlast us.

That night, as I settled under the covers, with the lights out, I heard our yellow Lab breathe as the wind announced the stars. There, in the silence that's never quite silent, I realized that, if there are at least seven thousand ways to speak, there are at least seven thousand ways to listen. And just how few we know.

The many ways to listen have been reaching into me for years. To *enter* deep listening, I've had to learn how to keep emptying and opening, how to keep beginning. I've had to lean into all I don't understand, accepting that I am changed by what I hear. In all, it's been an exciting journey, one that's made me more alive. I offer what I've learned and am still learning, not as a map or set of instructions but as one way to open our humanity.

To start with, we must honor that listening is a personal pilgrimage that takes time and a willingness to circle back. With each trouble that stalls us and each wonder that lifts us, we are asked to put down our conclusions and feel and think anew. Unpredictable as life itself, the practice of listening is one of the most mysterious, luminous, and challenging art forms on Earth. Each of us is by turns a novice and a master, until the next difficulty or joy undoes us.

In real ways, we are invited each day to slow down and listen. But why listen at all? Because listening stitches the world together. Because listening is the doorway to everything that matters. It enlivens the heart the way breathing enlivens the lungs. We listen to awaken our heart. We do this to stay vital and alive.

This is the work of reverence: to stay vital and alive by listening deeply.

The truth is we spend much of our time on Earth listening and waking. When awake, we come upon the risk to be honest and vulnerable in order to live life fully. If we get this far, we are returned, quite humbly, to the simple fate of being here. Ultimately, a devotion to deep listening remains the simple and sacred work of being here.

To awaken our heart through the reverence of listening strengthens the fabric that knits us all together. Why? Because as cells are nourished and cleansed by the bloodstream, the bloodstream depends on healthy cells. All work together to keep the body alive and whole. In just this way, the world depends on the dance between the individual awakened soul and the river of Spirit that feeds us all. The world needs healthy awakened souls to stay alive and whole.

Yet how do we inhabit these connections and find our way in the world? By listening our way into lifelong friendships with everything larger than us, with our life of experience, and with each other.

Our friendship with everything larger than us opens us to the wisdom of Source. This is *the work of being*. Our friendship with experience opens us to the wisdom of life on Earth. This is *the work of being human*. And our friendship with each other opens us to the wisdom of care. This is *the work of love*. While we may feel lifted or overwhelmed by each of these on any given day, they are intertwined and inseparable— three friends we need to stay connected to if we have any hope of living an awakened life. These three friendships—*the work of being, the work of being human,* and *the work of love*—frame the journey of this book.

In a daily way, listening is being present enough to hear the One in the many and the many in the One. Listening is an animating process by which we feel and understand the moment we are in: repeatedly connecting the inner world with the world around us, letting one inform the other. Listening is an ongoing way of relating to experience.

There are many interchangeable names for listening. The placeholder we call listening is merely the eyehole to the kaleidoscope; the shell we hold to our ear that somehow reveals the music of the ocean. It doesn't matter what you call it but that you find the entry that works for you. What matters is that you keep trying and keep putting your attempts together, that you gather your own understanding.

Though this book is called *Seven Thousand Ways to Listen,* there is obviously no secret number, no secret math involved. This is just a way of pointing to a path that has no end. As you read and gather notions of listening, I invite you to interchange them and grow your own sense of meaning along the way. For example, "Ways of Listening" might also be understood as "Ways of Keeping What Is True Before Us" or "Ways of Receiving" or "Ways of Entering the Unspoken."

I welcome you to this conversation between the stars, the animals, and the trees of language sprouting from the Earth. I invite you to engage in the work of reverence; in the work of staying freshly connected by entering your friendship with this mystery we call life. I invite you to listen in every way you can, for listening in all things is the first step toward friendship.

How to Use This Book

Over the years, I've found the genres of writing to be ancient tools in a timeless toolbox. Be it a story, a history, a metaphor, a conversation, a discussion of ideas, a piece of memoir, or a poem, I'm drawn, more and more, to use whatever the moment calls for. I simply try to stitch and braid whatever serves the mystery and the meaning. So I find myself exploring one encompassing form that includes nonfiction, fiction, scholarship, philosophy, and poetry.

I've also found that my life as a teacher and my life as a writer are twining and merging. For my utmost commitment is that whatever I discover and write be of use. Toward that end, I find myself creating

invitations for you, the reader, to personalize whatever you might find
meaningful. I began doing this with the meditations and invitational
exercises in *The Book of Awakening* and explored it further in *As Far As
the Heart Can See*. Each story in that book is followed by three kinds of
invitations: journal questions, table questions (for prompting meaningful stories and dialogue), and meditations, all intended to bring what
touches you into your day.

In *Seven Thousand Ways to Listen*, you will find reflective pauses
throughout. Each will pose one or more questions or meditations,
offered to initiate various forms of conversation as a way to locate what
has meaning in your own life. The placement and number of these offer-
ings follows the rhythm of what is shared. Sometimes sets appear at the
end of chapters. Sometimes a single question or meditation appears
at the end of smaller sections within a chapter. And sometimes one or
more appear in the middle of a story or discussion as a way to deepen
the conversation that follows.

I encourage you to use and develop the questions you are drawn
to, to change them and share them, as you are moved. Feel free to follow the sequence of chapters and questions or find your own rhythm
with them. You may want to go back and stay with a certain story or
question before moving forward. Find your own way to circle through
what is offered. I think of these reflective pauses as small gifts, like worn
shells washed up from the sea. Each found and polished and set in your
path so you might hold it to your ear and your heart, and *listen*—to
what they have to say of life, to what voices they stir within your own
depths.

THE
WORK OF
BEING

The Universe is a continuous web.
Touch it at any point and the whole web quivers.

—STANLEY KUNITZ

At a gathering in San Francisco, I met Marco, a careful and patient photographer from Santa Clara. When asked what surprised him during the last year, his voice began to quiver. He'd witnessed two breaths that had changed his life. His daughter's first breath. Then his mother's last breath. As his daughter inhaled the world, it seemed to awaken her soul on Earth. As his mother exhaled her years, it seemed to free her soul of the world. These two breaths jarred Marco to live more openly and honestly. He took these two breaths into his own daily breathing and quickly saw their common presence in everyone's breathing. Is it possible that, with each inhalation, we take in the world and awaken our soul? And with each exhalation, do we free ourselves of the world, which inevitably entangles us? Is this how we fill up and empty a hundred times a day, always seeking the gift of the two breaths? Perhaps this is the work of being.

BEYOND OUR AWARENESS

I WAS DRAWN TO write this book about listening without knowing that my hearing was breaking down. This holds a great lesson about a deeper kind of listening. For something deep was calling, drawing me to explore different ways of being. Life was offering me a chance to re-align myself with the world. When I say something deep was calling, I'm referring to that element that lives in our center, which overlaps with the essence of life itself. Like an inner sun, this common center has a spiritual gravity that pulls us to it. This unending pull to center may be our greatest teacher. It shows us a way forward by warming our hearts open, despite our fears.

The question under all of this is: how do we listen to and stay in conversation with all that is beyond our awareness? Many aspects of living continually bring us into this conversation: curiosity, pain, wonder, loss, beauty, truth, confusion, and fresh experience—to name a few. The way we think and feel and sense our way into all we don't know is the art of intuition. It is an art of discovery. *To intuit* means *to look upon, to instruct from within, to understand or learn by instinct*. And *instinct* refers to *a learning we are born with*. So intuition is the very personal way we listen to the Universe in order to discover and rediscover the learnings we are born with. As such, intuition is a deep form of listening that when trusted can return us to the common, irrepressible element at the center of all life and to the Oneness of things that surrounds us, both of which are at the heart of resilience.

I offer my own experience with hearing loss as an example of how we intuit ways of being before becoming fully aware of them. We are constantly drawn into our next phase of life, which is always beyond our current awareness. You might ask, how can we know what we don't know? Yet we don't know what we're about to say when our feelings and thoughts prompt us to speak. In this way, our heart and mind prompt us daily. Quietly, there's an art to reading and trusting the heart and mind. Together, they form an interior compass. Our mind maps out the directions, while our heart is the needle that intuits true north.

Though what is unknown is beyond us, what is ~~familiar is in danger of being taken for granted~~. And we live in between, on the edge of what we know. This is the edge between today and tomorrow, between our foundation and our tenuous growth. How we relate to this edge is crucial, another life skill not addressed in school.

The Center Point of Listening

Like everyone who begins to lose their hearing, I lost the edges first. Voices on the phone sounded a bit underwater. When Susan would speak to me from our living room, I knew she said something but her sweet voice broke up like a bad radio. I quickly grew tired of asking her to repeat herself. Soon I realized that, as I was struggling to keep up outwardly, I was also being asked to spend more time inwardly. This untimely shutdown of outer noise was forcing me to listen to a newfound depth.

Likewise, every disturbance, whether resolved or not, is making space for an inner engagement. As a shovel digs up and displaces earth, in a way that must seem violent to the earth, an interior space is revealed for the digging. In just this way, when experience opens us, it often feels violent and the urge, quite naturally, is to refill that opening, to make it the way it was. But every experience excavates a depth, which reveals its wisdom once opened to air.

I struggled with not hearing and resisted getting tested for months. I'm not sure why. This is a good example of *not listening*. I think I wasn't ready to accept this next phase of aging. Of course, whether I accepted it or not, the change of life had already taken place. This understandable dissonance of not listening affects us all. We add to our suffering when life changes and we still behave as if it hasn't. Whether facing limitations of aging or shifts in relationship or the wilting of a dream, we are often given hints of the changes before they arrive. It's how the angels of time try to care for us, drawing us to the new resources that wait out of view.

We are always given signs and new forms of strength. It's up to us to learn how to use them. Mysteriously, those of us losing our sight are somehow compelled to a deeper seeing, as those of us losing our hearing are somehow compelled to a deeper listening, and those of us losing heart are somehow compelled to a deeper sense of feeling—if we can only keep the rest of us open. That's the challenge as we meet life's changes: not to let the injury or limitation of one thing injure or limit all things. Not to let the opening of a new depth be filled before it reveals its secrets and its gifts.

My hearing had been eroding for years like loose shale falling from a cliff, a little more with each passing season, though I didn't realize it until enough had fallen away. It was the chemo I had over twenty years ago that damaged my ears. Designed to kill fast-growing cells, the chemo attacked the cilia that transmit frequencies in the inner ear. No one thought of this back in 1989, but those of us who have survived can no longer hear birdsong. So the cursed-blessed chemo that helped save my life has taken something else. How do I damn it and thank it at the same time?

It was a sweet day in summer when I finally sat in the tiny audio booth with a black headset while the kind audiologist whispered words like "booth," "father," and "river" in my ear. But my damaged cilia only caught the rougher consonants. A few times I didn't even hear her speak.

In a month I went to pick up my open-ear hearing aid, made for my left ear, beige to blend with my skin. When she tucked it in my ear, as if putting a wet pebble there for safekeeping, it felt incredibly light. I wasn't sure it was in. Back at her desk, she turned it on and asked, "How is that?" And hearing her voice sweetly and fully made me cry. I had no idea how much I wasn't hearing.

Not listening is like this. We don't realize what we give up until we're asked by life to bring things back into accord. Then it's disarming and renewing to cry before strangers who simply ask, "How is that?"

Now I go to a café near our house where the young ones know my name and make my hot chocolate ahead of time if they see me in the parking lot. What's beautiful is that they know everyone's name and everyone's drink. This is the sweetest kind of listening. And you'd think, having lost a good deal of hearing, that noise wouldn't bother me. But in fact it bothers me more. I find it overwhelms me. Even when I turn my hearing aid off. So I ask the kind young ones to turn the music down and they do this now, without my asking, as they make my hot choco-late. This too is instructive.

I realize that my balance point between inner and outer has shifted more toward the inner. That is, the center point from which I can listen in both directions has changed and my habits must catch up. This shift speaks to *a positioning of our listening in the world* that each of us needs to assess and reassess over time. As discouraging as it is that we can drift from this center point at any time, it's uplifting that we can return to that center point as well—through the practice of stilling our minds and being patient enough to listen to what is there.

To honor what those around us need in order to hear is an ordi-nary majesty. The young ones in the café are my teachers in this. Not only do they do this for me, but it's their ethic regarding everyone. It's *the relational environment they create*—a place to gather where everyone can hear. Their simple caring has made me ask, do I honor what those around me need in order to hear? Do I help them find their center point of listening? I ask you the same.

To Instruct from Within

What does it mean to follow our intuition? What kind of listening are we asked to engage in order to sense what is calling and whether we should follow? Even now, as I try to speak of this, I am stalled if I try "to think of what to say next." What is out of view only opens into some-thing knowable if I wait and try "to listen to what is there." If it takes a while, it's because some aspects of truth are shy like owls who don't like to be seen during the day. It seems that intuitive listening requires us to still our minds until the beauty of things older than our minds can find us.

Let me share a poem as a way to enter this more deeply:

THE APPOINTMENT

What if, on the first sunny day,
on your way to work, a colorful bird
sweeps in front of you down a
street you've never heard of.

You might pause and smile,
a sweet beginning to your day.

Or you might step into that street
and realize there are many ways to work.

You might sense the bird knows something you don't and wander after.

You might hesitate when the bird
turns down an alley. For now
there is a tension: Is what the
bird knows worth being late?

You might go another block or two,
thinking you can have it both ways.
But soon you arrive at the edge
of all your plans.

The bird circles back for you
and you must decide which
appointment you were
born to keep.

At every turn in every day we are presented with angels in a thousand guises, each calling us to follow their song. There is no right or wrong way to go, and only your heart can find the appointments you are born to keep. It's hard to take this risk, but meeting each uncertainty with an open heart will lead us to an authentic tomorrow. In the poem, however far you go to follow the bird is beautifully enough. If you simply pause and continue with your day, you will be given something. If you wander after its song a block or two, you will be given something else. If you discover that following this bird leads you to another life, you will be given something else indeed. Each point in the journey is an end in itself. One is not better than the other. Only your heart knows what to follow and where to stop.

Dag Hammarskjöld was the legendary secretary-general of the United Nations praised by President Kennedy as "the greatest statesman of our century." In his book of diary reflections, *Markings,* he wrote:

> *I don't know Who—or what—put the question. I don't know when it was put. I don't even remember answering. But at some moment I did answer Yes to Someone—or Something—and from that hour I was certain that existence is meaningful and that, therefore, my life, in self-surrender, had a goal.*

This gentle man had discovered the appointment he was born to keep. This brief and powerful reflection confirms that he had to listen to something he couldn't see and trust the certainty of his inner knowing to find his way. It's implied that some period of intuitive listening took place before he discovered the strength of saying yes.

No one can teach us how to intuitively listen or trust, but the quiet courage to say yes rather than no is close to each of us. It involves holding our opinions and identity lightly so we can be touched by the future. It means loosening our fist-like hold on how we see the world, so that other views can reach us, expand us, deepen us, and rearrange us. Saying yes is the bravest way to keep leaning into life.

Silencing the Tiger

Because the mind is a hungry tiger that can never be satisfied, that which is timeless swims in and out of our hands, bringing us forward into places we wouldn't go. So listening to what we're not yet aware of involves silencing the tiger and keeping our hands open so we can feel when something timeless moves through us. This can be difficult, for sitting quietly with our hands open in the middle of the day is suspect in our age. We can be misperceived as lazy or incompetent or not quite tethered to reality. But silencing the tiger in our mind and staying open is what keeps us connected to a deeper reality. By this, I mean the depth beneath all circumstance in which we experience a sense of meaning that doesn't change, the way gravity doesn't change though what it impacts changes constantly. Like inhaling and exhaling, the ways we silence our noise and open our heart are forms of deep listening that must be engaged if we are to survive.

What this means to each of us is different. For the furniture maker, it might be listening to the urge to carve curves in the legs of that very special table, though the design doesn't call for it. Curves might be what will heal him, though he doesn't yet know it. For my wife, who struggled with our move to the Midwest, it was listening, in the midst of her unhappiness, to a whisper that coaxed her to try the potter's wheel. Once her hands were guiding wet clay around the spinning center, she discovered her creative gift.

For me, it was listening to a fundamental uneasiness at being misunderstood that led me to pull a book from publication. I've worked with countless editors through the years and the tiger in my mind was roaring, "What are you doing?! Make it work!!" But something timeless had moved through my hands and it left me with an uneasiness that some part of me had drifted from its truth. I couldn't know that listening to that uneasiness and following it would awaken my next phase of authenticity, in which I would shed my lifelong need to explain myself. Finally, I could simply *be* myself.

In truth, my hearing loss has only pointed up the physics of listening we all face. For no matter if you are blunt in hearing like me or can hear a fox step on a fallen branch a hundred yards away, no matter our starting point or the acuity or diligence we bring, there is always something we can't hear. This leaves us with a need to approach the beauty that is beyond us with hospitality, a need to accept that there is more to life than we can know. This acceptance is imperative in order to live in the wonder and appreciation that Abraham Heschel speaks of in the opening epigraph of this book:

> [We] will not perish for want of information; but only for want
> of appreciation . . . What we lack is not a will to believe but
> a will to wonder . . . Reverence is one of [our] answers to the
> presence of mystery . . .

To limit existence to only what we know blinds us to the mystery of how we're all connected. This shrinking of the world has been the cause of violence after violence through the ages, as tribe after tribe and nation after nation has sought to preserve their limited view over all else. This is how important listening is. It is the beginning of peace.

I believe the humble approach to a greater life of listening begins with the acceptance that we hear more together. Accepting this, we are awakened to a committed interest in what each of us knows and wonders about. This committed interest in each other and the life around us is the basis of reverence.

Over time, I've found that the ability to listen for what we're not yet aware of has nothing to do with right or wrong, or good or bad, or neat or sloppy. In fact, judgments seem to make what is calling pull back, the way loud noises cause deer to retreat into the woods. This is why sitting in the midst of our own life with our swollen hands open will deepen our listening. Because a thousand possibilities to live wait for us to stop, so we can meet them in the center point of silence. Once there, we are touched by life directly, without the overlay of the lengthy instructions we've been given since birth.

To Remember How

So how do we lean in and listen to all that is not us, to all that is calling, to the particular angel waiting to guide us more thoroughly into who we are born to be? While we can share insights, only you can discover this for yourself. As you journey through this book, I encourage you to lean into your own sense of the unknown, to intuit and cultivate a personalized practice of listening to where life is nudging you and calling you. I invite you to listen to the part of you that life is trying to wake.

That threshold might be waiting just beyond your smallest curiosity. Your life could change by picking up a stone and rubbing it free of the dirt that covers its blue vein, which somehow reminds you of a dream you've forgotten. It helps to remember how, in a field with no one watching, the smallest wildflower reaches its tiny root into a dark it doesn't know and at the same time opens itself to a light it feels but can't yet see. And while the flower has no choice but to commit to this natural process, we as humans have a choice. Unless rooting and opening, unless listening to what is near but beyond us, we will forgo the soul's birthright to blossom.

In very real ways, we're drawn to what we need to learn. Often, it waits like a quiet blessing that we can easily ignore or just as easily open ourselves to, like that small wildflower. But for the soul to blossom, we must accept our deeper, humbler destiny. For the wildflower doesn't become rich or famous for blossoming. It doesn't live forever or become the greatest flower of all time. The wildflower's reward for trusting what it senses but doesn't yet know is to become what is was born to be—a flower whose inevitable place is realized in a small moment of Oneness, as it joins with elements that were here before it came alive and which will live on once it dies. This is the reward for every seed growing in the dark with no sense of what it will become. As a soul on Earth, this is all we can hope for, to feel the light and being of all time course through our veins while we blossom.

This is the closest we come to living forever. And after almost dying of cancer, after birthing and dying to many selves, after losing many and finding more, after feeling grateful for love wherever it might appear, I can bear witness that this deep listening at our edge is enough. I wish this for you though I can't tell you how to find it. At times, I'm not sure I can find it myself. We can only steer each other to our own inborn gift. For it's the gift waiting inside all our trouble that knows the way.

A Reflective Pause

A MEDITATION

- ○ Close your eyes and inhale slowly, feeling the path you are about to enter.

- ○ Exhale slowly and know that many hidden angels will call to you before you make your way home.

- ○ Inhale slowly and realize that your life will unfold between the appointments you know of and the appointments you will discover along the way.

- ○ Open your eyes and exhale slowly, saying yes as you begin.

JOURNAL QUESTIONS

- ○ Describe a learning you were born with and how you came to discover this. Where does this learning live in you now?

- ○ Describe your center point of listening. Where is the optimal stance for you from which you can hear both: yourself and eternity, and your loved ones and the world? How has this center point changed over the years?

TABLE QUESTIONS

To be asked over dinner or coffee with friends and loved ones. Try listening to everyone's response before discussing:

○ Consider how experience has excavated a depth in you. What has been opened in you? What is that depth asking of you beyond enduring the pain of having been opened? What is waiting there that might help you live?

○ Tell the story of a time when you were slow to listen to a change that was unfolding in your life. In retrospect, describe the signs you were given that change was happening and how not listening impacted you.

○ Begin to tell the story of your history with yes: your first experience of saying yes and where it led you, your first disappointment with saying yes, your greatest reward for saying yes, and your understanding now of what it means to say yes to life.

KEEPING WHAT IS TRUE
BEFORE US

Faith is not an insurance, but a constant effort, a constant listening to the eternal voice.

—ABRAHAM HESCHEL

EVEN THOUGH IT'S been twenty years since I was spit out from the mouth of the whale of cancer, it's never very far. Recently, I needed to have blood drawn for my annual physical and kept telling myself that was then, this is now. But in the early morning waiting room, I could feel my breath speed up, higher in my chest, and below any conscious remembering, the many waiting room walls began to appear, dark friends who say they miss me.

Once in the little lab room, a young woman wrote my name on a small vial, asked me to make a fist, and as she poked the needle in my vein, I looked away; swallowing my whole journey, which wants to rise through these little needle pricks any chance it can get.

It was over, for another year. I didn't realize it but I had been holding my breath, way inside. As I opened the door back into the world, I exhaled from underneath my heart and suddenly began to cry; not heavily but the way our gutters overflow in spring when the ice thaws all at once.

I was surprised. After twenty years, I thought the alarm of all that suffering and almost dying would be knit more quietly in my skin. How come it keeps bursting forth when I least expect it? I've been told it's a form of post-traumatic stress; a problem that can be addressed. As I drove to work, I made a vow to tend to this in the coming year.

The next day I was up early, before dawn, eager for my morning swim. On the way, I stopped at a light. There was no traffic. It began to snow very softly and the voice of the singer in the radio seemed, for an instant, to be falling like the snow on the windshield. It made me start to cry again in that overflowing way.

It's been a week since the little pinprick in my arm and I keep crying at simple things—the late cloud parting for the moon, the footprint of a small deer, even the fast-food wrapper on the sidewalk. With each small cry, it feels less a release and more like an irrepressible, unfiltered tenderness at being fully here. The more of these moments I experience, the less a problem it seems. For isn't this what I've been after: to be this close to life, to be pricked below the surface of things? Now it seems the damn needle is a gift! Now I wonder: isn't anything that keeps us this close to life a gift? Now I want to learn the art of puncturing whatever grows in the way in order to *feel* that moment where everything touches everything else. I'm coming to see that keeping what is true before us reminds us that there was never a better time than now.

This tripping on what pricks us is an age-old process through which we often stumble into moments of being fully alive. Though we often resist being opened this way, there are small pressure points of residual feelings that live in our bodies, small pockets of trauma that hold the sediment of the stories that have shaped us. We carry these residual feelings like emotional time capsules whose small doses of healing are released when we bump into life unexpectedly. It's natural to recoil from the rupture of these potent feelings but it's the meaning carried in them over the years that begins to heal us. Understandably, we avoid the sharpness of direct experience. But listening to the depth of feeling that surprises us and to the tears that want to surface is a significant way to tumble into the moment where everything touches everything else. Often, the only way to welcome this is to summon the courage to relax our heart back open after we in surprise and fear constrict.

Indigenous peoples have always had a fundamental understanding of direct experience. Consider the Polynesians, who believe that everything physical—stone, wood, a flower—has a numinous quality; that each thing on Earth emanates an inherent spirit that glows from within it. This is another way to describe the moment where everything touches everything else. We've come to call that inherent glow life-force or essence. When fully here, we touch what is before us—life-force to life-force, essence to essence. When asleep or numb or moving too fast, we only touch surface to surface. And without that glow of life-force, that glow of essence, things just get in the way. It seems that the *feel* of truth and meaning waits below the surface, and it's the heart of listening that allows the life-force in all things to touch us. It's our ability to listen that saves us from the sheer fact of things.

What often starts as a moment of unexpected feeling that startles us becomes, if leaned into, a deeper way of knowing. So how do we listen in a way that allows us to be touched by life? It helps to stay devoted to moving below the literal fact of things. For waiting under the surface, like an inner sun, the life-force or heartbeat of the Universe will reveal itself and connect us to the sheer power of what is vital in life— all through the heart and overflow of earnest listening, through a *being-with* that keeps us alive.

The Tuning of the Inner Person

U Thant (1909–1974) was a gentle seer. Born in Pantanaw, Burma, he became a diplomat and the third secretary-general of the United Nations (1961–1971). The first Asian to serve in this capacity, he was chosen when Secretary-General Dag Hammarskjöld was killed in a plane crash in September 1961. U Thant defined Spirituality as "the tuning of the inner person with the great mysteries and secrets that are around us." That tuning is a timeless art. No one can really teach it. And yet this is a helpful way to describe the work of being, which necessitates deep engagement and constant listening. The great Jewish philosopher Abraham Heschel suggests that the reward for such inner tuning is a sense of peace, and that by finding and inhabiting our place in the ever-changing Universe, we strengthen the fabric of life itself:

> *By being what we are . . . by attuning our own yearning to the*
> *lonely holiness in this world, we will aid humanity more than*
> *by any particular service we may render.*

Heschel implies that the world is not complete until fitted with our yearning; that just as the Earth would be barren without trees, plants, vegetables, and flowers, the holiness of the world, waiting just below the surface, will stay barren without the spirited growth of our dreams, creativity, generosity, and love. It seems that the first destiny of being here is to root our being in the world, that the world needs this as much as we need each other.

To Honor

How do we begin then to inhabit our destiny of being here? I believe it starts with reverence and listening, with honoring every bit of life we encounter. So at the deepest level, when I say *I honor you,* this means that, when I become conscious or aware of you, I make a commitment to keep that truth visible from that moment forward. To honor you means that what I've learned about you becomes part of our geography. It means that what has become visible and true *will not* become invisible again.

To honor myself, then, means that, as I grow, I *will not* ignore or hide the parts of my soul and humanness that become more present in me and the world. To honor myself means that I make a commitment to keep the truth of who I am visible; that I *will not* let the truth of my being become invisible again. Or if it does, I will stay devoted to retrieving it.

To honor God means that we vow to keep all that we become aware of in view; that we *will not* pretend to be ignorant of things we know to be true or holy. And if we forget or get distracted or derailed, we will stay devoted to retrieving the ever-present sense of the sacred.

So at the deepest level, the most essential level, listening entails a constant effort to *feel* that moment where everything touches everything else; a constant effort to live below the sheer fact of things. This fundamental listening invokes a commitment to keep what is true before us, so we might be touched by the life-force in all things. Such listening opens us to the never-ending art of tuning our inner person to the mysteries that surround us. We do this through the work of honoring what we experience, through the work of keeping what is true visible. All this is the work of reverence.

We will encounter many great listeners along the way, many great workers of reverence. To welcome you on this journey, I offer one great listener, known more for his understanding of gravity than for the deep quality of his ability to honor life: the legendary physicist Sir Isaac Newton. Near the end of his life, Newton declared with joy and humility:

> *I do not know what I may appear to the world; but to myself*
> *I seem to have been only like a boy playing on the sea-shore,*
> *and diverting myself in now and then finding a smoother pebble*
> *or a prettier shell than ordinary, while the great ocean of truth*
> *lay all undiscovered before me.*

Let us continue our walk along the sea.

A Reflective Pause

A MEDITATION

- Close your eyes, breathe slowly, and imagine the lineage of great listeners throughout time.

- Inhale deeply and feel their living presence.

- Exhale deeply and feel how such listening connects us all.

- Open your eyes and inhale slowly, honoring what you know to be true about your life.

○ Exhale slowly, honoring what you know to be true about those you love.

○ Enter your day committed to keeping all you are aware of in view.

JOURNAL QUESTIONS

○ Tell the story of a moment that surprised you with an unexpected flood of feeling and how this affected you.

○ Tell the story of one thing you know to be true and your history of keeping that truth in your awareness.

○ What does living below "the sheer fact of things" mean to you?

TABLE QUESTIONS

To be asked over dinner or coffee with friends and loved ones. Try listening to everyone's response before discussing:

○ U Thant's description of Spirituality as "the tuning of the inner person with the great mysteries and secrets that are around us" gives us an image of the individual in relationship to the whole of life.

○ Describe your own image for this relationship. Are we each a rung on an infinite ladder? A star in a constellation? A bird in a tree? A root growing in the Earth?

○ Share and inquire into each other's images of the person and the whole. Do not argue or compare them, just listen to them all.

○ Describe one aspect of your inner tuning that seems to be working well and one inner aspect that needs more of your attention.

THE GIFT IN RECEIVING

*Can you hold the door of your tent
wide to the firmament?*

—Lao Tzu

W E USUALLY THINK of giving as more important than receiving. Yet only by receiving light can flowers grow into their beauty and pollinate the earth. Only by absorbing rain can the earth grow what feeds us. Only by inhaling air can our bodies walk us to each other. Only by accepting each other's pain and vulnerability can human strength grow between us. In these ways, receiving involves absorbing, inhaling, and accepting the life that flows through us, between us, and around us. These are all deeper forms of listening.

On the surface of things, giving and receiving are about exchanges. I need. You give. I feel grateful. You feel good about yourself. I feel indebted. I give back. We take turns. But below the surface of things, giving and receiving become indistinguishable, and the aim is not to have or move things from one person to another, but to keep the gift of life flowing. The pulse of being alive moves like blood circulating in the body, and giving and receiving, like arteries and veins, are both necessary. For no one organ owns the blood. Rather, we are of one body. The gift of life, like blood, must keep flowing, if we are to stay alive.

The difference then between receiving and taking—between taking things *in* and taking things *from*—is crucial. To be sure, there's nothing wrong with taking something given by another. But when taking tight-

ens into hoarding, we stop listening, and the imbalance poisons us and
those nearby. We're always capable of both receiving and taking, and
so must guard against being one who just takes and acquires in favor of
developing our capacity to *take in* and transmit the life-force given; to be
a conduit rather than a repository.

The gift in receiving is that, through such openness, we apprehend
the world. Deep listening is a form of gifted receiving. When Lao Tzu
asks in the quote above, "Can you hold the door of your tent wide to the
firmament?" he is challenging us *not* to define the world by whatever shel-
ter we create but to let in the stars, to throw our tent of mind and heart
wide open in order to receive and listen to the flow of life. Of course, this
is not as easy as it sounds, but is as essential as light, rain, and air.

The Hawk, the Kiss, and the Glass of Milk

I was talking at a community college in the Midwest when the conversation turned to the sacred moment when giving and receiving are hard
to tell apart. A young, pensive man in the back asked if I could recall the
first time I experienced such a moment. I was amazed at how quickly
images and feelings came over me.

The earliest moment was as a boy, maybe nine or ten. I was by
myself ambling with a stick in the one patch of woods in our neighbor-
hood. It was the only place where none of the houses could be seen.
As I stepped on a fallen branch, a hawk swept before me, wings spread.
I gasped, and in that moment the sweep of the hawk's wings and my
sudden inhalation and the gust of wind carrying the hawk were all one.
I didn't even know what a hawk was. But that night, as I lay in bed, I
closed my eyes and each time I took a deep breath, I could feel the wind
sweep in my mouth. With each breath, I could see the hawk open its
wings above me. I hadn't thought about it till this young man asked,
but I've always had a kinship with hawks and wind. In the depths of
meditating, I have felt that inhaling steadily is taking in the wind of all
breath, and that breathing slowly is how the heart like a hawk glides
over all we feel.

Driving away from my talk at the college, I recalled my first kiss, while walking Chris home from Howard Johnson after our night shift. We were both sixteen and covered with dried ice cream. I remember the night air was cold. When our lips touched, slowly, tentatively, unsure what to expect, there was the soft moment of not knowing who was who; the brief instant when neither of us could hold on to who was kissing and who was being kissed.

But my first discussion of receiving as giving came during my junior year in college. My mother's mother lived alone in a hotel in Miami. We always called her Grandma Juicy because she loved orange juice. Grandma wanted me to visit her and kindly invited my closest friends. We had no money, but Grandma didn't hesitate to say, "No bother. Come. It'll all be arranged." I could tell that our visit meant a great deal to her. I knew it would mean a great deal to me. She was seventy-seven. I was twenty.

When I told my parents, they chided me not to freeload, not to take advantage of her. I thought about their position but felt in my heart that this was a once-in-a-lifetime chance to know Grandma. Though I had nothing material to offer, I felt committed to offer what little I had—my presence and my love. My parents and I grew heated about it all. It was a significant parting of values.

So during spring break, my friends Alan, Michael, Jack, and I piled into an old Fairlane with a corroded front left fender and bumped and coughed our way to Florida. We had no idea how long a state Florida is. In Jacksonville, we called Grandma to say we were right around the corner! Eight hours later, near three in the morning, we pulled into Miami and parked in front of her small residential hotel. The light was on. The doorman was waiting and knew us by name. She appeared in the lobby like a bent-over version of the Statue of Liberty. She'd rented a small apartment for us, down the hall from her. As we dropped our bags, there on the table was a plate of cookies and four glasses of milk.

During the week, we had our fun on the beach, but also entered Grandma's world. We went shopping with her, two of us on each arm, and she greeted her cronies like a matriarch whose sons had returned from a strange and silent war.

Our last day there, near sunset, she and I walked alone along the ocean and she went on and on about her life, her loves and disappointments. It was a privilege to hear her aging voice on one side and the ocean on the other. I'll never forget that walk. It seemed as if we were suspended for the moment on this sunlit strip of sand; out of time, free of pain and worry. She had the most peaceful look on her face and I knew then that I had come all that way to have this walk. Grandma not only taught me about generosity and the proper order in which things support people, but, for the first time, I was able to give when I had nothing—by receiving.

The Heart of God

What I learned on that walk along the ocean with Grandma, though it has taken almost forty years to articulate, is that there is a sliver of the beginning in each of us, and being infinite, it is totally forgiving of the blunders that bury it along the way. This sliver of the beginning simply shines in the center of our darkness, incubating its strength, waiting as it did before our birth. It can wait years for us to hear it, to receive it, to embrace it. It is as patient as time itself. I've felt it in those moments when giving and receiving become one. I heard the sliver of the beginning when I was surprised by the hawk. I received it when I first kissed Chris. And I embraced it when Grandma and I opened to each other before the sea. Much of my life has been trying to learn from such moments how we receive the truth of everything larger than we are. I'm humbled to admit that I haven't come up with much.

Two basic forms of awakening and receiving are always near. The mystery of revelation is the awakening through which our habits and frames are expanded by moments of wonder, awe, beauty, and love. And the weathering of erosion is the receiving through which we are broken open to deeper truths. Revelation always has the feel of epiphany; that is, it seems to happen all at once. It is the lifting of veils. One moment we are blind, the next we see. One moment we are numb, the next incredibly sensitive. But suffering and humility, like erosion, take time. We are worn to who we are meant to be. It is all any of us can hope for: to be revealed in an instant to life and each other and to survive the wearing away in order to behold what is soft and central and lasting.

It was on another shore, later in life, that I sat on a worn cliff on the south side of St. Martin in the Caribbean. I spent that afternoon in silence, just watching the vast ocean spray the stone and re-form itself, coating every surface, as if to soothe the stone's hardness. I came away convinced that the sea is a great teacher of receiving. Always rising and falling like the clear blood of the earth, the formless water receives everything that enters it. It rejects nothing. Always transparent, the open water gently covers everything; softening whatever it touches, giving itself completing without losing any of itself. The more I watched, the more I realized that the sea is both strong and gentle, sensitive and unwavering, it only takes the shape of what holds it or enters it. Whatever breaks its surface ripples through its entire being. So much like the heart of God. So much like the heart of experience, God's smaller face in the world. I came away with spray on my face wanting to be like the sea, to love like the sea: to receive and give myself to everything I meet, softening its way while making it glisten.

A Reflective Pause

A MEDITATION

- ○ Center yourself, and, as you breathe, feel your being rise and recede like an ocean within you.

- ○ As you inhale, welcome whatever is near. Receive it in the water of your being, knowing you can't lose who you are for taking it in.

- ○ As you exhale, let the water of your being touch whatever is near. Without any intent to influence or change what is before you, let your being soften the world.

- ○ Enter your day, ready to take in the world and, in exchange, let your being make the world shine.

JOURNAL QUESTIONS

o In the privacy of your own truth, describe a time you took
  something and how that came about. Describe as well a time you
  took something in and how that came about. Where are these
  things now? Which stayed with you longer?

o How would you describe the act of receiving to a child?

TABLE QUESTIONS

*To be asked over dinner or coffee with friends and loved ones. Try listening
to everyone's response before discussing:*

o Tell the story of a moment when giving and receiving seemed
  indistinguishable and what this moment has taught you.

o Who taught you how to receive? How have you received their
  teaching?

A REALITY THAT KEEPS UNFOLDING

The one moon reflects itself wherever there is a sheet of water,
and all the moons in the waters are embraced within the one moon . . .
One Reality, all comprehensive, contains within itself all realities . . .

—YOKA DAISHI

THE POET WALLACE Stevens was a constant deep listener. In 1923, Stevens wrote his legendary poem "Thirteen Ways of Looking at a Blackbird," in which he offers thirteen penetrating snapshots of the blackbird's place between what is visible and what remains invisible. The poem is instructive in two ways: it teaches us how to see and how to try. First, Stevens suggests that there is no one way to look at a blackbird. The blackbird exists in the mysterious sum of all these views. And each blackbird mirrors a part of the larger world, whose entirety can't be seen in any one view. Instead, we gather understanding toward a reality that keeps unfolding. Stevens also demonstrates that we have to keep trying and keep putting our efforts together. One pass at understanding will often be insufficient. This way of *gathering understanding* applies to everything, including the many ways to listen and love.

Here is a handful of ways to begin.

music

A Reflective Pause

JOURNAL QUESTIONS

○ Describe your own sense of what it means to listen.

○ Try to recall your first significant experience of listening. Who or what were you listening to? What did you hear and how did it impact you?

The One Breath

In the 1100s, the mystic Hildegard of Bingen defined prayer as "breathing in and breathing out the one breath of the Universe." This is listening with our entire being. It speaks to an immersion of attention that all the traditions aspire to; each claiming in its own way that peace resides in this completeness which arises when our individual sense of being merges with the ongoing stream of being that is the heartbeat of the Universe. Whether these moments arise from great stillness or great suffering or great love, they all seem unexpected and seem to depend on our ability to hold nothing back.

All the traditions suggest that breathing the one breath is our deepest home. We each have at least two moments of such completeness: during our first breath at birth and in our last breath at death. How often we stumble into this completeness of being during our time on Earth depends on our journey and our willingness to enter it.

In an effort to enter my own journey, I spent two weeks meditating daily on Hildegard's one breath. And somewhere in the second week, I had a dream in which the breath at birth met the breath at death.

In the dream, I was sitting in an open field without speaking for days. Finally, I began to wander. I came upon a huge tree to find Buddha beneath it. I could tell that many had come upon him in this way. He was just waking from a very long sleep and I happened upon him the instant he awakened. A light filled his face as he sighed. As I moved closer, he changed into a dying boy. This was alarming. As I put my hand on the tree, it turned into a fence of wire in Auschwitz. And the small boy, just as lighted as Buddha, was sighing his last breath which clouded in the cold.

In the days that followed, I kept breathing the one breath of the Universe, quietly thinking of Buddha waking and the little boy dying. I feel certain they both live in me, in you. We are both waking and dying in every moment, an inner form of day and night. Now I listen for Buddha waking and the little boy dying in the faces of strangers and friends tired enough to slow their breathing to the one breath that lifts us all.

Making Eyebrows in the Water

In central Alaska, there is a river that begins on the northwest slopes of the Alaska Range, and flows over 650 miles to the Bering Sea. The shores of the river are mostly thick with trees and uninhabited. These chilling waters are known as the Kuskokwim River.

John Larson, a *Dateline NBC* correspondent, was in Alaska covering a news story when he learned of an Inuit custom in which elders take their sons once a year to the mouth of the Kuskokwim River. Here the largest salmon return from the Bering Sea. The elders teach their sons that, if you watch closely enough, you'll see the biggest fish barely break surface, leaving an almost imperceptible wake. When the big fish break surface in this way, the Inuit say they are *making eyebrows in the water*. The slight break of surface is known as *the wake of an unseen teacher.*

When father and son alike see this wake, the harvest begins. This is a powerful metaphor for how we fish for what matters in our lives. We are always looking for the teachers that swim just below the surface, like the face of God skimming below the surface of our days.

The Inuit believe that, wherever the large salmon break surface, they leave traces of everything they've carried from the mountains to the sea and back. If a son can swim to the spot and drink, he will have the strength of salmon wisdom growing in his belly.

This Inuit ritual is another indigenous instruction for the great care and attention needed to see through to the essential realm of spirit that underlies everything. Though even when sighting what matters briefly, there is no guarantee that the deeper reality will surface in the same place twice. Still, it is the art of sighting the wake of an unseen teacher that begins the harvest. This way of listening below the surface of things opens a kind of education that is not really teachable, though we can bring each other to its threshold through love.

A Reflective Pause

JOURNAL QUESTIONS

- Like the ripple of a fish breaking surface, tell the story of something subtle that proved to be an unseen teacher.

- As your full view of a river would require you to walk its length, think of your understanding of the river of truth, and describe two or three views you've had along the way and what these views together say to you now about the nature of truth.

Keeping the Song Alive

The base of all Hebrew prayer is *to listen for the Oneness*. As Rabbi Alan Lew says, "There's a deeper speech that doesn't come from where normal speech comes from." So how do we hear this deeper speech of Oneness? We've already seen how we can gather many views of something true, not relying on any one; how, if stilled enough, our small breath can join the one breath of the Universe; and how tracking what lives just below the surface can connect us to the living Source.

If blessed, enduring and living our lives in the open wears us down to the bare speech of Oneness. In everyday terms, ordinary spirits—like the great salmon that return from the Bering Sea—can break surface with traces of the Oneness. This happened with a minyan of Jewish men in San Francisco who prayed together every day for much of their lives. After thirty years, several had strokes that impaired their speech. Yet when together—and *only* when together—they could still sing the prayers imprinted in their hearts. Did the source of song and their sense of community enable these men, after losing their speech, to keep singing in each other's presence? What kind of medicine is this whose serum is love and whose needle is time?

The Cherry Tree on Willett Street

For three glorious years, I lived on Willett Street in Albany, New York, in an old brownstone on the edge of a beautiful park, which I could see year-round from my bay window. Across the street was a very old cherry tree whose surprising blossoms burst for only a few days in early May.

The first year I called my dear friend Robert and my wife Susan, and we stood arm in arm beneath the tree, staring up into a swaying thicket of pink. Since it bloomed before everything else, the miracle of flowers sprouting from wood was shouting quietly. From that day, I watched the cherry tree intensely, in awe how quickly and easily it would let go of all its apparent beauty, as quickly gone as it had come.

There were times in late fall or winter when I felt as sudden in possibility, and as quickly bereft. I would go out in the rain or snow and place my hands against the trunk, as if asking for its counsel. And it always seemed to say in silence—*neither the fullness nor the bareness lasts, but we return.*

By the second spring, we anticipated the days of blossom. At first sign, we gathered and read poems to the tree and to each other. After the second blossoming, I saw the tree's bareness as a remarkable, enduring strength. Knowing this softness would return, and sprout from its woodiness, became a guide.

Susan and I now live in Michigan, but each spring Robert goes in silence to stand beneath the thicket of pink. And we call to hear how the tree has burst again in its fullness. We close our eyes as he tells us the story we want to hear, and we feel possible all over.

The Improbable Path of Yes

This is a simple story about a simple man, William Edmonson (1874–1951) who worked as a janitor in the South for much of his life. But one day in midlife, William had a vision in which he was certain that God had planted the seed of sculpting in him as he slept. And though he'd never sculpted anything in his life, he began chipping away at discarded blocks of limestone. With no formal training and with just a railroad spike and a worn hammer, he began to unveil remarkable sculptures, creating highly original tombstones, human figures, and arrowheads. His effort and the courage of his attention were shaping him into the sculptor he was born to be. There were many obstacles, many ways to say *yes, but* or *no, it's too late.* But there was only one clear and improbable path of *yes.*

I hold William Edmonson and souls like him as an encouragement to my own possibility, especially when I feel disappointed and tired. Stories like this remind me that, when touched by our calling, it doesn't matter if we've been prepared or trained or certified or if we've been delayed for years. What matters is if we can listen to our own unmitigated possibility with our whole being. For this will enable us to begin, the way one day of rain and one day of sun will start the flower in its destiny to bloom. In deep and unexpected ways, saying yes is a form of listening that brings who we are and what we experience into true meeting. Saying yes is the beginning of all flowering.

A Reflective Pause

A MEDITATION

- o With your eyes closed, inhale slowly and picture a cherry tree flowering in early spring.

- o With your eyes open, exhale slowly and picture your own unmitigated possibility beginning to flower like a cherry blossom.

- o With your mind open, hear the blossom within you say—neither the fullness nor the bareness lasts, but we return.

- o With your heart open, inhale and exhale slowly, saying yes.

what am I drawn to?

The Word for Listen

In Old English *hlysnan,* to pay attention, to wait for a sound or signal, to hear something. More deeply, the many ways we take things in. In Afrikaans, *luister.* How long does it take to listen when pain is all around us? In Albanian, *dëgjoj.* How do we listen to what lives below whatever name we give it? In Arabic, *náṣata.* In Bosnian, *slušati.* How do we hear what waits in the stories no one believes? In Bulgarian, *slúsham.* In Catalan, *escoltar.* Can we hear the sound of rain on cobblestone? In Chickasaw, *haklo.* In Czech, *poslouchat.* Can we hear the sound of light being folded in a river passing under a bridge? In Danish, *lytte.* In Dutch, *naar.* In Finnish, *kuunnella.* Can we listen like a hawk on a cliff, wings spread to the elements? In French, *écouter.* In German, *zuhören.* In Hebrew, *hikshív.* Can we listen till we hear the lost sigh of millions as a yellow leaf is blown across their soil? In Hindi, *sunnā.* In Italian, *ascoltare.* In Japanese, *kiku.* Seeing a plum, painting a plum, eating a plum: aren't these all forms of listening? In Kurdish, *guh dar.* In Lao, *fang.* In Latin, *auscultō.* In Lithuanian, *klausyti.* Can we listen for truth like music to come out of silence and return to silence? In Marathi, *aikaNe.* In Norwegian, *lytte.* In Persian, *guš dâdan.* In Polish: *słuchać.* Can we listen to each other the way veins listen to blood? In Portuguese, *escutar.* In Romanian, *asculta.* In Russian, *slúšat'.* Can we take in the spaces between all the things ever said? In Spanish, *escuchar.* In Swedish, *lyssna på.* In Thai, *fang.* Can we listen the way a cloud receives light and lets it through? In Turkish, *dinlemek.* In Ukrainian, *slúxaty.* Can we listen the way we breathe, inhaling everything and giving it back? In Urdu, *sunnā.* In Vietnamese, *nghe.* Isn't watching rice sleep in water a form of listening? In Welsh, *gwrando.*

Can you find your own word for listen? Say it twice.

Namaste

A Reflective Pause

A MEDITATION

- ○ Choose four words for listen from the preceding section that you are drawn to.

- ○ Breathe deeply and center yourself.

- ○ After each full breath, listen and say aloud each of these words.

- ○ Breathe slowly and voice your own word for listen, even if it doesn't make sense.

- ○ Repeat this process two more times.

- ○ Enter your day and watch something grow.

- ○ As you watch it grow, quietly voice your meditative words for listen.

TABLE QUESTIONS

To be asked over dinner or coffee with friends and loved ones. Try listening to everyone's response before discussing:

- ○ Speak of a time when you sensed the presence of life and death in the same moment.

- ○ Speak of a time when you were able to be more fully yourself in the presence of a friend or loved one.

- ○ The cherry blossom appears to say, "Neither the fullness nor the bareness lasts, but we return." Discuss what you think this means.

Anna
Boston

HOW DO WE LISTEN TO ALL
THAT IS NOT SAID?

There are no others.

—RAMANA MAHARSHI

I N MAY IN my fifty-seventh year, I spoke in an innovative series known as Narrative Rounds at Columbia University medical school in New York City. As a cancer survivor, this meant a great deal to me. It wasn't till walking through the halls that I realized that the medical school is housed in New York–Presbyterian Hospital, the site of a very difficult and important passage in my cancer journey twenty years ago. This was deeply moving and disorienting. It was here that skilled medical teams finally diagnosed the rare form of cancer crippling me, and here that my first chemo treatment was horribly botched because the detachment of their great intellects precluded hands-on care.

After a small seminar in the afternoon, I was in conversation with two medical students when one asked me how to listen to a patient who didn't want to talk. What a great question. It made me bypass all logic to recount this story from years ago.

I was strolling through Santa Monica. After a while, I landed in a street-side café where I watched the wealthy walk by the homeless, neither acknowledging the other, as if I were watching an overlay of people from different times inhabit the same street. Except this, of course, was the same reality. I actually saw a well-groomed man, in perfectly creased slacks and a satin shirt, step over a homeless person sleeping near a store window so he could get a better look at a sweater. He stepped carefully over the unwashed man's belly, taking his sunglasses off in midstraddle to catch the detail of the sweater's weave. The homeless man, used to being stepped over, didn't flinch or move.

I stayed there quite a while, not sure what to do or where to go. The sun came out and funneled into the alley across the street. There, it revealed another unseen soul in a wheelchair, his head leaning against the wall. Through the light traffic, our eyes met. For ten or fifteen seconds, the world stopped and opened. Neither of us looked away. In that long moment, I heard all he did not say. It pierced my heart. His stare intensified and I felt my shoulders drop.

Now my stare ached itself open and his shoulders dropped. And we knew in that long moment that we are the same; we just landed in different bodies on different sides of the street. The sun moved west. The clouds returned. And life resumed. He turned and wheeled himself away.

I have realized since that what matters gets covered quickly, but underneath all the noise and pain, we all keep searching for and running from this moment. It is the jewel inside every stone, the dark seed waiting for light, the heartbeat of everything waiting for a way to show itself in our hurried world.

This moment revisits me every time I feel alone or sad for no reason; every time I am with someone broken open by hardship or illness. This moment has become the aching atom of humanity which forever grips me with what it means to be alive. It is a silent moment that keeps speaking, which I have only begun to understand as I've re-engaged it over time.

By the time I finished this story, the student who'd asked the question seemed puzzled while the one who was listening seemed to understand. I thanked them for their care and left them to each other. We so need each other to understand anything worth keeping in the world. As I went to sleep that night, I dreamt of those two students in fifteen years, saving the lives of people like me, long after the stone of our time together will have sunk to the bottom of their consciousness.

The next day I went to Hackensack, New Jersey, to spend time with cancer patients at Gilda's Club, named after comedian Gilda Radner, who died of ovarian cancer in 1989—the same year the lymphoma spread to my rib, which was then removed. My time with the dozen women who showed up was raw and tender. We joked about veins too hard and worn to open for more and stared in silence into the center of our brief circle, knowing the gifts of this journey, which cost almost everything, are too rare to be captured in everyday speech.

And today, on the third day, I wake very tired and make my way through the steady rain to the International Center of Photography, on Forty-third and Sixth, just opposite Bryant Park, where I will be allowed to view the original photographs of Roman Vishniac. Of the 16,000 photographs he managed to take of Jewish life in Eastern Europe at great risk and with great difficulty from 1934 to 1939, only 2,000 survive.

I show my ID and go to the Exhibitions Department on the twelfth floor, where I am met by Ben, a kind young man devoted to preserving the truth of the past. I'd sent a list of prints I'd hoped to see, and Ben has boxes of originals ready. I am given white gloves, asked to hold each with both hands, and left alone with these sacred windows to a world long gone.

Not sure what I'm looking for, I begin to listen to all Roman Vishniac could not say with his brave photographs of a world now gone. I, an idiosyncratic, mystical, cancer-surviving poet Jew, am compelled somehow to the ruined temple of the past. I begin to hold these pried-open moments in my white-gloved hands.

A half hour in, I come upon a photo of a street in Kazimierz, the Jewish ghetto of Cracow, Poland, in 1937. It is another moment in an alley, this time sixty years earlier and two continents away. The day is gray, the walls roughed up and cracked, the cobblestone splattered with snow, a window at the end. In the alley, two people are about to cross each other's path. A man carrying something is walking away from us. He's short and stocky. We can't see his face. It's hard to tell what he's carrying, but he's holding on to whatever it is firmly, protecting it. Com-

common humanity

ing toward us is a woman in boots; her coat open, her head covered, her face slightly down. She is walking close to the wall nearest her, but her eyes are just lifting to look at the man about to pass her. The small lift of her eyes, looking sideways toward this stranger carrying something firmly, holds the center of the Universe open briefly. It is the reason for the photograph.

It is the reason for all photographs. The rest will fall away, but her soul, our soul, the filament of undying spirit reaching out through her cautious eyes to a familiar stranger carrying something home— this holds everything together. We are always doing this—carrying something past each other in small, lighted spaces between walls that are wearing down. These are the still fiery moments in the middle of everything harsh that we so easily miss, which reveal us to each other, which sustain us and rejuvenate our hope. These travelers are long gone. But the moment of this woman's eyes looking out into the life of another going the other way; this moment in which we know each other as lifelong pilgrims not sure where we're going; this moment never dies.

All these things are voices of the unspeakable: the brilliance and ignorance of the doctors who diagnosed me twenty years ago, the want of soon-to-be doctors to understand how to listen to all that is unsaid, the endless stepping of those who have over those who have nothing, the moment that life is held open by the stare of strangers through the human storm, and the cancered women wiping tears from each other's eyes in the New Jersey night.

This is why I have come to New York in May in my fifty-seventh year: to trip through all these moments, trying again to listen to all that is unsaid. It is perfect that, when I leave the International Center of Photography, it is still raining. As I fumble with my umbrella, getting wet anyway, I bow my head to the water from the sky meant to soften our minds. I stop trying not to get wet; opened one more time by the truth that we should always hold everything unspoken with both hands.

A Reflective Pause

A MEDITATION

- ○ Center yourself and look at your hands.

- ○ As you inhale and exhale, open and close your hands slowly.

- ○ Think freely of all the things your hands have touched in your life.

- ○ Inhale deeply and receive the life of touch your hands carry that can't be put into words.

- ○ As you enter your day, try to emanate what your hands carry without saying a word.

JOURNAL QUESTIONS

- ○ Tell the story of a silent moment that keeps speaking to you. What do you think it's saying? What keeps bringing you back to it?

- ○ Identify a time in the past you would like to know more about. When you can, find photographs or drawings of this time and look through them as you would a series of windows. Describe the life you find there and your relationship to it.

TABLE QUESTIONS

To be asked over dinner or coffee with friends and loved ones. Try listening to everyone's response before discussing:

- ○ Given the scene in Santa Monica where the well-dressed man steps over the homeless person, describe a time when you were the one who for the moment ignored the life around you and a time when you were the one ignored.

- ○ Tell the story of a recent conversation in which all that was unsaid was greater than what was said. Was this conversation deceptive or revealing?

BEING LOST

The moment we awaken to know that we are lost—to realize, as Jung says, that the ego is not master in the house—then we have begun the journey.

—HELEN LUKE

W HEN WE LOSE our map, our real knowledge of the path begins. It's humbling because we're forced to touch the Earth itself instead of our representations of the Earth. Humbling that, just when we lose our little plan of passion, the true impact of care overcomes us, because we are forced from our watch of longing along the shore to swim in the red tide of love itself.

As Helen Luke points out, the journey truly begins when we lose possession of what we thought were answers and are left to accept that we are not in control. Anyone who has lived through loss and been shaken of their grip will admit that beyond every answer waits a larger question, and beyond every arrival waits an unforeseen beginning. Being lost on the inner plane can be understood as a disorientation that is necessary as we are thrust from what we think we know into the vibrant field of all we do not know.

This is how being lost can be a prelude to a deeper way, because once we admit that we're not sure where life is taking us, then we are ripe for transformation. Then we are shapeable. When losing our way, we frequently retreat and withhold or take what we think is a safer path. This often complicates our confusion. An old woodsman told me that the reason most people get lost is because they don't go far enough. They doubt where they are and change direction too soon. Somehow we are called to lean forward by what little light we are given.

The great Jewish philosopher and physician Maimonides said, "We are like someone in a very dark night over whom lightning flashes again and again." Life does seem to dilate and constrict in this way. There are sudden comprehensive moments—lightning flashes—by which we can navigate for a while, sometimes for years. And the moods of confusion in between—those very dark nights—are where we need to practice patience. Too often, when drifting through a difficult passage of uncertainty, we become negatively self-centered and punish ourselves for not knowing more or not being more decisive. But if we take Maimonides's image to heart, this movement from lightning flash to dark night and back again is part of the journey, despite how hard we work. When the lightning flashes—in our mind or in our heart—we glimpse the hidden order and our changing place in it.

If we can see our way through the uncertainty of feeling lost, unexpected callings often present themselves. One stirring example is the story of Lorraine Hunt Lieberson (1954–2006), who began her career as an accomplished viola player. While on tour in Europe, her viola was stolen. Though she could have just replaced it, the theft threw her into a state of feeling lost and uncertain. She stopped playing for a while and then began to work with the only instrument she had left, her voice. Though she had sung before, she devoted herself to the instrument within her and, in two years, became the luminous mezzo-soprano she was meant to be.

A Reflective Pause

JOURNAL QUESTIONS

○ Describe a situation or aspect of your life for which the map you've trusted is no longer working. How might you honor it as you would an old guide who has brought you this far? How might you begin to explore and map the new land before you?

○ Describe your personal history regarding uncertainty and your response to it. How would you like your response to uncertainty to evolve?

waiting

The Pulse of Everything Living

As an undergraduate, I was seen by some as career-challenged because I had a difficult time choosing a major. I said I wanted to major in life. At first, people laughed, and when they understood that I was serious, they became concerned. But this inability to locate myself on the social map enabled me to uncover a deeper tie with the pulse of everything living, a tie that has nourished me my whole life.

I've found myself repeatedly at the threshold of authentic living, needing to acquaint myself with the discomfort of not knowing where life will take me. Enduring this uncertainty often allows a deeper order or way to show itself. Enduring this discomfort allows the deeper texture and meaning of life to discover us. It allows life's roots to spread and grow before our eyes, if we don't put ourselves too quickly in too small a planter.

Yet there is another definition of being lost that we must wrestle with, one that helps us find our way in the inner world. The word *lost* comes from the Indo-European root *leu,* which means *to loosen, divide,* or *cut apart*.

Understanding this root meaning can bring us to the center of our inner work, for it tells us that being lost has a quality of being divided or cut apart. So while *the outer sense of being lost* is not knowing where you are or where you're headed, and while the unknown secrets of tomorrow require us to withstand the discomfort of that, *the inner sense of being lost* is being inwardly divided or cut apart, and being whole necessitates healing these divisions.

This is a profound insight, for understanding where and how we are inwardly divided often leads to the center of our tensions. And inner divisions, unattended, widen into schisms that are difficult to cross. In significant ways, realizing and accepting where and how we are lost, or inwardly divided, can lead us right to the place where we must heal. Facing our inner divisions is the first step to knowing where we need to rejoin ourselves. You cannot set bone until you know where it is broken, and you cannot set upon the journey of individuation—of becoming a whole person—until you know where and how you are divided.

Getting There

The more I wander, the more I wonder.

—Tom Callanan

In every generation, the swell of humanity moves here, then there, like schools of fish being swept along. From inside each era, there is a push to reach, to move forward, to get there. Both to reach and move forward are natural and even essential, but to get there is an illusion. It is a supreme and painful irony that society, by its collective inclination, pushes everyone toward some imagined better place, when the heart of every spiritual path sheds everywhere else in favor of an illumined here.

Just where are we going? In the soul's journey, maps are just kindling, as are dreams; necessary but not always in the way we think. I'm not debasing the need to dream—every poem is the movement of a dream. I'm just asking that we hold our dreams lightly with humility. For it's using our maps and dreams like torches that lands us in the freshness of living.

I was thinking about all this while defragmenting my computer the other day. And while learning how to protect my computer against viruses, a screen came up that flashed: *Your definitions are 254 days old.* I immediately laughed and thought, yes, I need to stay current and check my definitions—*my maps of being*—at least once a year. Much of our trouble comes from the rigidity of obsolete definitions of self and world, which, like hardening arteries, are silent killers.

A Reflective Pause

A MEDITATION

- ○ Center yourself until you feel a sense of safety in the moment.

- ○ Breathe slowly and let yourself look at one old definition you carry. It might be how you view your own worth or how you inventory your likes and dislikes based on old experiences. *overly responsible*

- ○ Write this old definition down on a piece of paper and say it out loud for the last time.

- ○ Breathe deeply, set the old definition in a dish, and light it with a match, watching it disappear into the brief light that returns you to the undefined now.

Losing Our Context

It was mid-January and I was driving the back way to work. We'd had several days of light but steady snow and the trees along the road seemed to float under the whiteness. I began to think of my father, and for a few moments, while my hands were steering, I went inside to another place, searching for him in the remnants I carry in the back of my heart. When I returned to the snowy road, I wasn't sure which road I was on. Had I made a turn? Was I on Stadium Drive or Fourth Street? For a moment, I felt lost and had a rush of urgency. I passed a familiar stand of pines and relocated myself.

As I thought about those moments of free fall, I realized that I hadn't been lost. I had simply lost track of my context; that is, I'd lost sight of where I was coming from and where I was going. As for where I was, that was always clear. Though we're most comfortable thinking of ourselves as making progress from here to there—most comfortable working within our contextual dream—our personal context can box us in.

This now.

When I lost track of my context, I had to slow down considerably, but that allowed me to hear the snow falling on the covered branches. My way became immediate, and, if I hadn't relocated myself, my path would have unfolded: one step at a time, one turn at a time, one fresh experience at a time. Of course, I was relieved to remember my context and re-find my way. But this little moment exposed an underlying truth: that we often make up our context for the illusion of comfort that the days are orderly and progressing somewhere. They usually are, but not always toward the order we have imagined or ordained.

This little moment gave me much more compassion for those who suffer dementia or Alzheimer's. And yet, losing our context, losing our self-created map of where we're supposed to go, can allow us the grace of remembering that all we need is in the moment we find ourselves in. And that moment will lead to the next, if we listen to it. In fact, when feeling that your context has lost its meaning, when feeling trapped within the ambitious parameters you have spun, it helps to lose your map and return to the direct experience of feeling where your foot lands and what your eye sees. Following the immediate can break our patterns and restore wonder as our guide.

The Web of Tributaries

In my own life, I have detailed many maps only to abandon them along the way. When young, of course, I was pushed like everyone to move forward and get there, though I was never sure where *there* was. As a poet, this infected me with a want to leave a legacy of great work and carve a poem or two into the mountain along the way. But forty years on, I have found the reaches of mountains cold, unfit for love or the conversation of the ages. Now, I want only to give away all that I'm blessed to know and disappear in the stream.

Still I struggle. Here's another small story. I was on my way to the San Francisco Airport, en route to Santa Fe to see my dear friend Wayne. I was in the back of a shuttle listening to one side of a cell phone conversation being spoken in Chinese. I saw a large bird gliding over the highway and it occurred to me that while a bird starts out with a direction in mind, it simply rides the currents. As human beings, though, we somehow overreach the currents, imagining routes and timetables that we have no control over. We call these routes and timetables goals. If large enough, they become ambitions or aspirations. Then we adhere to them as if they came from God.

I constantly fall prey to this. Somewhere along the way, I learned or taught myself to prepare for every detail, which is fine. But at some point the preparations always turn into goals that must be fulfilled, or I have the feeling that something terrible will happen. Most of the time, this couldn't be further from the truth.

Whether the plans are to catch the shuttle at 9:20 and to sit in 4B on the 11:27 flight to Albuquerque, and then to go home on Monday at 2:30, or to go to school and get a master's degree and be married by thirty-five and rich by fifty, or to achieve a certain level of success, however you might plan—to tunnel our way through life toward intentions cast ahead of us as obligations is to actually bypass being touched by much of life. In truth, being single-minded is highly overrated. It often limits what we can learn from the world. For life is tangential and circulatory like the veins on a leaf or in a chamber of the heart. Or like the web of tributaries feeding water to a continent. The larger intention is to stay in relationship with everything that comes along, at least long enough to taste what is living.

For all my focus and conscientious planning, *unplanned unfoldings* are what have made me more human: the blind saxophonist down an alley in Greenwich Village whom I listened to until I wept; the trapped bird in the apse of the Duomo in Florence whose cavernous flapping made me realize my own entrapments. Waking from cancer, I fell into an unexpected loss of ambition, and the milestones by which I wanted to engrave my image on the world scattered. And, along the way, I've been surprised by the kindness of strangers who couldn't have found me in such need had I managed to stay on course.

As I arrived at the terminal, I felt like I owed the innocent driver more than I could pay for delivering me more deeply to myself. The large bird had vanished in a cloud and my mechanical bird was waiting. Standing on yet another curb with bags I couldn't remember packing, I realized that what has caused so much anxiety in my life of plans is the fear that, if thrown off course, whatever that means, life will leave town without me. How utterly silly. It's the other way around. God is fully wherever we are, and when our plans are bent or split or reversed by the unexpected appearance of life in its many guises, this is often where the learning begins.

A Reflective Pause

JOURNAL QUESTIONS

○ Describe a moment in which you briefly lost your context and what this did to you. What if anything was disturbing about this and what if anything was beneficial and growthful? How would you explain this experience to a friend?

TABLE QUESTIONS

To be asked over dinner or coffee with friends and loved ones. Try listening to everyone's response before discussing:

○ Tell two current stories about being lost in your life: first, in the outer sense of not knowing where you are or where you're headed, and, second, in the inner sense of being divided or cut apart from yourself.

Invite those listening to help you examine if and how these two ways of being lost inform each other.

Invite someone who has listened to imagine and tell the next chapter in your story from here.

○ Share one plan you made which turned into a goal that then had to be fulfilled. How did this goal grow in weight and take up more space in your life?

○ Share one unexpected unfolding that brought you closer to your own sense of aliveness. How did this lighten what you carry and take up more space in your life?

In the first six chapters, we've explored several forms of listening and how they can break our isolation so we can inhabit our connection with the rest of life. These forms of listening are key to our health. One reliable way to listen is to keep what is true before us. We can't do this all the time because we're human. So the practice of being human centers on the courage to return to what is life-giving. Returning to what matters involves setting aside our preconceptions and opinions so we can listen to life directly. When we can meet life with an open heart, receiving becomes indistinguishable from giving and we become conduits of grace.

Living this directly unfolds the work of being, where from time to time our individual breath coincides with the breath of the Universe. Listening this sincerely opens us to the spiritual gravity that pulls us to the common center of all living things. It is the pull to center that asks us to lean into all we don't know. Leaning into life is the work of intuition, the chance to discover the learnings we are born with, the way a seed discovers the flower it will become. The work of being is to listen our way into living our inborn nature, a beautiful beginning and end in itself.

This is a good time to ask: Are you holding your breath anywhere in your life? What will it take for you to breathe more deeply again? How goes your practice of emptying and opening, your practice of staying a beginner? Are you keeping what is true before you? Have you encountered a great listener? What can you add to your own practice of listening from their great example? How are you listening for the learnings you were born with? How close are you to your resilience? Is there a change you are resisting and not listening to? Are you letting the injury or limitation of one thing injure or limit all things? Who has your ear these days, the one in you who says yes or the one in you who says no? Are you listening to the part of you life is trying to wake? *Are you trying to hear all that is unsaid?* Are you open to the soft moment in the middle of everything harsh that will reveal us to each other? Which of your treasured maps is keeping you from the path you were meant to discover? *Can you endure your uncertainty until it shows you another, deeper way?* Do you know where and how you are inwardly divided? Do you know the center of your tensions? What old definition or plan can you put down that will return you to the freshness of now?

All these forms of listening are part of the work of being. I invite you to lean into them, to learn from them, to personalize your conversation with them. From here, we will explore deep listening, which invites us to experience the one living sense that connects all things. That living connection holds the history of presence and wisdom, which is the ocean we all drink from when forced to put our lips to the water of life.

IN THE PRESENCE OF SAGES

There are four types among those who sit in the presence of sages: the sponge, the funnel, the strainer, and the sieve. "The sponge," who soaks up everything. "The funnel," who takes in at this end and lets out at the other. "The strainer," who lets out the wine and retains the dregs. "The sieve," who removes the coarse meal and collects the fine flour.

—from the *Pirkei Avot, Ethics of the Fathers* (5:18)

THIS ANONYMOUS SAYING is two thousand years old, from a collection of sayings that have survived like driftwood on the sea of time. It is found in the fifth chapter of an early book known as the *Pirkei Avot,* which is Hebrew for *Ethics of the Fathers* (פרקי אבות). This is a book of maxims culled from the early generations of Rabbis between 70 and 200 CE, beginning with Moses. The *Pirkei Avot* is part of a larger book called the Mishna, which is a major part of the Talmud. The Mishna represents the first written collection of Jewish oral traditions. The Mishna has been called the Oral Torah. The *Pirkei Avot,* the Mishna, and the Talmud mark the trail of a long conversation among many voices over the centuries.

Whoever offered the preceding set of images or whatever group of seekers uttered parts along the way, the images alone tell us that taking things in has been essential to living from the beginning. Before we unfold the wisdom in these images, let's look at the notion of sage itself.

The word *sage* is from the Latin *sapere* (to taste) which comes from the Indo-European root *sap-* (to taste). In its original form, *sage* is a verb, a process or gesture by which we take in the world. It implies that we make sense of the world and find wisdom by tasting. While watching and thinking may be helpful, it is internalizing what we experience that opens us to wisdom.

Early references to *sage* as a noun, meaning *a person of profound wisdom,* are found in Hindu, Greek, and Chinese history. In Hindu literature, we find an early reference in the *Saptarishi* (Sanskrit meaning *seven sages*). The Saptarishi are the seven Hindu *rishis* praised in the Vedas, which never name them. *Rishi* refers to a Vedic poet called to compose the Vedic hymns. Mystically, a rishi is one to whom the Vedic hymns are revealed. It is implied that a sage is one who has been open enough to receive, taste, and filter the hymns of the Universe.

There is also an early reference to the Seven Sages of Greece. This highlights the ancient Greek philosophers: Thales, Pittacus, Bias, Solon, Cleobulus, Myson, and Chilon. The oldest mention of these sages is in Plato's *Protagoras*, where Socrates says:

> There are some, both at present and of old, who recognized . . .
> a love of wisdom, knowing that the ability to utter such [brief
> and terse] remarks belongs to a perfectly educated man. Among
> these were Thales of Miletus, and Pittacus of Mytilene, and
> Bias of Priene, and our own Solon, and Cleobulus of Lindus,
> and Myson of Chen, and the seventh was said to be Chilon of
> Sparta . . .
>   One could tell their wisdom by the brief but memorable
> remarks they each uttered when they met and jointly dedicated
> the fruits of their wisdom to Apollo in his shrine at Delphi,
> writing what is on every man's lips: Know thyself, and Nothing
> too much. Why do I say this? Because this was the manner of
> philosophy among the ancients, a kind of laconic brevity.

But as soon as Socrates names the wise ones, the sorting and debate over who is the wisest begins. Diogenes points out that there was great disagreement over which figures should be counted among the seven and disagreement over the number of sages. Some lists include up to seventeen individuals. Arguments arose: were the men cited merely shrewd and not wise at all? Soon the curiosity and wonder by which we receive and filter the hymns of the Universe were ignored as attention moved away from the tasting of life to debating who were the greatest tasters.

In how the Seven Sages of Greece were received, we can trace a fundamental shift in the meaning of wisdom and our approach to it. Now *sage* begins to refer to someone who *has* tasted, who has internalized the world and its many paradoxes. While we can certainly learn from such individuals, a significant change takes place that alters how we understand learning when the focus becomes the one who has tasted and not the practice of tasting itself. Now there is a middleman who expounds to others how they should live. Now there is the misguided belief that we can shortcut the process of *saging* and receive wisdom through one already wise. Much of the instruction of true sages throughout time has been to redirect seekers back to their own innate resources and their own firsthand experiences of the world.

In China, we find yet another early reference to the wise. The Seven Sages of the Bamboo Grove are a group of Taoist Qingtan scholars, writers, and musicians who came together in the bloody third century CE. The group needed to escape the intrigues, corruption, and stifling atmosphere of court life during the politically fraught Three Kingdoms period. They not only needed refuge from the dangers of society but longed for a company of spirit to make sense of the life they were given. They needed an interior friendship, a container that would keep them safe and let them grow. To create this container, they gathered in a bamboo grove near the house of Xi Kang in Shanyang, where they enjoyed each other's questions and lived a simple, rustic life.

These Sages of the Bamboo Grove were devoted to the engagement and joy of personal freedom, spontaneity, and a celebration of nature. Liu Ling, Ruan Ji, Ruan Xian, Xiang Xiu, Wang Rong, and Shan Tao were the other sages who made up the group. The friendship of the grove was described as "stronger than metal and fragrant as orchids." Their commitment to renew their direct taste of life, individually and together, enabled these friends to stay both strong and vulnerable. Their small, receptive commune enabled them to endure the heartless intrigues of third-century China by listening deeply to the nature of their own rhythms and the rhythms of nature.

The Hindu rishis showed us how to listen to the Universe itself, while the Greek sages showed us how to filter the lessons of living, and the Chinese sages showed us the sacredness of friendship with each other and nature. All worthy forms of tasting. All sources of wisdom. But as evidenced in ancient Greece, once we abdicate our own capacity to taste, we begin to sort and compare who is wise and who is not and what is wise and what is not. Once we value naming what matters over the experience of what matters, the wisdom itself is overlooked. When we grow small, the wisdom itself withdraws.

A Reflective Pause

A MEDITATION

- ○ Close your eyes and inhale slowly.

- ○ With each breath, imagine the Seven Hindu Rishis, the Seven Sages of Ancient Greece, and the Seven Sages of the Bamboo Grove. With each breath, bring your image of them into greater focus.

- ○ Open your heart and let yourself be drawn to one sage, for the time being.

- ○ Inhale deeply, and silently ask the sage you are drawn to one thing you'd like to know about life.

- ○ Open your eyes and enter your day. Be on the look for someone who might be a descendant of this sage.

- ○ Continue the conversation.

Saging

We are interested here in the timeless process of saging that is always waiting beneath the deification of the wise one. We are interested in the elemental process of tasting and internalizing the mystery of life. When we can restore wisdom as a process of firsthand experience and resist displacing our own responsibility to be a sage, we come upon the beautiful and luminous question: what do we listen to and how?

Being with this question enlarges the notion of sage—beyond the person worn into wisdom—to the aspects of Source from which the wise person tasted in the first place. Thus, when Buddha redirects his adoring students away from him and to the heart of all he speaks, he says that he and his teachings are merely fingers pointing to the moon. And when the Native American elder listens to the wind, he is listening to a sage-aspect of the Great Spirit. And when Rumi spins as the first whirling dervish, he is trying to lose his own frame of reference; to put down the habits of his knowing so he can taste freshly from the greatest sage of all—life.

Saging, then, is a fundamental process like breathing. It evokes a commitment to listen with all our senses and all our being until listening *is* tasting. Often, we can't do this alone and need the friendship of the grove to help each other find our way back to the oldest sage of all—the living presence of the Universe.

A Reflective Pause

JOURNAL QUESTION

o Describe your own significant experience of saging, of tasting life directly, beyond the instruction or teaching of anyone else.

If life itself is the sage and each of us in our journeys on earth is destined to taste of life directly, then how we listen and taste is a universal and personal art. From this unchanging truth, we can ask, how do we sit in the presence of sages?

Now to the wisdom in the images cited from the *Pirkei Avot*:

> *There are four types among those who sit in the presence of sages: the sponge, the funnel, the strainer, and the sieve. "The sponge," who soaks up everything. "The funnel," who takes in at this end and lets out at the other. "The strainer," who lets out the wine and retains the dregs. "The sieve," who removes the coarse meal and collects the fine flour.*

Simply and profoundly, it is the heart that can open itself like a sponge or a funnel or a strainer or a sieve. In the presence of life, with no one to interpret or explain the pain or wonder we trip upon, it is the heart that can absorb without preference; that can take in widely and let out narrowly; that can hold on to sediment or sift what is coarse, collecting what is fine.

Each of these ways of tasting has its gifts and its difficulties. But central to all is letting life move through us. For experience releases meaning as it filters through the living. Everything encounters life in this way: wind through trees, rain through roots, light through dark. Being human, we experience an unpredictable flexing and relaxation of the heart, the muscle by which we converse with the world. Depending on the day, experience will make our hearts open or narrow or hold on to or sift.

Let me tell you a story. There was a young man who was eager to learn all he could about life. He was sincere and devoted. Soon after leaving his family, he came upon a baker and became his apprentice. He watched as the baker used a sieve to sift and refine his flour and sugar. The young man thought, this is how I'll sift the best from life; separating what is gross from what is fine. This is how I'll learn and think and work and love; filtering out the unwanted pieces. But while his heart became schooled at sifting out what is harsh and indigestible, he found that basing his life on only what is fine can be dangerous, like building a house on sand. Once sifted, nothing was foundational and there was nothing substantial enough to stand on. His life became like powder.

In time, the apprentice left the baker knowing that sweet things are necessary but not enduring. In time, he came upon a winemaker and apprenticed with him. He watched as the winemaker let the blood-like wine ferment in large oak casks. After much waiting, he saw how the winemaker would strain the aging wine to catch the dregs and sediment, which had given it its taste but which themselves were undrinkable. Now he thought, this is how I'll strain the difficult lessons of life. This is how I'll let the lessons of pain and heartache age. This is how I'll strain what is drinkable from them. But the apprentice was surprised to watch the winemaker grow drunk from his own wine and saw how the pain and heartache surfaced anyway. So while it is possible and even admirable to strain out the broken pieces that life brings us, we still must guard against becoming intoxicated by the sediment of life.

And so the apprentice moved on. By now he was no longer young, but middle-aged. As he tired, he came upon a farmer who gave him some water. They struck up a friendship and he saw that the farmer was a master at irrigation, at funneling water into the root systems that braided his land. He stayed on to learn how wide openings can gather water, how narrow pipes can carry it, how smaller openings can feed the water to the things that need it. So now he thought, this is how I will live. I will no longer try to get things out of life, but live as an instrument, as a funnel myself. I will open my heart wide and collect the waters of life and carry them through me to water things in need. He thought, this is how I will be authentic and of use. And the apprentice stayed with the farmer for many years. In times of plenty, they fed many. In times of lack, they kept everyone in water. And it was good to be of use.

But over the years, the aging apprentice began to feel worn down by being a funnel, especially in the narrow part of him that carried love to others. Living like this had scoured his insides, and he felt, at times, that he was losing the depth and calm of the whole to this narrowing.

By now, he was an old man. And when his friend died, the apprentice sat under the largest tree on the farm and thought about his life with the baker, the winemaker, and the farmer. He thought about how his heart had been a sieve, a strainer, and a funnel. He could feel the gift of each and the cost of each. It was then that he left the farm and made his way to the sea, where he lived quietly, roaming the shore.

In his remaining years he befriended a sponge diver and became fascinated by the simplicity of sponges to absorb without preference and to give without holding back. He thought, this is where I've been led. This is how I'll live what years are left, accepting like a sponge and giving like a sponge. And so he spent his days being porous and cleansing.

As we need to sleep and wake, we need to taste all forms of heart. As we need to breathe, we need to presence and sage: to open and absorb and narrow and hold on to and sift. For no one can blossom the God within but you. So water what you know, even more what you don't know. Taste everything and be surprised.

A Reflective Pause

A MEDITATION

o Center yourself and imagine your heart floating like a jellyfish in the sea of life. Inhale and exhale and feel the currents of life brush up against you.

o Breathe deeply until your heart begins to flex. Note what this feels like. Note what your heart flexing does to your mood and body.

o Inhale and exhale again and feel the currents of life brush up against you once more.

○ Breathe deeply until your heart begins to relax. Note what this feels like. Note what your heart relaxing does to your mood and body.

○ Center yourself and realize that who you are at center doesn't change whether your heart, your mood, or your body flexes or relaxes.

TABLE QUESTIONS

To be asked over dinner or coffee with friends and loved ones. Try listening to everyone's response before discussing:

○ Give one example of how you filtered out an unwanted piece of life. What did filtering this experience do for you or to you?

○ Give one example of pain or heartache that you have strained from your heart and let age like wine but which has still been hard to let go of. What do you think this pain or heartache wants from you?

○ Tell the story of someone you consider wise and how they irrigated a path for you.

○ Discuss the current state of your heart and how it functions mostly: as a sponge, a funnel, a strainer, or a sieve? Which comes naturally? Which is most challenging? Considering how your heart functions, in what ways would you like to grow?

JOURNAL QUESTIONS

○ Along the way, we each discover a Wisdom Lineage we are a part of; a family of beings we are most at home with.

○ How would you describe the Wisdom Lineage you are a part of? What tribe of beings do you belong to?

○ Identify one constellation of your Wisdom Lineage by naming three beings, living or from the past, that you feel a spiritual kinship with and share why.

○ What is it about each—their life and work—that you count as part of your foundation and wisdom-worldview?

○ If you don't know your Wisdom Lineage: Who are you drawn to? How will you find out more about them? Go and find your teachers.

ENTERING SILENCE

We make a space inside ourselves,
so that being can speak.

—MARTIN HEIDEGGER

MOSTLY WE ARE caught in a storm of activity. For we live in the world, and are always drawn above and below and in between. Yet when we can stop talking, when we can stop mapping the chatter in our minds, when we can descend into that wordless current of being, we start to *see* Oneness. Helpful as this is, it is not enough. When we can summon the courage not to run back to the surface prematurely, we begin to *sense* and *feel* Oneness. When we can spend enough time below the noise of the world, even though we have to return, we might even say that, from time to time, we *live* in the unspoken. Then we might be blessed to *experience* Oneness.

To enter the unspeakable requires a quiet courage that points to what is often out of reach, though it is never far from us. Not unspeakable because it is awful, but because it lives beneath words. Not touching that silence and what lives there isolates us from the web of Spirit that connects everything. Then we lapse into what feels like a broken world of nothing. But entering that silence, the unspeakable shows itself as the thread of light that holds the web of life together. Feeling these threads, I am reanimated in a world where each small part contains everything.

The inner nature of things is always emanating and we relax our way in the world to finally receive it. I find that deep listening is such a relaxation by which I enter silence until what I hear enters me. Deep listening holds everything we know open till what can't be seen or heard is felt and received thoroughly enough to change our minds. Not only does it change the content of our minds, though that is significant by itself, but as water rushing through an inlet changes the shape of the inlet, letting what we hear enter us so completely changes the *shape* and *threshold* of our minds. Listening with this degree of openness can alter our experience of life. When we can relax our way in the world enough to truly receive, waiting is more than waiting and silence is more than silence.

Winded by my efforts to keep up or slow down, the turbulence of circumstance evaporates, and living is what's left. We all inhabit this spiral; an inner odyssey in which we take our turn as the warrior whose taste for the fight dissolves into a need for the ancient quiet. Some of us discover quite by accident or exhaustion that rising from the deep is our genesis, floating in the sun, our home.

Sitting till the things to be done dry up, till the voices urging they be done melt like ice in our minds, till the old hurts throb out of our bones, made harmless by the air, till all that we want has nothing left to shout at, till there is nothing left to reach for or with, and nothing left to let go of, till even our fear of death loses its tongue, and, with nothing in the way, the light of the world kisses the light of the heart and each breath shines.

In truth, our hearts keep moving through all these moods like whales who can't stay under too long or surface too long. Our destiny: to swim above, then below, only to break surface and depth again and again. And each time we enter the unspoken, we are allowed to escape the noise of the world so we might descend into the currents below speech where all hearts beat as one. Underneath everything, it is the beat of our hearts in silence that keeps the world going.

Never assume the song is gone because it's found its source in silence.

A Reflective Pause

A MEDITATION

- Center yourself and notice the noise around you and within you.

- Breathe slowly and reflect on what inner and outer noise covers.

- Close your eyes and listen carefully to the kind of inner noise you create and carry.

- Breathe deeply and try to name two ways you can quiet your inner noise in the next week.

- Open your eyes and commit to doing so.

JOURNAL QUESTIONS

- In the same way that entering the ocean calls us first to wade, then submerge, then move through the rush of surf, and finally lets us drift in the deep, silence calls us in increasing degrees to enter it more fully. What is your experience of this? At what stage of silence are you most challenged? At what stage are you at home? What keeps you there? What keeps you from going there?

TABLE QUESTIONS

To be asked over dinner or coffee with friends and loved ones. Try listening to everyone's response before discussing:

○ Describe a time when you changed your mind, your opinion, and what led you to do so. How did you grow from this experience?

○ Describe a time when you changed your mind more deeply, when the very way you perceive shifted, and what led you to this. How did you grow from this experience?

GOD BLINKING

When wiggling through a hole
the world looks different than
when scrubbed clean by the wiggle
and looking back.

M<small>Y DEAR FRIEND</small> Wayne Muller, author of *A Life of Being, Having, and Doing Enough*, speaks of the courage to see what's whole beneath what's broken. The French novelist and Nobel laureate André Gide also says, "If you go deeply enough into the personal, you reach the Universal." These insights imply that what's broken and what's whole are not forks in the road, but that one waits beneath the other; namely, a Universal Wholeness waits beneath our brokenness the way a torn seedpod lets all its seeds drop through its tear to germinate the Earth. A good deal of our suffering comes from not going deeply enough into the personal *to make it through* and so we get stuck between the surface and the deep. Often, the pain of being stuck makes us afraid to go deeper, which is exactly what we need to do in order to restore our inner health. So when stuck, we need to ask ourselves: Am I leaning *through* my brokenness *enough* to be touched and restored by the Wholeness of life?

The Sufi Master Ibn al-ʿArabī speaks of our journey to the Universal through the personal in another way. He describes the nature of human awareness as a moment-by-moment shift in perception. Like swimming in the sea, each stroke reveals a new vision and experience of life. In the moment that we move through what is broken and personal, we are lifted by a wave and sense the current underneath our pain. Yet in the moment that we are stuck in what is broken and personal, we are tossed under and experience what seems like God's absence in the drowning tumble of our pain. The seeming presence and absence of God unfolds moment to moment. We think God is blinking when it is we in our humanness and stubbornness who see, then don't. Being stuck in what is broken and personal is an unavoidable human mood. How long we live there depends not on avoiding feeling broken and personal, but on feeling it *deeply enough* to reach what's Universal in the heart of our very personal experience.

Perhaps the divine nature of things is disclosed to us through our humanity, moment by feeling moment, through the ongoing presence of the mystery we wake in and our intermittent reception of it. We could say that experience is the way God keeps breaking our trance so we might have another chance to be enfolded in the Whole. Our challenge is not to get stuck in between, but *to make it through;* not to dwell on how the world keeps tearing us apart, but to endure this holy process *deeply enough* that we are rearranged and imbued by life itself as we are put back together. All of which is happening to you and me as I reach for you through these words.

A Reflective Pause

A MEDITATION

- ○ Center yourself and imagine your life as a tree above ground.

- ○ Breathe deeply and imagine your soul as the roots of your life that keep you upright.

- ○ Breathe deeply and feel the life around you as the soil in which your life and soul are growing.

- ○ Breathe steadily and feel your personal place in all that is Universal.

JOURNAL QUESTIONS

o The French writer André Gide says, "If you go deeply enough into the personal, you reach the Universal." What do you think this means? How would you describe the difference between the personal and the Universal? If you can, describe a moment when you felt something personal to its bottom and how that depth of feeling opened you to a sense of the Universal.

TABLE QUESTION

To be asked over dinner or coffee with friends and loved ones. Try listening to everyone's response before discussing:

o The epigraph of this chapter speaks to the difficulty of wriggling through a tough place and the sense of clear simplicity that often waits on the other side. Tell the story of a tough place you had to make your way through, what that felt like, and what kind of clarity you earned on the other side. What did this experience teach you about how to approach tough places?

A CONVERSATION WITH
THE ELEMENTS

If you don't become the ocean, you'll be seasick every day.

—LEONARD COHEN

WE ARE SO close to the Earth that we often forget—it is alive. And the language of its aliveness is what we call nature. When we listen to nature, we are listening to the Earth. Of course, such a conversation takes time, because we are too small to readily grasp what the Earth has to say. The vast Earth has carried us our whole lives. Can we thank it? It has held up and endured everything for thousands of years. Can we ask it how? It speaks with a thousand tongues, none of which uses words. Yet, to build a relationship with that which holds us up seems essential.

But what can we hear? As the smog we've created prevents us from seeing the sky, the noise of machinery we've created prevents us from hearing the wind and birds and quiet teachers that have always been there. When I leave the mechanical hive, even briefly, I can tell that the horse runs to know its father, the wind. Just the other day, I took a walk where there is no pavement. I lost my way and followed two geese until I reached the end of my small logic.

A Reflective Pause

easy for me

A MEDITATION

o Go for a slow walk and let yourself be stopped by a stream or patch
of wind through an old tree. Pause at this whisper from the Earth.
Pause there and be still. Your stillness is a form of listening. Be still
until you feel the largeness of what carries you.

The Need to Be in the World

Have you searched the vastness for something you have lost?

—ROBERT SERVICE

As astronauts spend time in space, weightlessness causes muscle atrophy. With little or no resistance required to move, their muscles and
bones harden and retract. Astronauts in their thirties can return to
Earth with the bone density of people in their seventies. Specific biological and chemical reactions cause this, but in our conversation with
the elements, we can perceive something deeper: that yearn as we do
to shed the weight of the world, we need to be in the world to realize
our dreams. Just as too much gravity is oppressive and crushing, the loss
of gravity doesn't free us but causes us to atrophy and disintegrate at
an accelerated rate. Paradoxically, the only way to make it through the
weight of the world is to stay in the world.

An ancillary paradox is at work in the kinship between light and
dark. We yearn so hard and long to be rid of darkness. Yet without dark,
there is no shadow. And without shadow, there is no depth perception.
Without any depth perception, we have no sense of direction, no sense
of what is near or far. In our need to find our way, we are asked not to
bypass darkness but to work with it and through it.

Still, it is humbling to realize that, though we need the elements of
nature, we cannot survive their pure force. Ten years ago, I made my
way to the Continental Divide in the Rocky Mountains, through Estes
Park in Colorado. I've always been drawn to wide-open spaces and was

eager to ascend, away from the human tangle. But as I made it past the tree line into the tundra, the bareness was as cold and forbidding as it was magnificent. It made me dizzy.

I stopped and sat in the crook of a large rock overlooking a vast canyon. I sat there long enough to regain my balance. By this time, the glare of wonder had evaporated. Just then, a mountain jay teased its way near me, swooping higher in the mountain air, where humans can't go. At that moment I heard the jay and mountain air and the cold stone holding me say in utter silence, *Go back among the living where you belong.*

I was shocked, but it was true. It made me realize that we are welcome to make pilgrimage up this far in the thin majesty of things. We are welcome to be humbled and cleansed, but we are meant to live lower; moving among the roots and branches; following the elusive songs of birds and the tracks of shy animals; all calling us to remember our fundamental nature.

A Reflective Pause

JOURNAL QUESTIONS

○ Describe a time when you wanted to be free of the world and yet the only way out was through. What steered you back into the world? What helped you through?

Moving Through the Dark

In nature, we are quietly offered countless models of how to give ourselves over to what appears dark and hopeless, but which ultimately is an awakening beyond our imagining. All around us, everything small and buried surrenders to a process that none of the buried parts can see. We call this process seeding and this innate surrender allows everything edible and fragrant to break ground into a life of light that we call spring. As a seed buried in earth can't imagine itself as an orchid or hyacinth, neither can a heart packed with hurt or a mind filmed over with despair imagine itself loved or at peace. The courage of the seed is that, once cracking, it cracks all the way. To move through the dark into blossom is the work of soul.

Worn Open by the World

Like it or not, to be in conversation with the Earth is to be worn open by the world. We cannot escape the weight of the world, but must move through it. We cannot bypass our seeding in the dark, if we are to blossom in the light. And we cannot avoid the tangle of the living.

The pioneer in mind-body science Candace Pert suggests that, though the brain may be located in the skull, the mind is located in the entire person. As well, though the ear may be located in the side of our head, our ability to listen is also located in our entire person.

In the deepest embodied sense, the ability to listen and receive makes an inlet of us. Through our very lives, we each become a passageway of soul worn open as the world of being keeps interchanging with the world of experience, both sluicing through us. And as much as our intelligence feels compelled to sort these streams and to keep them separate, our job in being alive is to let them merge and shape us. In daily terms, the work of listening is to be constantly worn free of our preconceptions and preferences so that nothing stands in the way of our direct experience of life.

The Ethic of Wonder

Nature never did betray the heart that loved her.

—WILLIAM WORDSWORTH

Let me share three stories about wonder. First, there was a little boy, no more than five, who lived in a cottage near the sea, and when he slept, night after night, the roll and rush of the sea kept washing over his head. The boy grew up to be the pianist Michael Jones, whose music always sounds like the sea. Michael says, "I carry a sense of playing and being played." When asked, the pianist with the sea in his head says,

"We have two glorious tasks: to be a good steward of the gift we are given and to wait upon that gift. This calls for deep and constant listening, the way a wave listens to the deep."

The second story comes from my dear friend Megan Scribner, who grew up in the Northwest, in Walla Walla, Washington, which bears the name of the Native American tribe indigenous to that region. That part of the country is laced with a network of underground springs which surface into a system of fresh rivers. This deep presence of water, connecting everything below the surface, affects the way of life in this region. The name Walla Walla, which means *place of many waters,* is a reminder of this unseen connection. It approximates the sound that the many waters continually make if you close your eyes and squat near the rivers . . . *walla walla walla walla walla walla walla walla* . . . In naming things this way, the tribe and town bear the ethic of wonder, which is that things worth honoring are named twice. The Kooskooskie River is another example. The word *koos* means *water* and its repetition implies an emphasis on *very clear water.* In Idaho, this river is known today as the Clearwater River.

Simply and profoundly, things that matter are repeated as a way to bring our full attention to them, as a way to meet them. Such naming through listening is the beginning of prayer.

The third story comes from my friend Allan Lokos, who has devoted years to playing the Native American flute. There are many versions of the flute's origin, which essentially go like this: All the creatures had found their song, but the human song was missing. So the Great Spirit spoke to his friends. In time, a tree branch was hollowed by the long spirit, erosion, and holes were pecked in it by the small spirit, woodpecker. Then the big spirit, weather, caused the hollowed, pecked branch to drop in the path of humans. A young man came along and while holding the branch, a bird flew overhead and offered its call. In that moment, the young man thought the birdsong came from the hollowed branch. When he realized what was happening, he closed his eyes and, breathing across the holes, prayed for the birdsong to return. To his surprise, he birthed a song of his own. In this way, the long spirit, the small spirit, and the big spirit caused humans to discover their song.

The ethic of wonder is how we listen to the Earth: waiting for the gift until things that matter repeat themselves through our love, until we kiss the hollowed things put in our way. All this leads us to our song.

A Reflective Pause

A MEDITATION

This is a meditation that leads to a journal question, based on when the pianist Michael Jones says, "We have two glorious tasks: to be a good steward of the gift we are given and to wait upon that gift."

○ Go to a favorite place in nature where being quiet and still lets you hear your deeper self.

○ Breathe deeply and slow your mind open.

○ Inhale and exhale, forgetting your long list of things to do.

○ Breathe deeply and slow your heart open.

○ Inhale and exhale, letting your gift show itself.

○ Breathe completely. Do not run from your gift. Do not ask anything of it. Simply welcome it and, like the Native Americans in Walla Walla, Washington, honor your gift by naming it twice.

JOURNAL QUESTION

○ Later in the day, open a conversation with your gift by writing its name several times, as a way to invoke its presence again. Wait for your gift to appear and ask of it: How can I be a good steward of you? How can I bring you through me into the world? Journal what comes.

TABLE QUESTIONS

To be asked over dinner or coffee with friends and loved ones. Try listening to everyone's response before discussing:

o Tell the story of someone you have believed in and how you saw the blossom in them when they were just a seed. Describe the work of soul they encountered. Have they blossomed? In your opinion, why or why not?

o Describe a time when a preconception or assumption you had prevented you from listening more deeply. What did this preconception keep you from? How were you able to put it down?

ONE LIVING SENSE

Like a cell in the heart that doesn't know
it is carried by a body, we float, work hard,
and drift in a sea of life on which we depend.

HEARING HAPPENS PHYSICALLY when a signal is generated in the ear that gathers discrete pieces of information from all the senses and sends the aggregate to the brain, which creates a brief and comprehensive sound from it all. What we call listening is actually an innate process that integrates an array of sensations we encounter through different ways of knowing (sight, smell, touch, taste, *and* sound). What we hear is the sum of life's vibrations, which constantly arrive like waves that soak into a perceptual shore that the oldest traditions call the mind-heart.

A vibrant example of such fundamental hearing is Evelyn Glennie, one of the most innovative percussionists in the world today, who is profoundly deaf. She says she lives the rhythms and feels the vibration of the music, not instead of hearing but as the foundation of all hearing. Her gift comes alive from opening herself to where the senses begin as one integrated sense. She views the hearing world's insistence on separating the living whole as a disability:

> *For some reason we tend to make a distinction between hearing a sound and feeling a vibration. In reality, they are the same thing.*

It is interesting to note that in the Italian language this distinc-
tion does not exist. The verb sentire *means to hear and the same*
verb, in the reflexive form, sentirsi *means to feel.*

The gifted percussionist begins beneath her deafness and notes, "Deafness does not mean that you can't hear, only that there is something wrong with the ears." There is great wisdom in this, for we can just as rightly say that numbness or indifference does not mean that you can't feel, only that there is something wrong with the heart. And just as the senses are knit together beneath our sorry attempts to isolate them, so are the muscles of the mind-heart: joy, sorrow, wonder, pain, acceptance, and more.

Perhaps our want to separate and pull apart what we can't understand is a spiritual disability. The art of listening may be to gather meaning from all the senses rather than to isolate and analyze what we think or feel at any one time. Through the bird's song, the music of nature calls us to listen to the whole, while the biology of nature has us dissecting the bird's vocal cords to see how they work. Clearly, the way things work in the physical world helps us to build, repair, and survive, but deep health resides in restoring the one living sense through which we can feel and participate in the web of life.

Still, we do not engage the one living sense to simply better ourselves. We do so to enliven and grow the web of life. Though all the introspective practices can help us better understand who we are, there is another reward for being here authentically. Somehow, these virtues of openness—such as truth telling, integrity, kindness, and love—give us access to our place in the living Oneness of the Universe. It's taken more than fifty years, but I have learned that *experiencing* Oneness can let us know joy. And joy is not just self-serving, but a sign that the Universe is working. Joy is the hum of Oneness. Our aim is not just to "get it together" as an individual, but to be a clear, integral cell in the heart of the world that keeps the Universe going. Joy is a barometer that lets us know that everything is well tuned. The work of being is to participate in this larger harmony, where hearing and feeling are the same thing. The work of being is to inhabit our aliveness. In such moments, we become a conduit for the Oneness of life.

The Heart Must Be Tuned

*It is the attainment of harmony that is called heaven, and
the lack of it that is termed hell . . . The harmony of life can
be learned in the same way as the harmony of music . . . As
with everything else in a person's life, there comes a change
in voice with every step forward in spiritual evolution. [And
so] every experience in life is an initiation . . . Any pain or
suffering is a preparation, and just as one must first tune
a violin to play it, so the heart must be tuned in order to
express wisdom.*

—HAZRAT INAYAT KHAN

So often we run from feeling and yet it is only through feeling that
we can know the depth of life. Only through feeling can we hold the
smallest shell or bone and feel the tug of the Universe. Such raw being
aches, for, as the Buddhists say, the bareness of being here is so full. I
wake with this rawness and watching you sleep, I'm stopped before I
start. Before I dress, I lose why I'm going anywhere. Yet wherever the
day takes me—pausing to hold the groceries with the old man who
packs them or seeing the neighbor's child at the kitchen table doing her
homework as I walk our dog or pulling over to watch the small horse
breathe his cloud over the fence—everywhere the bareness illumines.
With no way to that bareness but through feeling and the listening that
feeling opens. Some say I get lost in this feeling, this listening. But only
if I think I know where I'm going, only if I think I know what I'm listening for.

Through this bareness of being, we refresh our openness and enliven
our innate connection to the one living sense. Through our unblocked,
sincere response to life, we can tune our inner person with the great
mysteries, as U Thant suggests. And in a daily way, through listening
and feeling, we can tune the heart in order to express wisdom, as Hazrat Inayat Khan suggests. This is the art we are born with and that we
travel through life trying to learn and relearn: to animate our bareness
of being through listening and feeling.

Underneath all instruction, the world waits, utterly as it is. We circle it in paths called centuries, from which we describe life as either chaotically thrown together or harmoniously designed. In each generation, we take turns guarding against this bareness of being and seeking peace in it. We take turns: preparing for when things fall apart, and discovering the mystery beneath all that falls apart, in which everything physical is just the tip of an ineffable Universe organized beyond our comprehension. Of course, no one will ever know the true anatomy of the Universe, but it is still important for each of us to explore our own bareness of being. Our fundamental relationship to everything larger than us or our blindness to it determines what kind of life is possible. Each of us must continually assess, without ever knowing for certain, which way the Universe appears to be unfolding. Is it breaking apart or coming together? Or is it a weave of both?

How do we respond to the tide of experience that sweeps into our ordinary lives? Do we respond to the unknown by being absent or being present? Do we hoard or give? Do we circumvent the truth or move through the truth? Do we withdraw and hide or stand in the open and seek connection? Do we view difficulty and suffering as isolating obstacles that exploit our weakness and stall our progress in life? Or do we view these incidents as transforming waves of experience that are part of an ongoing emergence of who we are? Do we believe that life is a-pulling-apart we must survive or a constant rearrangement and putting together that we must surrender to? Do we run toward or from the bareness of being?

A Reflective Pause

JOURNAL QUESTIONS

- o Describe one way that experience has tuned your heart and how your voice has evolved for this deep tuning.

- o Is there a feeling you are currently avoiding or running from? Why? What would happen if you let that feeling touch you?

My Own Path

I was born with the ability to see in metaphor. This has been my inborn way of relating to the living Oneness of things. From an early age, the world has spoken to me in this way. The analogous relationship of things has called, not in words, but in a silent language that has somehow shown me, however briefly, the web of connection under everything. This gift is a function of presence; when I am present enough, metaphors appear. They are my teachers. All of my poems are just notes from these teachers. Seeing how things go together sustains me. The moment of such grasping is like a synapse that is fired and life-force is released. Presence and time are servants of light. In the moment of seeing, enlightenment is an experience, no matter how brief, of the light within you or me coinciding with the light in the world. In moments of enlightenment, like moments of poetry or love, we both lose who we are and sustain who we are. In such moments, we are sent back into ourselves illuminated.

The fact that I have lived a life as a poet is a testament to my friendship with metaphor. Along the way, the life of poetry exposed itself as a life of spirit. This in turn is a testament to my friendship with the connectedness of all things. For metaphor exists to praise the Oneness of things. Ultimately, it doesn't matter if we write anything down or not. True poetry happens the instant the metaphor is seen. The rest is blessed labor to make the invisible visible.

As an interior form of nature, metaphor exists with presence *regardless* of whether we see it or not. It is there to be seen the way a vista is seen for the climb, but both the metaphor and the view are there even when we neglect the climb.

After a lifetime of climbing, it's clear that the human form of light is love. And only presence and time can comfort love into being, the way immense sunshine and heat cause the light within a seed hidden in the earth to seek its own nature and somehow break ground.

My own path of listening has led me here, for much of my life has been devoted to staying in conversation with everything around me—with the mystery, with God or Source, with the rivers of change, with you. As I get older, I long even more for the wisdom and companionship of other living things; to stay in conversation with all I love, with all I admire, with all who have suffered and given of themselves to stay alive and to keep life going. In many ways, our stories are part of one story. Our pain is part of one pain. Our surprise at the beauty and fragility of life is part of one chorus of awe. My passion now is to stay as close as possible to the pulse of what is kind and true; to stay in conversation with what happens there and to experience more and more ways to listen.

Over the years, the trail of these conversations has become the books I write. The further I go, the more of one water they are, as if each book is a different-shaped bucket which I haul to the sea, scooping what I can. Each book uncovers some learning that leads to the next. In this way, each book—like this one—is a teacher, leading me more deeply into the many ways of being here.

A Reflective Pause

JOURNAL QUESTION

o Trace your own history and evolution as a listener, describing three key experiences that have shaped what listening has meant to you and what you have heard along the way that has opened you to life and your place in it.

The Impulse Toward Unity

Pierre Teilhard de Chardin (1881–1955), a mystic who took vows as a Jesuit priest, was a student of the living Oneness of things. Trained as a paleontologist and philosopher, Teilhard understood life as an ineffable tapestry into which all forms of life are constantly weaving. In his writings, he describes this movement as part of our fundamental nature. He suggests that biological evolution is part of a larger evolution in which all life is converging toward an ultimate unity. The spiritual gravity we know as love draws us to that unity. "Sooner or later," Teilhard

declares, "we shall have to acknowledge that love is the fundamental impulse of life."

Artists and dancers know this at some level and search for it through their creations. As the legendary dancer Martha Graham said to Agnes de Mille in 1943, "It is your business . . . to keep the channel open." Out of such transparency of the human heart, things of value are created and *we* are created. Such openness requires two ongoing devotions: the risk to be, to slow to the pace of creation, where all things join; and the courage not just to *let* through whatever comes up, but to *sing* it through. The courage to voice what we experience, the way a coyote howls, out of a visceral joy at being a living thread in this living tapestry.

God is an infinite secret hiding in the open, waiting for each of us to slow enough to inhabit our aliveness through our bareness of being. When we can do so, we become conduits of spirit that continually converge toward an ultimate unity, as Teilhard suggests. This is how life-forms begin and continue: energy moves through particles, bringing them together, but it is the mysterious openness of the particle that enables the chain of life to assemble. And what is the human heart, if not the most mysterious and transparent particle of being known to humankind?

I'm reflecting on all this while driving home from work in the light snow, thousands of flakes drifting to earth, the car squeaking through them. Each flake like each of us, but together we form a mist of being that never dries. The snow leads me to the canopied trees. Some are growing and at the same time some are dying. Now I'm trying to imagine—*to listen to and feel*—all the trees on Earth that I can't see. They are anything but a still life. And for each tree, I try to imagine—*to listen to and feel*—each human life. Some of us are growing and some of us are dying. Such listening and feeling makes us lean into each other, makes us yearn to know our connection. Now I can sense all of life growing and dying at the same time and, yes, this growing and dying and yearning is the inhalation and exhalation of a living Universe.

If we listen close enough and long enough, we inhale and exhale in unison with the inhalation and exhalation of everything living. During a recital in Berlin, the legendary classical guitarist Andrés Segovia heard his guitar emit a loud cracking sound. He rushed offstage and, cradling his instrument, kept repeating, "My guitar, my guitar." Segovia soon learned that the man who built the guitar had died in Madrid. If dogs can hear earthquakes beginning at the center of the Earth and Arctic Terns can migrate halfway around the world, who's to say that the heart tuned to wisdom can't hear the one living sense that connects us all?

A Reflective Pause

A MEDITATION

- Wherever you are, center yourself.

- With each breath, become aware of the life around you.

- With each breath, allow the sensation of life birthing and dying at once to settle in your heart.

- Do not try to make sense of this, just feel it.

- Breathe fully and let the full range of life happening around the world at once move in and out of you.

- Notice how the touch of a living Universe makes you feel.

TABLE QUESTIONS

To be asked over dinner or coffee with friends and loved ones. Try listening to everyone's response before discussing:

- While a fundamental gift of the mind is to analyze, a fundamental gift of the heart is to feel. Discuss a time when you analyzed something instead of feeling it and where that led you. And discuss a time when you felt something instead of analyzing it and where that led you.

- Tell the story of a moment in which you felt the hum of Oneness.

DEEP LISTENING

Deep listening is more than hearing with our ears, but taking in what is revealed in any given moment with our body, our being, our heart.

—SUSAN McHENRY

IF THE PURPOSE and gift of love is to awaken and reawaken what is dormant within us, then when awake it is our responsibility to stay awake and keep the gift alive. We do this by deep listening. Not toward a goal or even toward a noble ambition but as a way of life, staying devoted to listening with our heart—*more than once, to everything.*

The faster we spin or are spun, the more we are thrown to the top where we grow mental and heady. When we slow or are slowed, things settle lower—in the heart, in the gut. As the Hawaiian elder Puanani Burgess says, "Your gut is where your best thinking happens. . . . [For] it is in the *na'au* (the gut/intestines) that we bring the mind, heart and emotions and intuitions and experiences together."

Deep listening mixes the grit of our humanness with the dust of the stars, retrieving in the exchange an indestructible and life-giving connection. The word *Brahma* in Sanskrit literally means *that from which everything arises, the Source of all.* Connecting to that living essence or Source is experiencing God through all the doorways life has to offer. The practice of connecting to the Source of all is participating in the world's soul. This is the aim of deep listening.

A Reflective Pause

JOURNAL QUESTIONS

○ From your experience, what is the difference between listening and deep listening?

○ From your experience, what does "participating in the world's soul" mean to you?

Below Our Answers

You can run around your mind three times, chanting on and on, and you still won't run out of assumptions.

—NANCY EVANS BUSH

Deep listening requires letting go of our internal argument with the world. Before we can truly listen, we must exhaust ourselves of our assumptions. In truth, if we are to ever glimpse the world outside the stubborn certainty of our minds, we have to put down our ready answer to everything. This necessitates an inner discipline so that I don't finish your sentence in my mind, or search my storehouse of opinions for a rebuttal or defense of the world as I see it. Letting go of my internal argument with the world means not pushing off of everything that comes my way. It requires my looking at you as a sudden fish that has surfaced from the deep. It requires bringing you water rather than my judgments.

Every time we speak, we have to discern: are we speaking honestly or just barking from our wall into all we are afraid of? And every time we receive, are we actually hearing the truth of another or are we preparing the next argument like a brick to strengthen our wall? We often wear so many opinions that wonder has very little chance of touching our skin. We all struggle with this. Yet the courage to be begins with the risk to let that instant of unknowing grow between what is said to us and our reflex to ready our response. Much of our isolation and sense of difference comes from our inability to slow down and let in what is before us. Regardless of the medium, this is the beginning of art, the honest listening, without pretense or judgment, to life as it meets us. Listening is not reacting or responding but meeting experience openly, the way a lake is filled by streams.

The German philosopher Georg Hegel (1770–1831) described the dialectic process whereby one idea (a thesis) truly engaged with another (an antithesis) can yield a third, new idea (a synthesis) that is born from both but which is wholly neither. This way of reasoning is often described dryly as a calculus of fresh thinking, but when we truly behold each other, it is nothing less than how our honest impressions of being alive birth insights of Wholeness that neither of us could have come upon alone.

Hegel's dialectic itself brings together elemental notions of experience that are found in sources as diverse as Buddha and Heraclitus. This means that life is constantly changing, and we and everything around us move forward by the push and pull of other life, which in the moment seems like obstacle after obstacle. This means that changes, one by one, lead inevitably to a series of turning points that challenge us to re-create who we are and where we're going. Hegel suggests that, while we can feel like we're chasing our own tail, the human path of growth is more like an endless spiral—similar but different as our lives unfold.

So the physics of deep listening is that we stumble beautifully into the spaces between our sufferings. This is why we dare to listen, so we might drop together into the truth that holds us all. In a spiritual sense, to synthesize means to discover the coherent whole of life that connects us by daring to mix our individual elements. The way blue and yellow mixed will make green visible, your heart and mine, mixed through true listening, will make visible the color of the Earth.

Pulling Threads

I want to speak about a particular way of listening that being a poet has taught me through the years. I confess that I no longer search for subject matter. As the years wear the faces off statues and the crests off warriors' shields, I have been worn of the lines between what is visible and invisible, what is objective and subjective, what is real and imagined. I can no longer distinguish between the life of poetry and the poetry of life—*Thankfully!*

This deepening into Wholeness has shifted how I encounter experience and the world. Now, I *relate* to what needs to be said more than author it. I walk down a street in summer and moments glow and call; each holds all of the mystery, the way one drop of ocean contains the entire ocean, the way one small act of love contains all the feeling of everyone who's ever loved.

The task now is to slow down enough and be present enough to enter each moment that calls. As if each enlivened instant—the sudden light on a crow's beak as it pecks the ground, the shadow that covers the sad girl's face as she stares into her half-eaten sandwich—each is a thread in the fabric of the Universe, each imbued and teeming with Spirit and wisdom. The task now is to be humble enough and attentive enough to pull the threads. And when I do, without fail, the threads unravel the cocoon of our own making that shrouds us from the mystery that is always present.

Who would have guessed? Nothing is wanting but we in our want. Nothing is fragmented but we in our isolation. Nothing is completely dark but we in our hesitation. So it turns out that the Universe—the endless fabric of now, the weave of all life, which is timeless—is the one and only subject. And listening for it, to it, with it, we are privileged to become glowing threads ourselves. All of us, God willing, here to unravel each other and to love back together what we find.

We are left with the beautiful chance to spill our presence into the world. In this way, we can irrigate each other. For each of us has a particular piece of wisdom that we might coax to speak. Each of us with a bit of eternity that, if not brought forward, will be lost; or at least stay silent during our time on Earth. This piece of inner wisdom that is in everything and yet which you alone carry doesn't have a name. We could call it your soul. So as you would honor a grandparent or teacher, how will you befriend that in you which has no name? What kind of relationship will you have with the oldest part of your life, so it might speak to you?

The One Note

We could call that from which everything arises the One Note at the center of everything. Some say this is the note we hear while being born, that we search for our whole lives. Perhaps babies crying at birth are trying to tell us the secrets of life in the only language they have. Perhaps this early cry becomes the song of the One Note that we spend our lives trying to rediscover.

The pianist Michael Jones reminds us that musicians and composers began with a need to find and play the One Note. Early on, composers used to go into nature and listen to farmers and peasants singing in the fields. They would then base their sonatas and symphonies on the common sounds they heard in how human beings worked in the earth.

In 1916, Anton Dvořák said that some fundamental aspect of music had died because, in the modern age, farmers had stopped singing and musicians had stopped listening. Dvořák and Michael Jones raise two questions that are crucial to how art has always served life. First, what is it about the cycle of experience—especially in modern life—that numbs us from singing while we work and from hearing each other? And even more important, what must we relearn in order to remember how to touch the Earth and sing, to remember how to listen to each other and turn that listening into music? Art has always helped us touch the Earth and sing. It has always helped us rediscover the One Note. Art, the great inner bridge that lets the song of inwardness sing us. In all its forms, art has always given us a way to recover from the numbness of experience.

During her travels to what was Yugoslavia, a friend wandered at night in the rubble of a Slavic town still smoldering from its latest ethnic battle. To her surprise, she came upon a sad, broken minstrel who played a one-string instrument in the rubble. The singer and the instrument were both called *Guzla,* a singer of tales. My friend listened as the one string and the one voice braided in drift through the night smoke. One string always playing the One Note. One voice always telling the One story. Many times in many ways. Don't we recognize each other when hearing this note? Isn't this the story of existence? Doesn't Spirit pluck its endless notes in each soul during our time on Earth? Aren't

common humanity

what it means to be alive

we reduced by pain and beauty to take our turn as a Guzla, a singer of tales? Aren't we stopped beyond memory, whether we admit it or not, to say to ourselves and each other, "I have found you. You have found me. I've known you for a long time."

A Reflective Pause

JOURNAL QUESTION

○ Watch someone doing something they love. Listen to the motion and rhythms of how they work. Name and describe the song of their work.

In Equal Measure

Like Newton's law of gravity, in which every action has an equal and opposite reaction, we can understand the degrees of listening in a similar way. In essence, we hear in equal measure to what we listen with. When we listen with our mind, we understand more of life. When we listen with our heart, we feel more of life. When we listen with our entire being and spirit, we are transformed and joined with life itself.

And so, life waits full-born in the moments of our lives. How we meet and listen to these moments unfolds the path of our own transformation. We can meet such a moment in our youth or in our thirties and carry it like a seed until experience waters that seed open many years later. Then, if blessed, the opening of that moment from the inside out might blossom our eyes, changing everything.

However we come upon it, to recognize and *see* such a moment can give us insight. This is valuable by itself. To relate to and *feel* such a moment can strengthen our heart through compassion and humility. This too is valuable by itself. But when we can *enter* such a moment, the world touches us with its unwavering illumination. Listening at such an intimate and complete level allows us the privilege of being permanently touched by what we encounter. When we can treat what comes our way not as an object but as a meeting with the living, then deep listening evokes a devotion that says, *Stay in relationship with everything.*

Destiny

If life is a river, then destiny is the unseen current that has come before us and that will continue after us. All we are left with is to find that current and to join it. This changes how I understand ambition. My ambition now is to listen for the water of time as it opens my gills, to feel the wind of truth as it bends my human grass, and to receive the ancient rain of insight as it softens my mind. All to create a pool in the center of my heart where strangers and friends alike can float and watch the stars.

A Reflective Pause

A MEDITATION

- ○ Close your eyes and center yourself.

- ○ Inhale cleanly and feel the current of all life, which is timeless.

- ○ Exhale cleanly and know that this current came before and it will continue after you.

- ○ Breathe fully and consider that how you join and move with this current is your destiny.

- ○ Open your eyes and enter your day, ready to find this current, ready to be unraveled of your plans, ready to love what you find.

TABLE QUESTIONS

To be asked over dinner or coffee with friends and loved ones. Try listening to everyone's response before discussing:

- ○ Do you have an internal argument with the world? What is it, where does it come from, and what does it do to you to carry it?

○ Tell a recent story of when you reflexively pulled an opinion out of your storehouse of opinions, shared it with others, and what that did to the conversation.

○ Describe a time when the truth of your heart mixed with the truth of another. Describe what your combined honesty opened.

○ Tell the story of one thread of attention you pulled and where it led you.

○ We are reminded here that there is "One string always playing the One Note. One voice always telling the One story. Many times in many ways."

Share a story in which you felt the presence of the One string or the One voice or the One story.

After everyone has had a turn, try together to describe the One string or the One voice or the One story.

○ Describe a time when you listened with your mind and what you heard.

Describe a time when you listened with your heart and what you heard.

Describe a time when you listened with your spirit and what you heard.

After listening to everyone, discuss the differences.

?

In the last six chapters, we've seen that taking things in—listening and internalizing what we hear with body and mind—is essential to living. The work of being reaffirms our own capacity for wisdom, which depends on our willingness to taste life directly. We have seen that the heart over time tries on many faces. In no particular order: it will sift the best from life; it will strain and filter the difficult lessons; it will give up trying to get things for itself; it will live as an instrument nourishing others. At times, the heart will live like a sponge, absorbing without preference and giving without holding back.

On the other side of experience, the heart meets its own wisdom when there is little left to say. It is here that we finally listen to silence. But having to live in the world, we spiral in and out of peace as our taste for the fight dissolves into a need for the ancient quiet, again and again. What sustains us are the moments with nothing in the way, when the light of the world kisses the light of the heart and each breath shines. This is the art we are born with that we travel through life trying to learn and relearn: to animate our bareness of being through listening and feeling.

Through "The Work of Being," we've been exploring our friendship with everything larger than us, which holds the wisdom of Source. Tending this friendship is the work of being. This is both personal and Universal and never-ending. Take some time to describe your friendship at this point with everything larger than you. How does Source speak to you? What do you hear? What has the living presence of the Universe said to you lately? If this presence seems distant, how can you move closer to it? How comfortable are you with taking things in, with internalizing what you experience? How can you face the pain of being stuck, which makes us afraid to go deeper? Have you let go of your internal argument with the world? Can you trust that the Wholeness of life waits beneath your arguments and your brokenness? Can you trust that you are not alone?

These are important inner tasks that we can't figure out alone. Do you have inner companions, friends you can talk to about the journey to be real? If not, what steps can you take to find a few meaningful friends? Can you refresh your ethic of wonder by listening to the Earth? Can you repeat what matters until it turns into a song?

All of this is part of the work of being. All of this is an invitation into a deeper relationship with life. All of this waits in the daily unfolding of our experience. All of this lives in the opening of our eyes, in the opening of our breath, in the opening of our heart. Waiting in each seeing, in each breathing, in each feeling.

We will be inquiring next into our friendship with experience, which holds the wisdom of life on Earth. This is the work of being human.

THE
WORK OF
BEING
HUMAN

I have lost so many, have lost so much, and each has been a breaking away, a letting go, the way clumps of earth that hold the river are worn free by the river. So the river of experience scours the small container that is our life deeper and deeper.

In Japanese mythology, the crane becomes immortal at the age of two thousand, when it is done being a crane. And the tortoise becomes immortal at the age of ten thousand, when it starts being a wave. So perhaps the purpose of experience is to wear us free of our names. Perhaps, underneath all the distinctions we can imagine—all spiritual paths are one, all philosophies are one, all occupations and passions are one. Perhaps all our ambitions and desires are like different cups dipping in the same well at center. And every name—every praise and blame—is such a cup, each holding the same sweet water. Perhaps it doesn't matter what carries us to and from that well but only that we drink. Could experience be for humans what erosion is for the elements? Is the purpose of experience, over a lifetime, to carry us to what matters and then wear us away till we become part of the sweet water the next generation drinks? If this is so, then what is the work of being human? There is no tangible answer, any more than we can ask fire why it burns. But like a crane flying steadily till its wings disappear or a tortoise swimming mightily till its shell wears away, we can live our way into knowing.

HOW WE LEARN

THE GREAT BUDDHIST teacher Pema Chödrön tells this story:
During the teaching known as the Heart Sutra, Buddha actually
didn't say a word. He went into a state of deep meditation and let
the bodhisattva of compassion, Avalokiteshvara, do the talking. This
courageous warrior, also known as Kuan-yin, expressed his experience
of the prajñāpāramitā (the perfection of wisdom) on behalf of Buddha.
His insight was not based on intellect but came through his practice of
deep listening. Then one of the principal disciples of Buddha, a monk
named Shariputra, began to question Avalokiteshvara. Inspired by
Shariputra's questioning, Avalokiteshvara continued. When the great
bodhisattva finished teaching, Buddha came out of his meditation and
said, "Good, good! You expressed it perfectly!"

The *how* of this story—how each person relates to the hidden
Wholeness of life and to each other—is a koan about education and
truth seeking; about how we learn and how we teach; about the sacred
relationship between teacher and student and the elusive nature of who
is teacher and who is student in any given moment.

At first, Buddha goes inward in deep meditation to experience the
underlying stream of life. Here immersion and absorption in silence
are the primary means of learning, and presence is the main means of
teaching. Then Avalokiteshvara somehow goes inward himself to the
vital space between him and Buddha, where he retrieves what he can of
all that is inexpressible and ciphers it into meaningful speech for the living. This suggests a devoted form of translation as the primary means
of learning and teaching. Finally, the monk Shariputra neither imitates

Buddha, holy as he is, nor is he blindly obedient to Avalokiteshvara, compassionate as he is. More deeply, Shariputra receives what he can and engages it through questions until he can hold it more personally.

When Buddha comes out of his meditation and says, "Good, good! You expressed it perfectly!" I like to think that the "you" is plural and refers to the honest exchange between Avalokiteshvara and Shariputra that pushes the stone aside so the seed Buddha retrieves can be planted.

The implication is that such learning flows in all directions: Shariputra's respectful questioning inspires the compassionate one, and the deep attempt to translate the presence of truth inspires the holy one, whose deep meditation inspired everyone in the first place. All the practices of lasting education are here: listening to the Source in silence; listening with heart to those who experience the Source and translating that presence into meaningful speech; and listening to the teaching, whoever or whatever may convey it, and furthering it in the world through deep questioning and honest dialogue.

In essence, the parable of how the Heart Sutra appears suggests that deep silence, deep speech, and deep questioning lead us to a depth of heart that lives below illusion. Each of us has *a deep listener* or Buddha within, *a deep speaker* or Avalokiteshvara within, as well as *a deep questioner* or Shariputra within. And living below illusion in the wondrous and gritty nature of things-as-they-are becomes our daily practice, by listening, translating, and questioning our experience.

We all take turns experiencing and translating and questioning. We even interchange these roles within our own lives. It is the way Spirit grows its presence in the world, a moment and exchange at a time.

A Reflective Pause

JOURNAL QUESTION

o Which part of you—your deep listener, your deep speaker, or your deep questioner—is the most experienced and which needs more of your attention? If each is a teacher, what has each taught you?

Deep Listening

We listen deeply by listening to the Source through immersion, absorption, and presence. The way Beethoven listened in the supreme silence of his deafness until the music of the spheres cascaded through as the Ninth Symphony. The way Einstein kept things in motion long enough to hear the whispers of relativity. The way the clairvoyant listens to the currents that run between the living and the dead, unsure of the signs they receive. The way the heart can feel the ache of another halfway around the world, unsure what brings such sadness. The way I knew my grandmother at ninety-four was waiting for me to come so she could die.

How might you practice listening deeply? We can always begin by allowing ourselves to sink into the depth of whatever moment we are in. For depth is ever-present. We don't have to travel to find depth. We simply have to relax our minds into the ground of where we are, the way roots unravel in the earth after a long, soaking rain.

A Reflective Pause

A MEDITATION

- I invite you to enter a space you are drawn to, a woods or open field, or to walk along a stream, or climb a height.

- Once in this space, slow your breathing till your entire being is one large ear.

- Let your inhaling take in all that you hear.

- Note what surrounds you and touches you, even if it defies normal hearing.

- If you can, breathe as one large act of hearing.

- Let your exhaling be how what you hear rejoins the space.

- When you encounter others in the days to follow, try to emanate what you have heard, not using words. There will be time enough to speak.

Deep Speaking

We speak deeply by listening with heart to the Source, no matter who or what conveys it, and translating that presence into meaningful speech. There are mythic examples, including Moses coming down from Mount Sinai and his brother Aaron translating the prophet's stammerings to the people in the desert. Or Jesus, whose spoken parables were passed from his disciples and followers to the eventual writers of the Gospels. Or Socrates, who wrote nothing himself though his singular student Plato captured and worked his teacher's wisdom. Or the mystic Rumi, whirling and whirling in order to listen below the habits of his mind while those who loved him scribed his poems. These are archetypes of the human journey writ large.

In quiet ways, we all take turns being the one compelled up the mountain. Or the one tempted in the desert. Or the one questioning the blind promises of the society he is born into. Or the one trying to spin free of his assumptions in order to see life afresh.

In our daily life, it might be as simple and profound as listening to a piece of piano music so completely that it enables you to speak from a place inside that has been covered over since you were a boy left all alone in the wonder. This happened to me when I started to speak of God as something larger than I could comprehend. It might come after surviving a serious illness, when thrown back into life, no longer able to pretend that expectations and judgments matter. Or words could suddenly rush from your mouth like a hive of bees drunk on the nectar they carry. And some of those near you will run thinking they will be stung. While others will stay thinking they have been given something incredibly sweet.

How might you practice speaking deeply? The first thing is to accept and work with what you hear. We so filter what we hear through what we believe that we limit what we take in to only what is familiar. This narrows our understanding of things as they are. I can hear thunder and not be that thunder, just as I can hear pain and not be that pain. And I can hear conflict and not believe in that conflict. Speaking deeply has something to do with letting things pass through our heart as they are, the way ink is pressed through silk to imprint a lasting design that we can wear.

A Reflective Pause

TABLE QUESTIONS

To be asked over dinner or coffee with friends and loved ones. Try listening to everyone's response before discussing:

o I invite you, in the next week, to stop and listen without expectation to another person; to their words, below their words, to the space that surrounds them, to the presence you feel once they leave. Can you listen to the silence beneath their presence?

o Don't speak of these listenings for several days. Let them steep in you like green tea.

o Once their presence and meaning have brewed, sit with a loved one or friend and convey what has touched you. What might such an experiment teach you?

Deep Questioning

We question deeply by listening to what is offered and surfacing its meaning and usefulness through further questioning and honest dialogue. The way Audubon questioned the flight of birds through his endless sketching. The way Gandhi questioned the authority of a century by walking barefoot to the sea. The way the maid Janabai became a great teacher and poet while grinding wheat in fourteenth-century Pandharpur. The way great healers tune in to the braille of the body with their fingers. The way my friend's small child wants to know why the colors of the leaves don't splash into each other when they mix on the ground. The way the same child as a teenager will ask me the same thing about all of our feelings. The way the old woman who survived the war would listen to those who sought her out and by evening sigh, "What you say is true. But every trouble wants to draw the very best of you into the world."

How might you practice questioning deeply? Think of a deep question as a door that opens between you and what you experience, not as a veiled way to criticize or take things apart, or as a strategy to bide some time till we can pursue our own agenda. What can you ask that will open that door? What can you ask that will let you enter what has been opened? A sign of a good question is that the questioner is more alive for having asked it.

A Reflective Pause

JOURNAL QUESTIONS

○ I invite you to listen with your heart till you admit to a question you are currently carrying. Call to this question honestly so it might open like a door in your life right now. How can you use your sincerity to open it further? What does it feel like to enter this door? What is it opening?

Part of the mystery of Oneness is that, like the sun, its light is everywhere and yet we need to grow toward that Oneness to know its light. To open our experience, we need to enliven our deep listener, deep speaker, and deep questioner. These skills are as essential as waking, breathing, and eating.

A Reflective Pause

A MEDITATION

○ Wait a week and retell the story of how the Heart Sutra came to be to someone you care about.

RESTORING CONFIDENCE

Help me resist the urge
to dispute whether things
are true or false
which is like
arguing whether
it is day or night.

It is always
one or the other
somewhere in the world.

Together, we can penetrate
a higher truth which
like the sun is always
being conveyed.

THIS POEM CAME to me during an unclear time when I was letting
go of God as a directive force and discovering God by many names
as the mysterious atmosphere in which we all live. My inability to see
clearly led me below my own conflicting opinions into the sea that
holds all thoughts. From that comprehensive sea, this poem came one
morning in a whisper. It has helped me greatly. Through holding it and
reciting it and turning it over, I have discovered that losing confidence
has to do with being drawn into surface listening, which splits me into
dualistic thinking, and restoring confidence has to do with resisting that

draw until I can listen my way more deeply into the realm where things are always joined as part of a living Oneness.

This led me to learn more about the word *confidence*. The Indo-European root of *confidence* is *bheidh,* which means *to trust and abide,* from the German *bīdan, to wait trustingly.* The word *restore* means *to bring back to life.* Restoring confidence then has something to do with *bringing our trust back to life.* This presumes that we will lose our trust in life and therefore need to understand the practice of restoring that trust. Being human, we all suffer this drift into confusion and are all uplifted by the steerage back to an aligned clarity. This cycle is part of our growth, part of our incarnation as human beings: glorious, painful, mysterious, frustrating, and unavoidable.

The Practice of Not-Knowing

> The deepest words
> of the wise . . . teach us
> the same as the whistle of the wind when it blows
> or the sound of the water when it is flowing.

—ANTONIO MACHADO

To bring trust back to life requires the deepest sort of listening. I'm still learning how to listen in this way. Even after sixty years, it feels elusive, as the most important teachers whisper behind the wind to ensure that we give ourselves totally to discovering their secrets. Two such teachers are not-knowing and paradox. Essentially, I have learned that true knowledge that can help us live waits on the other side of our ability to hold two things at once that are both true. One aspect of true knowledge that came to me through my experience with cancer is the paradox that we need to die in order to live. I am still trying to understand the daily meaning of this.

But let's talk a bit about paradox. Where conflict is the tension created by two mutually exclusive choices (You can't be in two places at the same time), paradox is the tension of seeming opposites which we need to endure till we can fall beneath the illusion of their separateness into the living truth of how they inform each other. (In our heart, we *can* be in two places at the same time.)

Paradox means *beyond belief,* from the Greek *para* (*beyond*) and *dox* (*belief*). I take *beyond belief* to mean more than *unbelievable,* but rather *beyond our current understanding of things.* This is not just abstract information. Engaging paradox is crucial because, without the courage and patience to listen below the surface of things—without the ability to wait trustingly—we are never baptized into the full depth of life. In just this way, I was drawn through cancer beyond belief, beyond my understanding of things, into the painful and liberating journey of dying in order to fully live.

A Reflective Pause

JOURNAL QUESTION

○ Tell the story of how some aspect of who you are has fallen away and died and what new way of being has replaced it.

It seems our capacity to withstand the tension of opposites is key to entering paradox, and key to that is becoming comfortable with the space of not-knowing. Understandably, most of us are uncomfortable when things are undefined, when things are not clearly to or fro, up or down, left or right, or right or wrong. But the deeper truths always take time to reach us, and it is our job to enter a practice of waiting openly—which involves enduring the tensions of not-knowing. This requires a crucial, ongoing effort *not* to prematurely name or define what we encounter in life. The truths that matter require us *not* to form opinions or beliefs hastily. On the contrary, we are asked to allow time to surround us with the Wholeness of life, to take the time required for the paradox of truth to show itself.

All the traditions confirm that paradox is not the end but the beginning. It is the threshold of transformation. When we can lean into the realm in which all things are true and stay there, however briefly, we find ourselves in the midst of that higher truth in which it is always day or night somewhere in the world. My own experience has made me realize that it is not enough just to see paradox; we somehow need to inhabit it and even embrace it. Despite my efforts to resist this not-knowing, I have exhausted myself into an alarming but ultimately beautiful surrender to the *experience* of paradox. And being in relationship with paradox is what leads us into transformation.

So where do we begin? It seems that the practice of not-knowing begins with a trust in the unnamable space that holds us, in the mysterious atmosphere in which we all live. That seems to be the true space of listening and learning, where our brief experiences of life in its totality, whether harsh or calm, will not fit into our tidy little maps of perception. Until I had cancer, until I found myself close to death, I had, in very typical fashion, thought of life and death as two different continents, one leading to the other. But almost dying thrust me below these distinctions, below the map of names. And in that tide of pure, unnamable experience, life and death pooled together; indistinguishable, one *informing* the other. Being spit back into the days like Jonah from the mouth of the whale, how can I return to the map I was given that presumed they are different?

After all this way, I can only affirm that this trust in not-knowing has always been essential. Yet where are we educated in this? Where are we taught to withstand the surf and undertow of ambiguity and confusion long enough till we can drift in the majestic swell that sages and poets of all traditions have called the unity of life?

A Reflective Pause

A MEDITATION

- ○ Sit in a comfortable place where you feel safe.

- ○ Inhale deeply and, for the moment, forget where you have come from.

○ Exhale deeply and, for the moment, forget what awaits you when you leave this meditation.

○ Follow whatever light is near you and remember that not-knowing doesn't always lead to fear.

○ Be thankful for the patch of light before you.

○ Breathe freely and try not to name or define what is before you.

○ Breathe slowly and practice not-knowing by receiving the many truths that exist at once, the way an inlet accepts water from any direction.

○ When you stand, leave your opinions in the light.

○ Enter your day with a commitment to deepen your trust in life.

TABLE QUESTION

To be asked over dinner or coffee with friends and loved ones. Try listening to everyone's response before discussing:

○ Discuss a situation you lived through in which the truth involved more than just your point of view. How do you understand what happened?

HONEYCOMBS AND
THINKING-STRINGS

"My body needs strength so I can hear my thinking-strings,"
said Grandfather Mantis, while eating honeycombs.

THIS DECLARATION IS from a South African tale in which
Grandfather Mantis needs to hear his thinking-strings in order to
figure out how to keep the aging sun up in the sky. Embedded in this
moment is an entire philosophy of life and a description of how one
form of life renews another in a mystical chain of being that keeps the
world going. Honoring these connections can renew us when we feel
too tired to go on.

The story unfolds as the creatures begin to miss the sun's warmth,
only to discover that the aging sun is tiring from its daily path across
the sky. They turn to Grandfather Mantis for a solution since he has
a gift for surviving. Now Grandfather Mantis realizes that, in order to
think clearly, his body needs strength, and for that to happen he needs
nourishment. So he takes his sandal and slaps it to the earth, at which
moment the sandal becomes a dog that runs straightaway to retrieve
honeycombs for Grandfather Mantis to eat. Eating the honeycombs
strengthens his body, which enables him to hear his thinking-strings.

That his thoughts come to him through thinking-strings implies
that ideas are retrieved, not created. Refreshed and strong, Grandfather
Mantis listens and then charges all the creatures to lift the tiring sun at
dawn, just before it wakes, and to give it a boost up into the highest

sky. They all do this and, once aloft, the sun is carried by the higher current, back and forth across the sky, until its warmth is again available to all.

Within this story, the immediate remedy for a waning life-force resides in the trust that each part of life affects all the others and that each part has a role to play in keeping the other parts well and functioning. The underlying secret to releasing that remedy seems to be the realization that no living thing is the sole author of its vitality—life-force flows from one living thing to another. So when feeling weary and out of sorts, the first thing we can do is to see where our connecting points to life are dislodged. This is no different than checking if the plug is cleanly in the socket when the lamp begins to flicker.

A Reflective Pause

JOURNAL QUESTIONS

Now feeling trapped

○ Describe the last two times you were weary and out of sorts. Explore if the things that made you weary have anything in common. What restored your energy in each case? Explore if the things that restored you have anything in common. How would you name and describe the source of your energy and vitality and what you do to connect with that?

not honey we get

The story reveals some fundamental understandings about what is nourishing, how we think, and how we stay warm and lighted. In order to think clearly, Grandfather Mantis eats honeycombs. Now, honey itself is that sweet thickness produced by bees from the nectar of flowers. Thousands of bees belonging to a hive gather the nectar from thousands of flowers blooming in spring. They then bring that nectar back to the hive where, in the center, they create honey. In the center of the hive, they store the honey in an amazingly thin-walled honeycomb that they construct of beeswax. Elsewhere in the honeycomb, the larvae of unborn bees are incubated.

Empathy

So when Grandfather Mantis eats honeycombs to strengthen his body and think clearly, he is eating this entire process. He is eating the flowers breaking ground on the other side of winter and the nectar forming in the heart of every flower. He is eating the search of a thousand bees scenting after the nectar and their bringing it back to the center of the hive. He is eating the mysterious way they turn that nectar into honey and the hive's industry at turning their wax into a honeycomb. He is surrendering to the fact that, in order to be strong and clear, we need to internalize the unending way that the variety of life is tripped upon and gathered and worked into one thick sweetness.

It is the strength gained from *taking-such-Wholeness-in* that allows Grandfather Mantis to hear his thinking-strings. Just as the Greek aeolian harp was placed on the top of a mountain till music was revealed by the wind moving through its strings, this South African tale suggests that the mind doesn't really originate thoughts, but places itself in the open so the larger forces can play our mind's strings. Like Grandfather Mantis, our job is to hear the thoughts and insights plucked on our thinking-strings.

This tale implies a way of life that involves taking in how the world works in order to be strong enough to hear the forces of life pluck our thinking-strings and make music in our minds. And all toward what end? Nothing less than keeping the sun in its course across the sky. We need everything and everyone to keep everything going. By helping each other, we can re-enter the strongest currents of life and be carried along. This is how the parts keep the Universe whole, and how the Whole keeps the parts vital.

All this is embedded in these two lines from a South African tale. Both astonishing and affirming, it suggests that what nourishes, strengthens, and warms us comes *through* us, not *from* us. How we live our lives evolves very differently if we accept this premise. All this has implications for how we listen, love, and live.

Of course, it's not as simple in our daily lives. Unlike Grandfather Mantis, we can't have someone else engage in all the processes of life and simply imbibe the result. We have to experience these processes ourselves. That's what eating the honeycombs really means! And if the world works this way, then listening is more a matter of letting things enter and combine than sorting and analyzing. And loving is more a matter of being a conduit than a mirror. And living is more a matter of keeping everything connected than fending off life with our will.

With this in mind, the story uncovers a set of self-reflective questions: Have we endured and faced our pain? Have we softened that pain till it forms a nectar in our heart? Have we offered it up? Have we shared it with others or kept it to ourselves? Have we searched for the pain softened in others? Have we turned what we've been given, through friendship and love, into honey? Have we worked our experience into a honeycomb in which to carry the sweetness we've distilled? Have we eaten what we've earned or just looked at it? Have we used the strength that comes from all this to place ourselves in the open so the larger forces can find us? Can we hear what moves through our thinking-strings? Have we interpreted that music well?

These are not easy tasks. Is it any wonder we need each other to make it through? So if you're willing, I may turn to you when stuck or sputtering, to see if I've retreated into that stubborn belief that we're the sole authors of what we need. If you're willing, we can slap each other's sandals till they become dogs that will retrieve the sweetness we've misplaced. If you're willing, we can help each other put the sun back into the sky.

A Reflective Pause

A MEDITATION

○ Place some honey on a plate and sit in the sun, if you can.

○ Breathe deeply and center yourself.

○ Inhale slowly and remember that when Grandfather Mantis eats the honeycomb, he is taking in everything that created the honeycomb.

○ Exhale fully and lift some honey on your finger.

○ Close your eyes and eat the honey from your finger.

○ As you taste the honey, remember that the word *sage* means *to taste*.

○ As you taste the honey, know you are taking in the nectar that formed in the heart of every flower.

○ As the sweetness coats your throat, know you are taking in the search of a thousand bees scenting the nectar and bringing it back to the center of their hives.

○ Inhale deeply and know you are taking in the mysterious way that nectar is turned into honey.

○ Open your eyes, knowing that you carry a timeless sweetness.

○ As you enter your day, be ready to gently kiss something or someone along the way.

JOURNAL QUESTION

○ Tell the story of one painful experience you've turned into honey and how that sweetness, once eaten, led you to find more light.

TABLE QUESTIONS

To be asked over dinner or coffee with friends and loved ones. Try listening to everyone's response before discussing:

○ Tell the story of Grandfather Mantis to a child in your life and, without interpreting it in any way, ask your young friend to explain the story to you.

○ Tell the story of an insight or understanding you came upon that has been helpful, that you discovered more than created. How did it come into your life?

GOING BACK INTO THE FIRE

Let the gifts stitch or cut the web,
let what needs to come together or break apart,
come together or break apart. Let the miracles,
even the ones we don't want or see, unfold.

LESIA WAS SEVERELY burned in a gas fire when she was nine. Her traumatic fear of fire grew to dominate her life. If someone left a gas grill on while eating, she began to sweat. More than thirty years later, Lesia woke with the notion that she must go back into the fire in order to replace that awful life-changing moment with another.

She worked with firefighters who set up a controlled fire. She wore a fire suit and walked into the flames and just stood there, at first feeling alarmed by her fear, which had enveloped her for so long. Slowly, her fear started to melt and she began to see through the intense heat. The world was waiting beyond the flames. She opened her palms and watched the tall flames curl around her fingers without being able to burn her. As she walked out of the fire, she could feel the wall of heat part and rejoin behind her. As the coolness of simple air surrounded her again, she could feel her heart—cramped so far inside for more than thirty years—begin to relax, even expand.

For Lesia, the fire was actual. For many of us, our pain is real enough, but the fire is often a wound or fear that keeps burning us up. This is why we need a controlled fire to go back into without getting hurt. It is difficult to listen to life, each other, or the voice of Spirit, if everything is muffled and distorted through the constant flames of pain or fear.

Don was driving home with his wife, both in their early thirties, a loaf of bread and a gallon of milk in the backseat. It was late afternoon on a fall day. The light was edging the almost brilliant leaves when a truck driver, searching to find a country station, swerved, tried to stop, but hit them squarely on the passenger side. Their car burst into flames. Don was badly burned and his wife died. Now in his seventies, Don has remarried and is a grandfather of four.

A few years back, he was driving by himself to get fresh tomatoes from a nearby farm stand and the light of late summer brought it all back—his first wife's presence, the almost miraculous light, the sudden impact and explosion. He pulled over and wept. And for some reason, he sought out that truck driver. It took a while, but somehow he found him.

They shared some coffee and the old driver fiddled with his napkin. It was clear he'd never recovered either. Finally, Don took his hand, the one that was tearing at the napkin, and muttered, "I forgive you." The old trucker broke down, confessing that he hadn't driven a truck since. The two went for a ride in Don's car. In silence, they watched the sun coat the fields and felt the current of life still holding them up and their hearts slowly opened to each other. Finishing the story, Don stares off. After a while, he punctuates the silence by admitting, "I just had to let him off the hook before I die."

Lesia and Don are great and humble teachers, both in what they have to say and how they came to it. For is there anything more brave or kind that we can do for ourselves or the world than going back into the fire and letting each other off the hook before we die?

But How

It is said that souls intent
on living will reach deep into
their wound and bring out the
fire living there, which out in
the open turns to light.

It is said that those intent on
making things better will reach
deep into their minds and bring
out the fire there, which out in
the open turns to truth.

It is said that those who love
like rain soothe every fire.

There are still fires I'm afraid to go back into and people I struggle with,
unable to let them off the hook. As important as these thresholds are,
I don't know how to cross them. The fear of being hurt unspeakably,
again and further, is at the core of my inability to reclaim the hurt parts
of my soul. I fear that whatever fire I need to go back into will devour
me alive this time, and fear that in order to forgive I may not survive the
re-feeling of that initial violation.

Still, it is imperative to hold sacred the most uplifting ways of being
on earth, even though we have trouble living those values day to day.
Otherwise we construct cold and even cruel philosophies to accommo-
date our limitations. Otherwise we can minimize or nullify compassion
as something not worth teaching, because we have trouble remembering to be kind.

The truth is that life will break us and burn us at some point on the
journey. This is not pessimistic or cynical but descriptive of the geography of being alive. It is part of how we are transformed by the journey.
Yet when we're broken or burned by events, we feel betrayed by God.
When we're broken or burned by people, we feel betrayed by other
souls.

Cancer was the event that broke and burned me, and though I've
been transformed, I am still afraid to go back into that fire. And I've
had my share of being broken or burned by others. Too many stories
to unfold here, but there has been the broken promise, the surprising
act of self-interest, the taking of something that was dear between us,
the public denial of our closeness. Yet living long enough, I've seen how
I've betrayed others, not meaning to. And so in the privacy of my heart,

I have softened and let my love of those who've hurt me reappear like spring, though I am afraid to move through the painful storm of facing them.

Just what then does it mean to you *to go back into the fire*? And what does it mean to you *to let someone off the hook before you die*? For this process is as personal as it is universal. And yet, an essential paradox underscores these efforts for each of us. While going back into the fire and letting someone off the hook seem like destinations, places of resolution to work toward, inwardly they are more like sacred forms of exercising the soul that can clear the sediment of a life so we might breathe more cleanly.

In this, we have no way of knowing what the destination looks like or feels like or when we may reach such resolution. Like meditating till you are free of all thought, you may focus intently on that aim while tripping on a moment of bareness that changes everything. So while you may have some specific fire you need to go back into, you may or may not actually re-enter it as Lesia did. And while there may be a specific someone you need to let off the hook, you may or may not actually speak to them as Don did. Still, a sense of completeness may be possible, as grace follows its own mysterious logic, which brushes us without revealing itself.

A Reflective Pause

JOURNAL QUESTIONS

These are challenging questions, so take your time and enter them when you are ready. Explore whichever of the two sets calls to you first, saving the other for another time within the coming year:

o What does it mean to "go back into the fire"?

o Tell the story of someone you admire and how they went back into the fire.

o Describe a fire you need to go back into.

○ What does it mean to "let someone off the hook before we die"?

○ Tell the story of someone you admire and how they let someone off the hook before they (both parties) died.

○ Describe someone you need to let off the hook before you die.

E dai—And Then?

While mystery tolerates our planning, it waits for us to enter. Often, planning is a form of guessing that makes us feel better as we enter the unknown. For sure, it always helps to see what's before us and around us and within us. But fear makes us puzzle this information into a picture of what will happen that often hardens into an expectation. And expectations tend to make us feel better on the way toward them and not so good when we encounter what really unfolds as we step through them. So perhaps all we can do is look around and take the next step.

When in Brazil, my friend David encountered the phrase *E dai* (ay-die-ee), which is Portuguese for "And then?" Regardless of the story told or hardship conveyed, the custom is for the listener to ask after a while, "*E dai?*" with a tone that implies, "And so? What now?" Literally *e* is *and* and *dai* means *from there, from a place near you*, as in "What is just beyond where you are?" or "And so, what is your next step?"

The phrase *E dai* invokes three successive meanings, often asked by the one who will hear you out: First, *I hear what life has given you. E dai? And so, what does this matter? What does this mean?* Second, *I see where you are. E dai? And so, from there, what is in front of you? What is just beyond where you are?* And third, *E dai? And so, what now? What is your next step?*

In a deeply practical way, this custom invites us to locate ourselves in any given situation from the inside out and from the largest frame of reference possible to the immediate circumstance. Before we overreact or react prematurely to whatever situation we find ourselves in, it helps to ask, *E dai? What does this mean in the journey of one life in its time on Earth within the larger journey of all life across all time?* Such consideration will affect whether we respond at all or in what way. After locating the event in the largest frame, it helps to look at the particular situation and determine, E dai? What is in front of us? Will the ground before us bear our weight? Should we back up? Should we sidestep the situation? Or should we stand firmly where we are? Both the larger and more particular context help us to ask and know, E dai? What is our next step?

In most cases, urgency is not an issue. In most instances, we have time to engage this situational inventory, which practiced enough becomes automatic, like breathing. And in those few cases where we need to act quickly, we are challenged to trust our intuition, dared to enter the moment without hesitation. From inside such moments, time often slows down and opens up, becoming timeless. This is what people report after moving through physical crises, that the event seemed to unfold in slow motion.

For each of us, going back into the fire, letting each other off the hook before we die, and helping each other take the next step—these are acts of love that require courage and compassion. They are profound gestures that change both the giver and receiver. They can change the landscape of a life. The great analyst Erich Fromm spoke of love in this magnitude as "the active power that breaks through the walls that separate one human from another . . . [It] unites us with one another." To listen with your heart will change everything, regardless of what you've been told.

A Reflective Pause

TABLE QUESTIONS

To be explored with a trusted friend or loved one. Have one of you ask and listen to the other, then get together another time and switch roles:

○ Describe a bridge, wall, divide, or unknown edge that is before you.

○ Have your trusted other say and ask of you the following, giving you time to respond to each:

- I hear what life has given you. E daí? And so, what does this matter? What does this mean in the context of your entire life?

- I see where you are. E daí? And so, from there, what is in front of you? What is just beyond where you are? Where is solid ground?

- E daí? And so, what now? What is your next step?

WHAT HAPPENS WHEN YOU REALLY LISTEN

A mind that is stretched by a new experience can never go back to its old dimensions.

—OLIVER WENDELL HOLMES

S O MUCH DEPENDS on whether we see everything we meet as alive or inert. When we meet things, looking for the life they hold, we tend to listen and receive. We tend to engage and join. When we meet things as lifeless and inert, we tend to observe and manipulate. How we move through the world depends on whether we view everything we meet as self-contained or as containing all of life. If I see a stone as merely an object in the way or as some weight I can use, I am drawn into a limited plane of living that is governed by problem solving: this piece fits here, this one does not, this piece will help me get over there, this one is in the way. Being so strategic may shorten my to-do list, but it doesn't open me up. With no sense of how things are connected, I may move things along without ever being touched by life.

But if I can hold that stone with enough presence and attention to realize its journey over centuries, how it wasn't always solid, how its minerals coalesced, how it felt the thud and press of every horse, car, and road placed above it, I might feel a deeper connection to the Earth that might broaden my perspective beyond the confines of my individual life. ~~One of the purposes of listening is to break our self-reference.~~

Listening beyond our own silhouette, each thing we encounter *is* alive—be it a stone, a dragonfly, a symphony, or a peach. And each thing in its aliveness encodes and mirrors the whole of life in its own way. ~~When we can listen, each particle of being, no matter how small, invites our presence and attention, so we might hear and feel the Universe through it.~~ Despite our physical explanations, this is what enables us to hear the ocean when putting a shell to our ear or ~~all of humanity when holding someone with a broken heart.~~ As the visionary William Blake wrote, "To see a world in a grain of sand . . . Hold infinity in the palm of your hand." *empathy*

When relating to what we encounter, ~~we become more possible ourselves; able to grow from what other things see and feel.~~ But how does a stone see and feel? Well, that's the work of openness, isn't it? To discover and inhabit many ways of listening, not just those we call human.

Time has made me accept that I can't possibly know or absorb the Oneness of things all by myself. In this way, listening becomes a partnership by which we listen and converse *with everything*. And this conversation with everything—yes through words, but more through presence and attention—becomes the partnership by which we keep everything joined. So, I invite you into this conversation that has been going on since matter first conversed with space. I invite you to immerse yourself—through words and beneath words—in the deeper, fresher, eternal ways of listening that keep us alive.

A Reflective Pause

JOURNAL QUESTION

o Tell the story of your own example of coming across a small part of life that, by giving it your attention, opened up a larger sense of life.

What Presents You?

Being authentic opens us. There is no getting around this. When being authentic, we often come close to what matters, even hold it in our hand, and just as often put it down. This is not because we are dense, though sometimes we are, but because it is hard to sustain our presence. Often, we don't listen or give our attention long enough to know the secret is in our hands. Sometimes we revert so quickly to the habit of our seeing that we miss the resources coming our way.

I was co-leading a retreat in British Columbia with the great storyteller Margo McLoughlin. After Margo read the Hindu folktale "What Happens When You Really Listen," we asked our companions to journal on what they were hearing at that moment in their lives. After a while, one woman said that she began to wonder, "What prevents me?" But when she went to write this, she actually wrote, "What *presents* me?"

At first glance, this seemed a slip of the pen, a brief mental lapse. She deemed it another small failure of attention on her part. But the appearance of *presents* instead of *prevents* was an answer to her question. As long as she could stay open to the possibility that some deeper voice—perhaps her inner teacher, perhaps her very soul, perhaps the Great Spirit itself as Native Americans would say—was asking her to shift her perspective.

Listening to the gap between *presents* and *prevents,* she began to realize that she was being asked to stop immersing herself in self-recrimination and to stop problem solving. Rather, she was being asked: What *presents* you? What *bestows* you? What *tenders* you? What *makes you known*? It seems dangerously simple: If we ascribe everything we hear as coming from us, we hear very little. When we allow the other voices of life to move through us, we begin to truly hear.

When we listen with our heart, we allow the reality of things to touch us below our identity. When we listen below our identity, who-we-are is in-formed (formed inwardly) by the depth and breadth of things. This inward formation opens the depth of heart with which we listen. And on it goes. So how does true listening affect our relationship to the world? How much of your pain do I need to hear before I hold you? When do I see the TV news as real? How do we listen deeply enough to act in the world?

A Reflective Pause

JOURNAL QUESTIONS

This is a journal question that leads to a table question. Invite a trusted friend or loved one to do this with you:

○ Begin a dialogue with your deeper self. Begin by asking your soul, "What prevents me?" Without thinking out a response, free-write your inner reply. Then on a new page, ask your soul, "What presents me? What bestows me? What tenders me? What makes me known?" Similarly, free-write your inner reply.

○ Put these responses aside for a day. When you return, highlight the phrases and insights that inspire you or trouble you. Copy them onto another page and try to unpack their meaning, as you would a passage found in an old book discovered in the attic.

TABLE QUESTIONS

○ Bring your soul responses to "What prevents me?" and "What presents me?" and your work with this material to your trusted friend or loved one.

Discuss this experience and what insights or questions it surfaced for you.

Listening for the First Time

In the Hindu folktale Margo told that day in British Columbia, a lazy, inattentive husband is sent by his cultured wife to see a weeklong performance of the *Ramayana*. During the opening performance he falls asleep, and before he wakes sweets are placed in his mouth. He tells his wife that the *Ramayana* is sweet to behold. She is pleased. The next night he falls asleep again, and a boy sits on his shoulders to view the stage, leaving before the man wakes. This time he tells his wife the *Ramayana* is heavy to endure. She thinks him reflective. The third night he dozes on the floor, and a dog pees on him before he wakes. He tells his wife the *Ramayana* smells like urine! She senses the truth. His lethargy is exposed and they return together for the fourth night of the epic.

Now he is in the front row with nothing between him and the tale of Rama being brought to life. For the first time he gives all his attention to the story and forgets he is in a theater, forgets it is a performance. He is *in* the story. Just then, the narrator speaks as Hanuman the monkey god, just back from leaping across the ocean to take Rama's ring to Sita. While leaping over the waves, the ring slipped from his hand and fell into the ocean. Hanuman is distraught, doesn't know what to do. While the narrator keeps wringing his hands, the husband, who is listening for the first time with all his heart, calls out, "Hanuman! Don't worry! I'll get it for you!" He then jumps onstage and dives into the ocean, finds the ring on the ocean floor, and brings it back to Hanuman. The narrator is dumbfounded to have a ring in his hand, and everyone, including the man's wife, is spellbound to see the fresh listener standing onstage, dripping wet.

This is what happens when you really listen. No getting around it. Magic happens. And the listening itself draws us below familiar logic into the realm of resilience embedded in our hearts. Another story. I know a tall, gentle man. He's been a teacher his whole life. After bypass surgery to repair his heart, he was drawn to take up the Native American flute. He was captivated with its flowing sound and immersed himself in learning how to play, in trying to play with others. After a year, he returned to his cardiologist for a checkup. His doctor was amazed to find his heart strengthened and his lung capacity increased. His blood pressure was low and his pulse was strong. The doctor queried him, "What have you been doing? Have you been exercising? Running?" It took the gentle man a while to make the connection, but then he smiled, went home, and continued to play his flute.

The mystery and power of life is always before us, though we often walk by it. I was in Barcelona in 2004, drifting down La Rambla, a tree-lined street in the heart of the city filled with markets and vendors and countless mimes, impeccable mimes. Not far from the Plaça Catalunya, I was stopped by two mottled angels, frozen as statues. Even their eyelids were painted, a metallic gray. The smaller angel had her hand out. If you put a coin in her hand, they both would move, gracefully, majestically, and the smaller angel would bless the giver of the coin. We all thought it clever, well done. A small crowd gathered and through our legs, a young girl came running with a coin from her mother. She was so excited to come upon two angels. She put the coin in the smaller angel's palm with such belief that the young mime believed she had something to bestow. And with a quiet bow of reverence, she blessed the child, who all alight, skipped away. The angels turned again to stone. The crowd moved on. And I fumbled in my pocket for a coin, desperate to be blessed.

A Reflective Pause

A MEDITATION

- o This is a walking meditation, to be done in the world.

- o During your travels—to work and back, to the store, getting the mail—dwell on one thing or person longer than usual.

- o Breathe deeply, and with that breath, try to inhale their point of view.

- o Without interacting or reacting to this thing or person, simply open your heart in their direction.

- o Listen in this way until you feel something stir within you.

- o Return to your day.

- o Later, in the evening, make a cup of tea, and with each sip bring the presence of this thing or person up from your heart before your eyes.

TABLE QUESTIONS

To be asked over dinner or coffee with friends and loved ones. Try listening to everyone's response before discussing:

o Bring to mind a person or idea or piece of music you had to listen to more than once before being touched by their full presence and meaning. What enabled you to truly feel their presence? What happened when you really listened? What did that feel like?

BEING ARTICULATE

A GOOD FRIEND ASKED, "Have you always been this articulate?" I was surprised, like a worker bee lost in the work, startled by the fact that he's been slowly producing honey. My first thought was that it's been a life of working through words to reach all that is unsayable. This is the nature of art. The only things worth saying are those that are unsayable. But before my mind could answer, my heart leapt out with "Only since I've found the courage to say what I see."

This wonderful question on a cool spring day on a well-worn path opened me to voice something I think I've always held quietly true: that being articulate is not a facility of language but a fidelity to vision. And so we are all articulate when finding the courage to say what we see.

This presumes some other things: that everyone has a vision, a perspective, a view of reality and eternity; and our job of being is to discover through experience the particular language we are each born with; so that we might find and inhabit our common place in the living Universe. We do this by voicing what we see in our firstborn language.

A Reflective Pause

JOURNAL QUESTIONS

This is a journal question that leads to a table question. Invite a trusted friend or loved one to do this with you:

o What does having a "firstborn language" mean to you?

○ For one day, practice "saying what you see" to yourself; that is, take the time to write down and affirm your own direct experience of life and the feelings and thoughts that living generates.

TABLE QUESTIONS

○ With your trusted friend or loved one, share what you think your "firstborn language" is. Then discuss your day's worth of "saying what you see," including what insights or questions it surfaced for you.

The Latin origins of the word *articulate* have a split history. The Latin *articulas* means *joint, to attach by joints*. But the word that grew out of this, *articulare*, means *to separate into joints*. Quite a different story. Throughout human history, we have separated when our original intent was to join. Other fields offer more dynamic definitions: *Articulation* in anatomy refers to the location at which two or more bones make contact. *Articulation* in sociology refers to the process by which particular communities personalize and apply cultural forms and practices for their own use. And *articulation* in music refers to the continuity between multiple voices, notes, or sounds.

Under our sophisticated forms of separating, the work and joy of articulation is the fresh movement toward that ever-present place where two or more hearts make contact, where we learn from each other in order to keep the song alive. A conceptual and verbal bias in our culture reserves *being articulate* as a descriptor for only how well we write and speak. But there are as many languages as there are callings, and we can learn from each of them. One is not superior to the other. The woodworker, the gardener, the horse trainer, the gravedigger—each has their own language to discover, an experience at a time. The bird is articulate in how it twigs its nest, the wind in how it lifts a willow, the tide in how it softens what it touches while taking nothing. The cliff is articulate in how it finds its smoothness through the years. And under our feet, the Earth is articulate in how it spins on its axis without any of us feeling it.

The articulation of the sea is strong and gentle at once, reflective and clear by turns, accepting and softening of all that enters it, giving all of itself and losing none of itself day after day. My first teacher in how to listen was the sea. I still want to listen like the sea.

Years ago, before I understood any of this, I was visited by a poem which held part of my firstborn language. In it, I was practicing saying what I see. I cite it here:

INHABITING WONDER

If the sun thinks
by radiating light,
its language is warmth.

If the ocean thinks
by undulating its mass of waves,
its language is wetness.

If a tree thinks
by converting light to sugar,
its language
is the sprouting of leaves.

If the wind thinks
by moving unseen
through everything,
how it bends us
is its tongue.

I am tired
of only thinking like a man
and pray for the courage
to radiate, undulate, sprout,
and move through
everything
unseen.

Saying what we see, openly and without judgment, is imperative if we are to grow from aspects of life that are not us. Paradoxically, saying what we see is a fresh way of listening. It is how the soul puts things out in the open so we can begin to make sense of them. It is the first step in bearing witness.

A Reflective Pause

A MEDITATION

This is a walking meditation that may take several days:

○ Sit quietly and center yourself. As you inhale, consider all the different ways that life on Earth speaks. As you exhale, try not to impose your human speech on everything you meet.

○ During your day, stop in the sun and feel its warmth and try to let yourself radiate warmth.

○ The next day, center yourself and enter your day. Stop near some water, put your hand in it, and feel its wetness undulate in waves. Try to let your care for the world undulate softly.

○ The next day, center yourself and enter your day. Stop near a tree or bush, put your hand on it, and imagine how inside it is turning light to sugar, and try to sprout your pain into sweetness.

○ The next day, center yourself and enter your day. Stop and listen to a patch of wind, feel the wind rush by you, and try to re-enter your day as quietly as the wind, as unseen.

○ On the final day, inhale slowly, letting these other forms of speech mix with your own.

In trying to understand what it means to live on earth, we've seen that experience for humans can be what erosion is for the elements. Try as we do to fight it, we are worn to our beauty, a season at a time. Being human, we get hurt and lose our trust in life and therefore need to understand the practice of restoring that trust. This requires a crucial effort not to prematurely name or define what we encounter, not to form our opinions or beliefs hastily. Instead, we are asked to allow time to surround us with the Wholeness of life, so the paradox of truth can show itself. In time, we may need to go back into the fire to retrieve the fullness of our heart. In time, we may need to let others off the hook before we all die. In meeting what we're given, we can use lasting practices to return us to what matters. They include deep listening, deep speaking, and deep questioning: listening to the Source in silence, listening with heart to our experience and translating that teaching into meaningful speech, and rooting ourselves further in the world through honest dialogue. In time, it becomes clear that we need everything and everyone to keep everything going. By helping each other, we can find the strongest currents of life and be carried along.

This is a good time to ask: What do you do when you're weary? What do you do when beauty is close and you feel numb? If every part of life keeps the other healthy, how can listening, speaking, and questioning keep you in this living remedy? How firm is your trust in life these days? If wavering, how can you restore that trust? Are your connecting points to life dislodged? Are you being moved along or are you being opened up? Have you softened your pain till it forms a nectar in your heart? Have you eaten of this nectar? Have you searched for the pain softened in others? Have you eaten of their nectar? Are you letting fresh experience enter *and combine, or are you obsessed with sorting and analyzing what comes your way? Are you able to listen and receive, or are you observing and manipulating? We all do both. Rising up and falling down, we all are left with the risk to place ourselves in the open so the larger forces can speak through our mind. We all are left to ask, day to day: from where I am, where is solid ground?*

Sooner or later we are shown that life is one ongoing conversation. And none of what matters reveals itself unless we stop to listen. In this way, listening becomes a partnership by which we listen and converse with everything. So I invite you to explore the one conversation. When you feel you can't listen any more, listen some more. When you feel you can't take any more, let more in. When you feel you can't give any more, let one more thing go. All of this is the work of being human, from which no one is exempt.

From here, we will explore the call of the soul, which is the call of our aliveness that never rests. From here, we will explore the many seasons of listening we move through in our time on Earth.

THE CALL OF THE SOUL

Ufunde uze ufe!

—Zulu for *Learn until you die!*

I T HAD BEEN a difficult time in my fifty-ninth year—loss, pain, demanding transitions—when a good friend asked, "Are you feeling as much impermanence and fluidity as it sounds like you are?" I loved her for asking such a question, for not only seeing me, but the larger landscape. I looked over her shoulder at the brilliant leaves drifting off the trees begging for winter. And I thought, yes, that and more. I had grown weary from trying to sort my lot of catastrophes, from trying to make sense of events and turns, from imagining plans and backup plans. Out of exhaustion, I finally just opened myself to everything; not trying to draw any conclusions but to receive it all the way the mouth of a river receives all the river carries, letting it mark and groove my bottom. This seems a better way to meet experience. Not with ignorance or denial but with a felt acceptance that this too will shape me.

It was then that I chanced to learn that the Greek root of *rhapsody* means *stitch* and *sing*. I found this stunning and thought, isn't this the art of being human, the ongoing act of stitching and singing? Isn't rhapsody the moment we fall into, when here enough and honest enough to stitch ourselves back together? And doesn't the feeling of being stitched back together release our common song?

All this made me realize that there's a difference between *the soul's calling* and *the call of the soul*. Both are needed. Both are invaluable. Both are ever-present and elusive. I know now that the difficult time I still find myself in is, in some ways, a shift from my soul's calling to the call of my soul. Let me describe the difference. While the soul's calling helps us discover our life's work, the call of the soul is a continual call to aliveness. Both are important. Like being and doing, like giving and receiving, these two deep calls are inextricable aspects of the energy of Oneness, a spiritual form of wind and calm.

This leads to a story of friendship and trees. During the last year I've been crossing this threshold, not sure into what. I feel a need to get closer to the Source, to open myself to other forms. Like William Edmonson, the southern janitor who sculpted limestone, I am drawn to sculpt, though I too know nothing about it. I want to sculpt wood. Some part of me wants to hold a piece of wood older than me till it conveys some sense of what the wind and rain have said to it for years. Some part of me wants to chip away to see what's in there.

My good friend George knows a lot about wood and the land. He and his wife, Pam, lived in Nova Scotia, where they built their own home and tilled the land with horses. Now they live near us, off Riverview Drive, where they have a deep and giving garden, where George has a woodshop, where the land opens to a forest. Last week, when walking the land as he does, he came upon an old twin cherry tree, close to two hundred feet tall. One side had come down in a storm about a year ago.

So off we went on a fall day down the path from his garden into the woods; stepping over briars and clearing broken limbs till we got to the fallen cherry. We walked the length of that majestic tree and cut some logs, then walked deeper into the woods. My muscles were sore, but good-sore. I couldn't stop smiling. As our feet were stepping down twigs, George said, "When a tree is very young it's covered with limbs, but as it grows older most of its limbs die and break off." We stopped by a mature oak, and I put my hands on the bark of this very old, straight tree, light flooding its length, and felt the wisdom of its years. It struck me squarely: trees in the forest start out *reaching for the light* and end up *standing in the light*. Once standing in the light, there is less need to reach.

I feel this happening to me. The ways I've reached into the world are dying and breaking off. I'm losing limbs. This is not sad, but developmental. After all these years, I'm reaching less and being more. Can it be that the more we stand in our being, the more the mystery comes to us?

This reaching for the light is at the heart of the soul's calling. It's how we wake to fulfill our purpose and find our place in the world. But once finding the light and growing in its presence, we are left with the call of the soul to simply live in that aliveness. Of course, these twin calls are happening continually and are constantly informing each other. One can lead to the other—within an hour, a day, or a lifetime.

I just know, after all this way, that the deeper place inside that doesn't change serves as a conduit to an Original Presence that keeps calling to us. This is the light of Spirit. Its illumination calls to our soul. And what does it ask of us? In our own particular, authentic way, to keep reaching for that Original Presence that doesn't change and, being blessed to find it, to stand there in the open and simply be.

A Reflective Pause

JOURNAL QUESTIONS

○ If the soul's calling is about the work we are drawn to in the world, and the call of the soul is about staying close to our sense of aliveness, describe one kind of work you are drawn to now, and one thing that brings you alive today. How do they inform each other?

○ In order to stay close to our aliveness, we must keep inquiring into what is real and sacred. Speak in detail about your own history of inquiring into what is real and sacred.

Five Vows

How then do we reach for the light and stand in the light? In the face of life's vast, impenetrable power, how do we not vanish? How do we not let existence crush us? How do we live in the open together? How do we—today, now, in every breath—try, by being real, to find our membership in the cosmic and global community that is greater than any one self? How do we listen for and follow the soul's calling and the call of the soul? Our partnership with these twin calls is an ongoing process.

I suggest that we don't achieve or arrive at these states, but that we keep enlivening the presence of our soul by staying in relationship with ourselves, each other, and the Whole. We all stumble in and out of this stream of presence, but I try to keep some vows that seem to help in a daily way. I invite you to personalize your own sense and practice of them.

First, I try *to stay visible.* I don't mean that I draw attention to myself, but that I try not to mute or withhold my presence and care. This involves a rigorous practice of self-honesty, for I can stand in a room full of loved ones or strangers and no one will know if I am present or not. We also think of being visible as being capable of being seen, but as important is the often neglected fact that, unless we are visible, out in the open, *we can't see.* Being invisible limits our vision. So I try to live in the open and meet everything with the strength of vulnerability, the way salmon swim upstream belly first.

As well, I try *to stay committed to looking.* This centers on facing life and accepting things as they are. Often, the storms of experience will turn us away or throw dirt in our eye or place obstacles in our path. But our part in this eternal dance is to keep getting up and turning back around, to wipe flecks of fear from our eye, and to stay in relationship with our obstacles until they tell us why they've come. *trap*

I also try *to stay committed to the moment.* The moment is our constant guide. It is the doorway to all that matters. And slowing our presence to meet the heart of each moment opens us to the mystery and power of life. As Russell Means of the Lakota tribe says, "Just because someone has invented a clock doesn't mean you have to hurry through life." When we rush by the moment, any moment, we miss the deep aliveness that is always waiting to show itself. So often, when feeling bereft, we chase what we think is special, when that deep aliveness is waiting in the moment we are in.

And I try *to maintain my friendship with all that is eternal.* We have all struggled to untangle strings of Christmas lights and found one old bulb that doesn't want to light. Then we jiggle it loose, examine it, and screw it back in, just to watch it spark. But cleaning it off sometimes refreshes the connection. Keeping our connections clean so we can stay lit is what maintaining our friendship with the eternal is all about. This involves the many things we've been exploring that slow us down enough to be touched directly by life. In his book *The Dream of the Earth*, Earth scholar Thomas Berry speaks of this clean and open connection between living things as *the call for mutual presence*.

Finally, I try *to stop rehearsing my way through life*. This is as important as it is elusive. With our overactive minds, we consult our experience and prepare for everything. While this is a highly efficient tool of survival, if given too much primacy, it can prevent us from being touched by anything new. Always anticipating what is coming prompts us to rely on a prepared response. Anticipating too much, we can catch ourselves crying ouch *before* we're even touched. Eventually, this leaves no room for surprise. Being hyper-vigilant makes a net of the heart and a goalie of the mind—deflecting everything that comes our way, good or ill.

Only you can imagine how these things live in you. I urge you to create your own practices by which you can know what the Original Presence of life is saying to you. How might you open yourself like a river bottom to all that life wants to rush through you? Are you reaching for the light or standing in the light? What has each given you? Who are you and what is it you feel called to do with who you are? How can you know your work in the world and your place in life? And most important, how can you learn the art of rhapsody, stitching up all that's been torn, so we can thread our experience into a common song?

A Reflective Pause

TABLE QUESTIONS

To be asked over dinner or coffee with friends and loved ones. Try listening to everyone's response before discussing. In your conversation circle, respond to one of the following:

○ Tell the story of a recent effort you made to stay visible with who you are.

○ Describe a recent situation that had you get up, wipe the dirt from your eye, and keep going.

○ Tell the story of a time when you chased after something, only to find that what you were looking for was close to you.

○ Describe a connection to Source you need to clean. How will you do this?

○ Describe a situation in which your anticipation and preparation became a rehearsed response. How did this benefit you? How did this hurt you?

SEASONS OF LISTENING

*If your mind isn't clouded
by unnecessary things,
this is the best season of your life.*

—WUMEN

HOW MANY KINDS of seasons can we experience? It was twenty-four years ago today the tumor vanished from my head. What kind of season is this? What have I heard in a quarter of a century of listening? So many things have come and gone, including family, loves, and friends who grew in different directions. Even the face of my mind and heart has changed, the way a cliff is worn over time by the sea. Perhaps this is the most devoted form of listening, when we are shaped over time by what we hear.

I only know there is a time to listen to the whole and a time to listen to the part, a time to listen for how things go together and a time to shut out everything so we can hear what lives beneath our masks. We listen differently if in a quiet wood or on a city street, if eager for daybreak or longing for sunset. We listen one way to what we've lost and another way to what we've found. I know what a roller coaster of feelings and thoughts the days can become and want to affirm that no one feeling or thought holds the future, though each tries to convince us that it does. Our soul—with its insistence on finding the still point from which it keeps rising—carries us through the seasons of our lives.

This still point under all that keeps moving waits under every season we can imagine. It is the silent center that keeps us sane. It helps to remember that the Earth is the still point around which the seasons turn. Likewise, the seasons of our lives have a common immovable ground, around which the weather of our lives unfolds. We all have different names for this immovable ground, but I call it spirit. Each passing year, we are asked to return to the ground of our spirit in order to go on. Each passing year, we are asked to listen like the seed for our crack of light in spring, to listen like the brook for our soft gurgle in summer, to listen like the leaf for our orange face in fall, to listen like the snow for a quiet place where we can powder down and rest.

The Fifth Season

Though I am well and hope to live many more years, I am sixty and entering what the Chinese call the Fifth Season. In Chinese lore, the Fifth Season is late summer, when the glare is gone and only the color of things as they are can reach us. It takes all the seasons to become this bare. All the turmoil to be worn of edges. All the loss to hold on to nothing. All the seasons to wear our hands open. Landing here, I no longer want things. I only want moments. In the sun. In the rain. With you. When confused or sad, I only want to look to what is and tumble into joy. Together. Alone. I want to put down all I've been carrying.

Like the squirrel that doesn't know what to do with all it's gathered, we have all this knowledge. What do we do with all this knowledge? What kind of listening sources us back to what matters?

The Fifth Season of late light marks what the Chinese call the Heavenly Pivot, a turning point in life in which knowledge is worn into knowing, watching into joining, seeking into being, and struggling with truth is worn into inhabiting the truth of struggle. The Heavenly Pivot is a time of transformation that helps us make sense of our experience. All seasons lead to this season, all experiences to this understanding of experience. So whatever cycle of seasons we find ourselves in—from one identity to another, from innocence to maturity, from arrogance to humility, from codependence to individuation, from numbness to compassion, from apprentice to master, from master to beginner—we are being steadily prepared for the Fifth Season, being slowly stripped of our resistance to the Heavenly Pivot.

A Reflective Pause

JOURNAL QUESTIONS

○ Every life has its seasons. Describe the cycle of seasons you are in now and how these seasons are impacting you.

○ In Chinese lore, the Fifth Season is late summer, when the glare is gone and only the color of things as they are can reach us. This Fifth Season is also known as the Heavenly Pivot, a turning point in life. Describe your own understanding and experience so far of the Fifth Season and the Heavenly Pivot. Describe the turning point you are approaching.

The Still Point

He was one of those rare irrepressible talents, like lightning in a bottle that only wants to break what carries it. Such immense gifts have seasons of their own and are often harsh on those who don't know what's busting out of them. His alcoholic father was an adequate musician. When he discovered his son's gift, he pushed him relentlessly, though the boy was only five. His father would come home late and drunk, sweep in like a storm, and make him practice on the piano till morning. He'd stalk what was wanting in his own gift and press his young boy to find it, punishing him mercilessly when he made mistakes.

There was no still point for the gifted child. The only peace he knew was from his gentle mother, whom he would describe later in life as his best friend. He was the lost pearl among seven children, except when his father, drunk and sinking, would ride his son's gift to quiet his own lack of worth. It was hard for the boy to hear his own mind. At the age of seven, the boy gave his first public performance. Before the age of twelve, he published his first musical work. Within the year, he was earning a living for his family by playing the organ and composing.

Early on, the immensely gifted boy was listening to the waterfall of music cascading out of the eternal silence while holding off the storm of the world. He kept working his gift as his gift worked him. He kept searching for the still point, not to retreat from life, but from which to engage the music of life more directly.

We each can relate to the tension of this life position. For regardless of the nature and size of our gifts, we are always holding off the storm of the world to hear the music that runs through everything. Always like the child, holding off the voices of others to hear our own voice. Always holding off being like the father, holding off looking with anger for what we lack in others. We all face this tension in what to listen to: the storm or the music, the gift waiting within or our seeming lack of worth. These are seasons that compete for our care: the season of noise, the season of harmony, the season of self-acceptance, and the season of endlessly comparing ourselves to others.

Soon the gifted child left home and began to study with the giants of his time. The lightning within him was striking its way out. He was growing by leaps. When seventeen, he was called home because his mother was dying. Now there was a sadness to counter his gift, to feed his gift. At first he tried not to listen to his grief, to listen only to his gift. But soon he learned that this is the purpose of all gifts: to carry our grief, our joy, our humanness, and our confusion and wonder before all that is unknown.

The Storm

The precocious son of the alcoholic musician was Ludwig van Beethoven (1770–1827), one of the great composers in the history of music, whose gift burned so fiercely that his unstoppable creations inspired—and even intimidated—generations of composers and musicians. While few of us are born with such raw immeasurable gifts, each of us is born into the same journey of life. We all find ourselves in the same tensions between the storm and music of life, between meeting the grief inherent in living and discovering the usefulness of the gifts we carry.

Of all the maladies that could befall a gifted musician, Beethoven gradually lost his hearing. Whether famous or anonymous, whether things come easily or with difficulty, we each face tight passages in our journey in which what we need to be who we are is challenged. If you're a mountain climber, it might be a serious injury that forces you to stop climbing. If you build things, it might be arthritis in your hands. If you're a painter, it might be a film of cataracts veiling what you see. If you're a poet, it might be the threat of brain surgery that will compromise your memory and speech. But time and time again, we experience the unexpected re-emergence of life-force that is born from the friction of our gifts against what gets in the way.

Beethoven is a heroic example of this. In his late twenties, he began to complain of a ringing in his ears that made it hard to hear music of any kind. It was hard to distinguish between instruments. Music was rushing endlessly within him, but his ears were no longer the instrument through which he could hear the world. He was also having trouble tracking what others would say and started to avoid conversation. Having experienced the slow decay of my own hearing, I can only imagine how painful this was for someone born to meet the world through music.

The young composer was experiencing early signs of tinnitus, which is usually described as a ringing noise but can take the form of a high-pitched whining, hissing, humming, or whistling sound. Some have reported hearing a constant ticking, clicking, or roaring. Others have heard the likes of crickets or locusts in the back of their heads. Still others describe it as a whooshing sound, as with wind or waves. An odd vigilance of focus and surrender is necessary to keep this constant inner noise from dominating your days.

In our modern world, our chance at listening deeply to the music of life, our chance at hearing the call of our soul, is greatly compromised by the constant ringing in our ears that comes from the endless bombardment of voices and images from all over the globe. Without the human context or time to internalize them, we experience a psychic form of tinnitus that blunts the heart from working properly as the miraculous perceptual organ that it is. But unlike physical tinnitus, we can re-find the still point from which we keep rising and regain our footing in that immovable ground of spirit that somehow lets us begin again.

Beethoven couldn't begin again. He had to move forward. The lightning of his gift had no interest in his growing inability to hear. Like Van Gogh, who would arrive at this precipice almost ninety years later, the gift would use the composer up in making itself known to the world. Imagine the internal pressure building in the young musician, discovering the scope of his immense talent and at the same time discovering that his chief access to that talent, his hearing, was breaking down.

In 1801, Beethoven confessed to his friends in Bonn that he was severely frightened of becoming deaf. Increasingly, the music he would hear cascading out of the eternal silence would be clear enough to pierce the soul. And increasingly, any attempt to play it or share it would be garbled with the imprecise static of his impending deafness. In the coming year, he became depressed. It felt impossible to go on. He left Vienna for a time and withdrew to the small Austrian town of Heiligenstadt, where he thought of suicide. How could he live in this constant taunt: being a conduit for such unprecedented music and never being able to hear it in the world?

But something happened in the cottage at Heiligenstadt. Perhaps the lightning he was carrying wouldn't let him go. On October 6, 1802, Beethoven wrote his Heiligenstadt Testament, a letter to his brothers, Carl and Johann, in which he confesses his despair at the unfairness of life and at the relentless advance of his deafness, a journey he doesn't want to live through. But then the letter becomes a testament to the music coursing through him. And with an inexplicably willful surrender, he vows to overcome and persevere, to ride his gift as far as time will allow. Beethoven never sent the letter, but kept it hidden for the rest of his life. It was discovered in March 1827, shortly after his death.

Beethoven's great music came out of this acceptance of both his gift and his humanness, out of this messy mix of will and surrender. He resolved to live for and through his gift. He agreed to be ground into

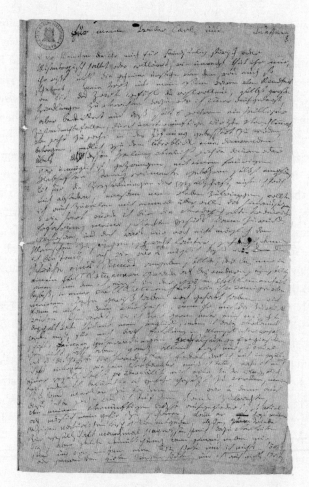

Beethoven's Heiligenstadt Testament, 1802

deafness while releasing as much music as he could from the still point that was spreading its silence over his entire life. He threw himself into his work for the next twenty years, creating nearly a hundred unprecedented compositions ranging from the sonata for piano *The Tempest* (Sonata no. 17 in D Minor, Opus 31, no. 2) to the unparalleled Ninth Symphony with its "Ode to Joy" (Opus 125, in D Minor), which he composed completely from the precipice of silence.

The Tempest was composed during the turbulent Heiligenstadt period, and while it was suggested that the sonata was inspired by Shakespeare's play, Beethoven never referred to the piece this way. The storm this music circles seems more internal. I asked my good friend the classical bassist and teacher Anders Dahlberg about *The Tempest,* and we went for a drive, listening to it in the middle of a snowstorm. Anders spoke with passion between the movements: "It's as if he starts out trying to solve a dark internal question. Who knows what it might be. He tries to solve it by getting louder, then softer, going higher, then lower. . . . But the problem keeps returning. It's a problem that won't go away. Perhaps it's his loss of hearing. Perhaps it's the relentless fragility of life. . . . Whatever it is, it's a problem to live with. For a time this seems possible, but the problem keeps returning. Though life is still possible. Yes, life goes on. We go on." It is an anthem for us all. This thoroughly human and affirming piece ends with a quiet, snow-like return to the eternal silence that sees us through the storm.

The Ninth Symphony premiered in Vienna on May 7, 1824, in the Kärntnertor Theater. For Beethoven's first stage appearance in twelve years, all of Vienna crowded the house. While the intense composer was conducting center stage, the performance was quietly directed on the side by Michael Umlauf, the theater's Kapellmeister. Umlauf instructed the singers and musicians to ignore the totally deaf Beethoven, who was quickly turning the pages of his score and beating time for an orchestra he couldn't hear.

Violinist Josef Böhm who played that day gives this account:

> Beethoven directed the piece himself . . . he stood before the lectern and gesticulated furiously. At times he rose, at other times he shrank to the ground, he moved as if he wanted to play all the instruments himself and sing for the whole chorus.

At the end of the symphony, as the audience erupted into a standing ovation, Beethoven was several measures off and still conducting. It was then that the contralto Caroline Unger walked over and gently turned the disoriented master to face the crowd. Seeing their reception and hearing nothing, he began to weep.

Conversation Books

Beethoven kept conversation books, in which he would ask visitors to write what they wanted him to hear. These books became a Talmud of sorts, in which the conversation and questions of a lifetime were put back and forth, seldom with answers—just open discussions of music and voices, and pushing here and there for insights into life.

The more we accept our very human frailties, the more we need to stay in conversation with all of life's agents. We need our own conversation books to investigate and inhabit our very real relationship to life. Paradoxically, we need a space to talk things through, alone and together, while we search for the wordless still point within. More is at stake than we think. So I invite you to start your own conversation book of what you hear when you enter the unspoken, a journal of your seasons of listening, a journal of this conversational space that is yours and everyone's.

And in that private yet universal space, what was Beethoven listening to as he drifted further into silence? What did he hear that enabled him to persevere, and how can his example help us now? Though we are rightfully in awe of his great music, it is the instrument revealed by his living that is at the heart of our discussion. No matter what we are put here to do, no matter what obstacles we face, Beethoven's commitment *not* to leave this life, his commitment to keep working, despite his increasing experience of loss, is directly transferable to all our lives.

This is the challenge to the living: to take what we hear, despite our diminishments, and make whatever music we can for as long as we can. Our challenge is to *keep* listening, to *keep* meeting life. Like salmon who turn to swim upstream and gulls who turn to fly headlong into wind, it is *meeting* life that enables our moment of flight. It's our courage and resolve to listen *through* our diminishments that reveals the finer truths we earn, the way the hollow of a tree reveals the song building in the wind. And it's the rush of spirit through the hollow in our humanness that reveals the song of life.

Earlier I quoted Evelyn Glennie, the near deaf percussionist, U Thant, the Burmese secretary-general of the United Nations, and the great Sufi teacher Hazrat Inayat Khan. Each described what opens at the bottom of every experience when we can meet the still point. Through this meeting, we can enter a bareness of being that refreshes our innate connection to the one living sense that informs all things. Through our unblocked, sincere response to life, we can "tune our inner person with the great mysteries," as U Thant says. And in a daily way, through listening and feeling, we can "tune the heart in order to express wisdom," as Hazrat Inayat Khan suggests.

This bareness of being is opened to each of us when we are forced or willing to remove our filters and *feel* what we hear and meet. Beethoven is a touching example of an ordinary person with an extraordinary gift whose experience forced him to live very close to this bareness of being. This can be both painful and rewarding. That the gifted boy in a broken man's body could, after all his suffering, birth a piece of music such as "Ode to Joy" is proof that an atom of resilience waits like a seed in every soul come to earth.

Our filament of light is carried in the frailest human form, until our acceptance of both storm and silence ushers us into the Fifth Season, where the glare is gone and only the color of things as they are can reach us. Perhaps this is the central work of being human. I'm not sure. I'm just inspired to lean more fully into life, to listen a bit further, to welcome the bareness of being when I stumble into it. But I believe if we can lean on each other from time to time, we can put down all we're carrying and help ready each other for the Heavenly Pivot.

A Reflective Pause

A MEDITATION

- ○ Go outside if you can or sit near a window. Breathe slowly and watch the season you are in unfold around you.

- ○ Close your eyes and look within. Breathe slowly and watch the inner season unfold before you.

- ○ Inhale and listen for the still point under all seasons.

○ Breathe deeply and listen for the filament of light that lives in you. Feel it brighten the closer you are to the still point.

○ Breathe deeply and feel your very human form encase the light that lives in you.

○ Calm yourself and listen to the seasons you are in, the body you are in, the light rising within you.

○ Now open your eyes and go to your conversation book and begin today's entry with the line "My gift and my humanness meet in me. I know this because . . ."

TABLE QUESTIONS

To be asked over dinner or coffee with friends and loved ones. Try listening to everyone's response before discussing:

○ Tell the story of a time when you felt the tension between holding off the storm of the world and listening for the deeper music of life. How did you cope with this? What did this experience teach you?

○ Tell the story of a time when you felt the tension between your grief and your gift, and the story of a time when your grief deepened your gift.

○ Beethoven's struggle to listen for and create music through his deafness illustrates the paradox of limitations, how a constraint in one direction can intensify a gift in another direction. Tell the story of a time when something limiting in your life actually opened you to a deeper form of listening. What did you hear?

○ As moving as his music is, Beethoven's courage in accepting both his gift and his humanness is equally inspiring. Tell the story of someone you admire who has demonstrated a similar courage of acceptance. Describe a place in your life where you are being challenged to invoke such an acceptance.

OUTWAITING THE CLOUDS

The role of spiritual practice is basically to exhaust the seeker. If the practice does what it's supposed to do, it exhausts our energy for seeking, and then reality has a chance to present itself.

—ADYASHANTI

I'VE LEARNED A great deal drifting in and out of wakefulness over the years. In the beginning, I used to *do* a lot of things—write, play music, draw, garden—one after another. But along the way, it stopped being about creating things and started being about the space that is opened in the act of creating. Now the experience of creating brings me such joy, because somehow I came to realize that it is the space that creating *opens* that saves me, not what it *produces*. Now it doesn't matter if I finish anything. I just need to be in that space. In that holy interlude, I am grounded. Only when in conversation with *what-is-eternal* am I able to stand in a fundamental knowing that is unshakable. When I stand there, I feel calm. When I stand there, I'm attuned to different weather.

Eventually, whatever our devotion, because of our devotion, the practice we commit to is used up like wood in a fire. Even the fire is used up in the creation of heat and light. And what is care but human wood? Time and again, I keep learning that, for all my effort to shape and create, it is I who am shaped and created for my engagement with life.

A Reflective Pause

JOURNAL QUESTIONS

- ○ Tell the story of one lesson that awaited you on the far side of the exhaustion of your will.

- ○ How has this experience affected your understanding of will?

Recently, I was in Sausalito, having breakfast in the valley, looking at the sculpted hills against the morning sky. As happens, things begin to speak. This is what I heard:

ON THE RIDGE

We can grow by simply listening, the way the tree on
that ridge listens its branches
to the sky, the way blood
listens its flow to the site
of a wound, the way you
listen like a basin when
my head so full of grief
can't look you in the eye.
We can listen our way out
of howling, the way the heart
can soften the wolf we keep
inside. We can last by listening deeply, the way roots
listen for the next inch of
earth, the way the old turtle
listens all he hears into the
pattern of his shell.

That morning, my understanding of listening expanded and I was reshaped yet again. It sounds simple and obvious but it takes time to listen; time for the deeper things to show themselves. Just as we can't see all the phases of the moon on any one night, we can't hear the phases of truth or the heart unless we listen for how the truth of feeling grows full and dark and full again over time. Patience, the art of waiting, is the heart-skill that opens the world; the way opening our eyes is necessary in order to see.

Deep listening also takes time because things get in the way that we must allow to pass. When we outwait the clouds, we can feel the sun and see the water bead on the hosta. When we outwait the clouds, the birds in our heart come out and the webs in our mind become visible.

That morning in Sausalito, I learned that listening this deeply *is* an act of creation that shapes us beyond our will. I've always been taught that first you listen, then you act. This of course gives time for compassion to rise in the heart. But I'm also discovering after all these years that listening deeply over time is one uninterrupted growing—*one continuous act.* In this way, the tree on that ridge bending to the wind till it grows to the bend *is* how it listens over time. And *in* the act of receiving our darkest cries, the heart begins to soften the howl of our wound. The old turtle is mastered by time, until moving at the pace of being *is* how it listens. Loving you over time, I take you in, until watching you sleep in the hammock is enough to break my heart into blossom.

Always running counter to this deep listening is the noise of the modern world, where the tasks and passwords keep multiplying. The lists seem endless. You have your own. First it's the dishes and laundry. Then gas and electric. Now the motherboard is on the fritz. And the Facebook page was hacked into. And the automatic deposit stopped being automatic. And the transfer didn't transfer. And the laundry is still piling up. And at work there are spreadsheets that take so much time to spread.

As I get older, I fear these lists will keep me from what matters. I want my best energy to go to being alive, to staying alive. Early before work the other day, after checking my list, I stumbled into this poem:

COMING OUT

While there is much to do
we are not here to do.

Under the want to problem-solve
is the need to being-solve.

Often, with full being
the problem goes away.

The seed being-solves its
darkness by blossoming.

The heart being-solves its loneliness
by loving whatever it meets.

The tea being-solves the water
by becoming tea.

While there is much to do, we are not here to do. I keep forgetting
this. And remembering it somehow rearranges me where I can't see. To
be sure, this is not about shunning doing or not living in the world. That
would be like saying "I'm not going to breathe." So given that there are
endless things to do, how do we hold this? Is life no more than the all
too brief pause between the completion of one list and the beginning
of the next?

It's much like living in a body. We can't ignore what carries us or we
will die. But if the body's a temple, what are we devoted to while living
in it? This brings us to the work of reverence: to solve our darkness by
blossoming and to solve our loneliness by loving everything.

I was teaching in the spring in the Pacific Northwest. In that sweet
group, a woman who lives on a small island taught me that *serene* means
clear, bright, and unclouded. In deep ways, practicing serenity is outwaiting the clouds. So let us say that outwaiting the clouds is the patient,

slow process of awakening that innately takes time and can't be rushed, while parting the veil is the work of moving through illusion. We are constant students of both.

A Reflective Pause

A MEDITATION

- In deep ways, practicing serenity is outwaiting the clouds.
- Let's practice serenity.
- Whether inside or outside, sit where you can see the sky.
- Breathe slowly and center yourself.
- Watch the clouds drift as you breathe.
- Imagine the sun endlessly on the tops of those clouds.
- Imagine the truth of being endlessly on top of all your troubles.
- Inhale deeply and practice outwaiting the clouds.
- Exhale deeply and realize that you can outwait many of your troubles.

TABLE QUESTIONS

To be asked over dinner or coffee with friends and loved ones. Try listening to everyone's response before discussing:

- The poem "Coming Out" contains the lines

  Under the want to problem-solve
  is the need to being-solve.

  What does this mean to you?

- Give a recent example where, in addressing a problem, a form of being would have served you better than an act of doing.

- What is your relationship with lists?

APPROACHING THE DARK ACRE

EVERYONE HAS A dark acre between their days and the Source, not dark as in evil or forbidding, but dark in the way that the canopy of a forest filters out light. Crossing this acre is knowing who you are. Some call that crossing introspection or facing oneself. Most of us are forced to cross that dark acre because of some loss or hardship. Others cross that inner forest by following their creativity. Writers write their way across, singers sing their way across, and painters paint their way across. But this journey is not reserved for artists. It is everyone's journey and, regardless of how, crossing that dark acre is the only way to find a home that lasts.

Another way to speak of this crossing is what the Hindus call *parting the veil of illusion*. In Hinduism, Maya is the goddess of illusion. The word *maya* means *illusion*. It is believed that anything added to reality, to the truth of things as they are, is illusion. This veiling power of illusion creates the differences known as "me" and "mine." Maya, the power of illusion, creates the ignorance of the individual self that thinks it is separate from the rest of life. The unity of life fragments into self-centered thinking by the layering of illusion.

We can look at the world through the veils of illusion, with all its possessiveness and isolation, as the prevailing story of conflict across time. And we can look at the interrelated unity of all life that waits beneath our illusions as the perennial, transforming story of spirit and love.

Encountering Illusion

What do we do when we encounter illusion? Every spiritual path has tried to address this question. No one has solved it, but that doesn't mean the human experiment has failed. Encountering illusion is part of the human journey, part of our spiritual geography, and what we do with illusion is instrumental in whether we are transformed in our time on Earth.

If we think of illusion as a persistent fog, what do we do when we encounter fog? The first thing is to stand still till we can get our bearings. We try then to discern if the fog is temporary or something we have to live with. If permanent, do we live with it or live somewhere else? If we must start over, what is the pilgrimage that will help us leave the fog? And if the fog is localized, how do we outwait it? But what if the fog is a cloud in our eye, or mind, or heart? What if we carry the fog with us?

Though the practices that speak to these questions go by many names, standing still until we can see is at the heart of all meditation and prayer. And discerning what we have to live with is at the heart of accepting things as they are. Based on the truth of things, we enter the practice of discerning right action: do we live with what is before us, try to change it, or live somewhere else?

The pilgrimage of living with things as they are, changing what is, or starting over is at the heart of humility and a Beginner's Mind. When the fog of illusion is localized, the practice of serenity outwaits the clouds, while the practice of love and compassion burns off the fog. But when the fog is a cloud in our eye, or mind, or heart, then we must remake how we see, how we think, and how we feel. We must be born anew through a process of self-transformation. This has never been something that can be taught. We can only believe in an unclouded life and keep each other company along the foggy way.

A Reflective Pause

JOURNAL QUESTIONS

○ Explore one time in your life where you experienced some sense of
illusion by which you were distanced from the truth of things. How
did this happen? What did this feel like? How did you finally part
the veil of this illusion? Perhaps you are still trying. If so, what do
you need to do next?

Preparing to Listen

If meditation is the practice of opening the eye, contemplation is the
practice of seeing once the eye is open. Together, meditation and contemplation offer us a perennial way to become unclouded. In this, meditation and contemplative practice are not just about stress reduction but
more about an initiation into a softer, clearer, more durable engagement
with being alive. Once entered, they lead us to resources that can help
us outwait the clouds in our life and the fog of illusion we encounter.

Meditative traditions—within Hinduism, Zen, and Christianity to
name a few—encourage a disciplined practice that helps us create still
points from which to live more peacefully in the world. If lived in, any
practice is eventually used up and incorporated into an authentic way
of being in which practice and living are inseparable. Yet even with the
best of intentions, my efforts to practice anything—meditating, writing, reading, swimming—have often through their own noble momen-
tum crowded out life. So I need to remind myself repeatedly that the
goal of all practice is to help us *live*.

Acting on What We Hear

We are asked to practice serenity by whatever means until we can dis-
perse the fog of illusion, whether the clouded veil comes from others or
from a making of our own. But as powerful as such seeing and hearing
is, it is not enough and we are faced with the need to *act* on what we see

and hear. Then we are asked, even demanded by the one life we have, to *live in accord* with what we come to know is true.

This has always proven to be a crucial turning point in the human journey. Each of the mythic lives immortalized in story and the inner unfolding of sages and saints throughout time has such a turning point. As a young man with great promise, Prince Siddhartha had to leave the world that was being prepared for him, leave his family and position, in order to search for the very nature of existence. His courage in acting on what he heard as true led him to become Buddha. Moses had to leave his life as Pharaoh's son to enter the desert where he at last found God. Still others had to stay and remake themselves where they were. Rosa Parks felt the need to stay in her seat on that Alabama bus. And Nelson Mandela felt the need to stay in a homeland that imprisoned him for twenty-seven years.

But this turning point is not just for heroes. These legendary figures are often so lionized that we lose sight of the difficult human part of their journey and how it mirrors our own. I doubt that Buddha knew he would become Buddha or that Nelson Mandela knew he would become the first post-apartheid president in South Africa's history. This crucial turning point in every life requires great courage and heart when no one is watching.

Ultimately, it's not about leaving or staying, but opening the door that waits between our soul and the world; the door that the storms, human and natural, always close and which truth and love always reopen. In opening that door, no matter how often it closes, we are challenged to live the one life we are given.

A Reflective Pause

A MEDITATION

o The practice of right action involves discerning when to live with what is before us, try to change it, try to change ourselves, or live somewhere else.

○ With this in mind, wash your face slowly and dry it slowly.

○ Sit feeling the coolness on your face.

○ Inhale deeply and center yourself.

○ As you exhale, allow a point of confusion or difficulty in your life to rise before you.

○ Inhale deeply and circle this difficulty with an open mind.

○ As you exhale, simply feel the density of the difficulty.

○ Inhale deeply and try to discern if the density is located in you, the situation, or the time.

○ As you exhale, simply feel what draws your attention most.

○ Rise and enter your day, doing nothing but holding this intuitive information.

○ Revisit the difficulty tomorrow with an intention to discern right action for yourself.

TABLE QUESTIONS

To be asked over dinner or coffee with friends and loved ones. Try listening to everyone's response before discussing:

○ Share the story of a friend or loved one who, in your opinion, is fogged in—emotionally, mentally, or spiritually. From your vantage point, what kind of pilgrimage might guide them from this fog? Accepting that you can't do this for them, can you respectfully be of some help?

○ Share the story of a practice or hobby you committed to in order to help you live more fully and how it moved you both closer and farther away from your life.

UNTANGLING THE NET

IN HIS EARLY work in Mexico, the leading peace builder John Paul Lederach asked a town full of ordinary people what words they use to say they are in conflict. After forty minutes of lively cross talk, they came up with almost two hundred different phrasings. Two Spanish words for conflict stand out. The word *desmadre,* which means *motherless* (*without a mother*), and the word *enredo,* which means *the net is tangled.* The root of the word *red* means *fisherman's net.*

John Paul describes the fisherman's long history of untangling his net that informs this Spanish expression:

> *Enredo,* to be all tangled up in a mess, figures among the most common of the Spanish synonyms for conflict. The core word around which *enredo* emerges—*red* or net in English—relates literally to a fisherman's tool. Here people envision conflict like a broken and completely tangled fishing net, the way it looks after coming through a particular hard session at sea. Interestingly, the work of response and repair requires the patience of the fisherman's hands. If you have ever watched a fisherman, having completed his early morning foray into the sea and his catch removed, sit with his nets in a small boat in the late morning or into the afternoon, you will have the key image. Patiently, he unravels the tangles, repairs the torn areas and makes the rope-web whole again. And once whole, thousands of knots, points of contact and connection hold the individual strands together.

Enredo as a vision (for healing) begins and concludes with a focus on the relational context and quality of the collective whole. A fisherman does not "resolve" a tangle. He restores the connections and relationships, bringing back to life the very fabric and function of community.

Consider the assumptions at work here. You don't cut a tangled net, you unravel it. For without a net, you can't eat. Only when too tangled do you cut it, but then you weave another. Likewise, being motherless implies being lost, having lost our connection to the center, and refinding that central connection is the work. So resolving conflict hinges on untangling the net by which we feed each other and on restoring our central connection. Both efforts address the relationships that live beneath the circumstances of any immediate conflict.

When we in the modern complex say *we are in conflict,* the focus is on the impasse. The emphasis is on the brokenness, not on the oneness that was broken. But if we can say, with the fishermen, that *we are motherless* and *entangled,* we are pointing to the state of Wholeness from which we've fallen. The emphasis is not on blaming the conflict on anyone. Nets left in the sea long enough will tangle. It's part of what nets *do.* And being human, unraveling knots is what *we do,* once we get past the blame game.

John Paul goes on to say that, in areas of conflict around the world, he often asks, "When did your conflict begin?" He usually encounters three levels of response. The first typically cites the start of violence or disruption. The second begins to describe the patterns that led to the violence or disruption. The third and deepest reply starts to examine the long history of who we are. He notes that it often takes as long to get out of a conflict as it did to get into it. For this reason, the deeper the inquiry into the question, the deeper the chance to transform the relationship.

The aim of spiritual practice, no matter its form, is to untangle the nets that living snares us in. But though we can learn to untangle specific situations, even get good at it, life on earth is a never-ending weave of becoming tangled and working to get untangled. And deeper than any coping skills we might learn is our acceptance of the weave of tangle, which is closely tied to the rhythm of being whole-hearted and half-hearted. Like dilating and constricting and inhaling and exhaling, this opening and closing of our heart is necessary to stay alive. None of these states—being tangled or untangled, being whole-hearted or half-hearted, being open or closed—is a place we can permanently stay. When we are half-hearted, we tangle the net. When we are whole-hearted, we untangle the net. But the weave of tangle never ends.

A Reflective Pause

A MEDITATION

- Sit near water or near a large tree with leaves.

- Breathe deeply and watch the movement of the water or the movement of the leaves. Notice how untangled they are.

- Breathe fully and feel where you are tangled. This is the feeling of being half-hearted.

- Breathe slowly and let the slowness of your breath untangle your heart.

- Breathe fully now and feel where you flow like water and lift with the ease of leaves. This is the feeling of being whole-hearted.

- Enter your day, stopping when you feel yourself tangle, knowing that your slow breathing can untangle the knot in your heart.

JOURNAL QUESTIONS

- Give a history of your relationship to conflict. How do you address conflict? How do you carry it? What does conflict do to you inwardly? What would you like to learn about conflict?

Conflict

Like everyone else, I tend to avoid conflict. Even though I've learned to face it and see it through, it's always hard. It's easy to blame this tendency on our fight-or-flight reflex, but the strength of its presence in our lives can be blamed on our silent reinforcement of this avoidance as a strategy for survival and even as a principle by which to live. Avoidance of conflict is even seen as polite or dignified in some regions of the world.

Somehow we think if we avoid the conflict, we avoid the tangle. This is the root of denial. Imagine the toddler who breaks his cereal bowl and then covers his eyes to make it go away. To think we can avoid the tangle is just as infantile. Yet we all do it.

Just last summer, someone hurt my feelings. Our relationship was immediately tangled. I was caught off-guard and pulled back into my hurt. Every time we saw each other, I could feel the pull of the tangled knot between us. More than this, I realized his capacity to be cruel. Our relationship has changed. This of course happens and sometimes needs to happen. But though I removed myself from a hurtful relationship, I never faced the conflict between us. Even more instructive is the fact that by not facing this conflict, I let my self-esteem get tangled with his cruelty. Now, months later, I feel the pull of this knot in my self-worth which, if honest, traces back to the illegitimacy of the hurt I received and how I let it take residence inside me. Now I'm spending time alone with my tweezers of introspection, trying to untangle this small but irritating knot in my heart that is taking up more space and attention than it deserves.

The longer we ignore the tangled net, the harder it is to untangle. We've all struggled with the tangled hose or extension cord left in the garage and how it braids and seems to tighten into itself. It doesn't take long before my frustration in trying to free the coils has me slamming the hose or extension cord on the garage floor, as if that will break the tangle. It's important to recognize that avoiding conflict increases our own capacity for violence born out of frustration and impatience at a situation we've ignored for too long.

When fishermen spread their nets, they each take one end of the net and back away from each other until the net is fully open. Then they can see the knots and tangles more easily. Once they've repaired it, they walk the open net into the water together. What this tells us is that even when having the courage and commitment to face conflict, we need enough distance between us so the net of relationship can untangle and open fully. Once untangled, the net is used to gather food from the deep. Likewise, the net of relationship is untangled *so it can feed us.*

I'm trying to learn the patience of a fisherman, trying to see what is tangled—within me and between us—and slowly and gently undo the knots, one by one. All to make the web whole again. So when I find myself in difficult standing with someone, I try to approach that person, if it's safe, to take their hand, look them in the eye, and as I would invite someone into a space I seldom share, I aim to say softly, "Our net is tangled. Can you feel it?"

A Reflective Pause

TABLE QUESTIONS

To be asked over dinner or coffee with friends and loved ones. Try listening to everyone's response before discussing. These table questions offer you the chance to discuss a conflict you are currently a part of, in preparation for an invitation, when ready, to address that conflict directly with the person involved:

o Give the history of a conflict you are currently a part of.

o How is your relationship tangled and off-center? What areas are torn?

o Identify some steps you could take to unravel the tangle, repair the torn areas, and make the web whole again.

o Invite honest feedback from your listeners.

o When the time feels right and you feel strong enough and brave enough, approach the person you are in conflict with.

○ Begin by sharing the Mexican fisherman's understanding of conflict.

○ Then, if you can, say softly, "Our net is tangled. Can you feel it?"

○ Invite this person's view of how your relationship is tangled, torn, and off-center.

○ With the patience of a fisherman's hands, let your heart tell you what comes next.

PLAYING HANDS WITH GOD

I can't go on. I go on.

—SAMUEL BECKETT

TRUMAN CAPOTE SAID, "More tears are shed over answered prayers than unanswered ones." He suggests that we don't really know what to ask for and that we think what we want is what we need, only to find that want and need are two different masters. I would add that prayer, below all words, is really listening, not problem solving when we're backed into a corner.

To pray comes from the Latin *precari,* which means *to ask earnestly.* So prayer *is* tied to asking questions. Only in our desperation does it turn to asking *for* something. When we break, some run, some watch, but those broken know it is the beginning of the deepest question, which my good friend Wayne Muller has framed as "How then shall we live, knowing we will die?" Asked in earnest, this question becomes a prayer whose inhabited depth becomes a way of life. In these waters, living as an unanswered question *is* a prayer that, more than rescuing us in times of need, brings us closer to life. Now I understand. When one of us is cut or lets fly a song of truth, we all bleed the faceless face of God.

A Reflective Pause

A MEDITATION

○ Sit quietly and begin praying, whatever that means to you.

○ As soon as you find yourself asking for something, stop.

○ Inhale deeply and begin again.

○ Begin as many times as necessary until you sink below your problem, your fear, your want to be rescued, and simply pray by listening.

○ Resist the urge to ask for something. Just listen your way closer to life.

○ Ask earnestly for nothing until you feel safe in the miracle you carry by being alive.

Reconciling Our Humanness

When we can live earnestly in question, we are presented with many hints or thresholds into Wholeness: through wounds, through wonder, through revelation, through silence, through dreams, through paradox, through the love of others. How we relate to these hints or thresholds has much to do with whether we will reconcile our humanness on Earth.

As Carl Jung makes clear in his *Answer to Job:*

> It is the task of the conscious mind to understand these hints. If this does not happen, the process of individuation will nevertheless continue. The only difference is that we become its victims and are dragged along by fate towards that inescapable goal which we might have reached walking upright, if only we had taken the trouble and been patient enough to understand in time the meaning of the numina that cross our path.

So the work of being refined while alive will go on of itself, whether we are willing or not. What is at stake is our peace. *To reconcile* means *to reunite, to bring back together, to restore relations, to accept, to harmonize.* Being human, we are constantly broken apart by experience. To reconcile our humanness means we are ever learning how to accept our suffering and to restore our Wholeness. We are often distracted into thinking we can solidify ourselves against being broken or that we can sidestep suffering. Both are impossible. We are fated by this incarnation to come apart and to be put back together. It is the opening and closing along the way that holds the secrets, and there is no other way to that wisdom than to be fully human and to accept where that leads.

A Reflective Pause

JOURNAL QUESTION

o When broken, we're presented with many hints or thresholds that lead us into Wholeness: through wounds, through wonder, through revelation, through silence, through dreams, through paradox, through the love of others. Share the story of how an experience with one of these helped put you back together and reconcile your humanness.

Now Everyone Is Right

My good friend Bob went to see his eighty-nine-year-old mother in the hospital. She loved to play poker. It was Thanksgiving and she, all agitated, greeted him with some urgency, "I'm playing hands with God! Can't you see?! I don't want to be playing hands with God! But there He is! And now *everyone* is right!" This was a shocking yet profound encounter which she couldn't stop repeating. She had dropped through the seam of her days into a deeper reality in which each person's view contributes its rightness to our fundamental understanding of life, the way each wave contributes to our understanding of the ocean.

Quite often, in approaching death, our elders are thrust through the tension of opposites, as if stepping off a cliff, and there the endless delineations between right and wrong and good and bad pale compared to the great unity of things which we all can feel, but not always understand. This abrupt awakening is not reserved for the elderly. Often, in crisis, in illness, in love, or in great unexpected joy, we stumble there.

When we've been taught to see everything as a choice between an upward and narrow path to success and a downward path of mistakes to failure, the awakening that everything is holy, that every path is right, can be disorienting. Whether we realize it or not, we are always playing hands with God and everyone is right.

In my own life, I was busily working to change the world when cancer stopped me and I woke up to the humble realization that the world was changing me. In my pain, I looked at my fellow patients surviving under their invisible weights and at the soft and chiseled nurses tied to removing those weights. In my pain, I realized that, indeed, everyone is right—and everyone is hoping that the turned-over card that God is holding on their behalf is an ace. But when we are opened by suffering, a mix of humility and desperation makes whatever card we hold glow so brightly that the faces of Kings and Queens become our faces—and miraculously *every* face holds *everything*. And whether we live or die, it becomes blessedly clear that every one of us is a gift and every card is an ace.

The Majesty of Being Human

The fragile, resilient miracle of life is unrepeatable. We all know this at some level. That we exist at all is a stunning improbability, given how many attempts nature needs to create one ounce of nectar. Yet we tend to fall asleep to the beautiful fact of being alive.

In actuality, a naked look at the countless ways that seas erode shores, that dreams feed the fires of eternity, that experience wears down our human pride till we are smooth and precious, an uncluttered look at the way things are scoured apart only to be pressurized back into being—all this makes living a humble and spectacular affair.

More than consciousness, what makes the human spirit truly heroic is the irrepressible instinct to face all of life's tides with an open heart. The heroic fact that we can be worn by these mighty, overwhelming currents and still pucker open and find a way to sing—this is the majesty of being human.

A Reflective Pause

TABLE QUESTIONS

To be asked over dinner or coffee with friends and loved ones. Try listening to everyone's response before discussing:

○ Describe an encounter with someone who seems to have dropped into a deeper reality. Though their surface behavior might appear illogical, explore what they've said or done as you would a riddle. Assume there is wisdom there and seek to understand it.

○ Take turns describing the majesty of being human as you experience it.

Then take one phrase or image from each person's sharing and write everyone's phrase or image on one piece of paper without identifying who spoke what.

Read aloud your collective poem on the majesty of being human.

KNOWING WHERE WE ARE

TWENTY-FOUR YEARS AGO, I drove from Albany, New York, down the thread of the Taconic Parkway to Kingsbrook Medical Center in Brooklyn, hugging the curves in early spring, wondering if this would be the last time I would see Grandma. When I arrived, she was sitting on the edge of her bed, her bedsore heels bandaged, and I imagined her immigrant heels were sore from ninety-four years of arriving. We were happy to see each other, and when I realized she hadn't been outside in months, I wheeled her down to the courtyard where the sun was waking all that had survived winter.

What happened there began my understanding of being lost and being centered and how often one is a threshold to the other. Driving home that day, I spoke the following poem into a tape recorder, only to discover at a rest stop that it hadn't recorded a thing. And so, having to say it all again, I began to *feel* the place where Grandma lives in my heart. Having to say it again, the truth of Grandma reached me, and so, through my tears, I was *inside* what I was saying, this time scrawling it on a napkin the way a caveman, brushing close to the pulse of life, must have scratched his fragile feeling on the wall of his cave.

Here is that feeling, that poem:

To Live Out the Gift

In the sun, in the yard
between the brick towers
where orderlies eat hard rolls
and yawn; in the sun
with her rubber brake on
and her footplates heating;
in the sun, for the first time
in seven months, she beams back
to the fresh earth she has not yet forgotten.

In the sun, in the yard
of the facility, she says,
the warm breeze brushing her face,
"I want to go home."
I wheel her around.
She says the trees are beautiful,
the clouds are beautiful.
She says the pansies and stray
wounded hungry cats
are beautiful.
She thinks the dirty bricks
are beautiful
as she inhales the light
and sighs, "Why can't I go home?"

Her white hair is swept in a wave
and she is healing in the sun,
and I start to feel
we are home.

She closes her eyes
and the heat is laced with bees
and the warmth and buzz drape

her strong near-century lids
and she smiles, then looks beyond the garden
and says, with a laugh, "Where are we?"

I start to retrace the day,
to frame her in, but the sun
like a knell of God overwhelms us,
and I rub the wind from her face.

She takes my hand, washing it
in the dish of air between us,
and says, serenely,
"I don't know where we are."
And I confess,
all organs of memory
in my throat,
"Neither do I."

I have replayed that moment with Grandma many times. I had been so prepared by my family to expect that she was slipping in and out of lucidity that I first heard her question, "Where are we?" as sad static in the breakup of an elder's mind. But quickly a deeper reality prevailed.

Here I was, thirty-six, sitting in the sun with a woman almost three times my age, a woman who had taken almost a hundred years to make her way from Russia to this small courtyard in Brooklyn; almost a hundred years through the full cycle of her life as a lost Ukrainian girl who didn't know English, as a young woman in love in America, as a tired mother during the Great Depression, as a midlife sister to those who died in Buchenwald, as a widow who never adjusted to the loss, and as a grandmother who never stopped telling us we were why she came.

Here, this ancient one looked like a cliff of heart worn of its many languages. Here in the sun, after all this way, watching an ant eat a small flower, she asked after a century of living, with deep profundity and humility, "Where are we?"

Often, I replay her chiseled face asking and my harried listening as a recurring dialogue between soul and self, between the center of my being and the center of my doing. It has become a way to check my course. In those rare moments of hard-won peace, my spirit asks, "Where are we?" and my very busy self is forced to look up and break its stride and reassess a pilgrim's progress.

And from that simple, profound moment, I hold these utterances like oracle bones:

> Why can't I go home?
> Where are we?
> I don't know where we are.
> Neither do I.

These four statements have become points of an inner compass that, when revisited and felt, help me discern if I am lost or centered. To carry these utterances honestly can open me, in any given moment, to what is keeping me from being fully at home in my skin and from my place in the Universe.

Now I can see that, without realizing it, this experience with Grandma began to set my course. From my visits with her at the end of her life, I began to shape my own inner practice of authenticity. Even the struggle I went through that day, to express my feelings in this poem, provided a lesson in *how* to live out the gift. At first, I felt that a difficult day had been made more difficult because the stupid tape recorder wouldn't work. But speaking my heart while driving home, then having to stop and, through my tears, do it again, was not just bad luck, but the chance to surface the gift of Grandma slow enough and deep enough that I might be affected by the experience, and enlarged by the truth of what she means to me.

That the tape recorder wouldn't work was really a blessing, for it forced *my spirit* to record her wisdom in the tissue of my heart. In this way, I saw the wisdom in speaking over writing, and now I understand why Homer, blind as he was, tripped about the Greek countryside reciting the *Odyssey* over and over. It is what we all are humbly asked to do, if we are to know what it means to be alive: to tell the story of our suffering through our blindness, over and over, until it reveals its secret melody.

Today, I can say that through the many trials and sheddings I have undergone since Grandma's death—through cancer, through the death-storm of one self that has cost the love of some and birthed the love of others, through the crests and swells of life's constant arrival—I have been lost and centered many times. I am not the same man who wheeled Grandma in the sun that day, though I am the same soul. And though I still don't know where we are, it is this deep and humble sort of not-knowing that puts us back in touch with the very pulse of life.

A Reflective Pause

A MEDITATION

- Breathe quietly until you feel centered.

- Inhale fully and ask yourself, "Where am I?"

- Feel your immediate surroundings.

- Close your eyes and inhale fully, asking yourself as you look inwardly, "Where am I?"

- Feel your inner surroundings.

- Open your eyes and breathe quietly until you feel where you are both inwardly and outwardly.

- Breathe deeply and open yourself to all of time, asking yourself, "Where am I?"

- Feel your place in eternity.

JOURNAL QUESTIONS

- Describe a time when you had to say or do something more than once and what that led to.

- What does "being home" mean to you? What part of "being home" do you carry within you? When do you go there?

TABLE QUESTIONS

To be asked over dinner or coffee with friends and loved ones. Try listening to everyone's response before discussing:

- What does "to live out the gift" mean to you? Tell the story of someone you admire who is an example of this.

- Go and sit with an elder and ask what they see after their long climb through life.

- Wait a week and go and sit with someone younger and share your story of visiting this elder.

Like being and doing, like giving and receiving, we've seen that the soul's calling helps us discover our life's work, while the call of the soul is a continual call to aliveness. Both are important. And key to living in the world is our vow to listen for the Original Presence that keeps everything alive. Despite the turbulence and unexpected turns we face, our friendship with that Original Presence lets us know where we are. In truth, we don't achieve aliveness, but we keep enlivening the presence of our soul by staying in relationship with ourselves, each other, and the Whole—until the glare is gone and only the color of things as they are can reach us. This is the season waiting under all seasons. And regardless of our good fortune or trouble, we are always holding off the storm of the world to hear the music that runs through everything. As harsh a teacher as experience is, our greatness as human beings is the unexpected re-emergence of life-force that is born from the friction of our gifts with what gets in the way.

Deep listening takes time, and the more we accept our very human frailties, the more we need to stay in conversation with all of life's agents. This brings us to the work of reverence: to solve our darkness by blossoming and to solve our loneliness by loving everything.

Through "The Work of Being Human," we've been exploring our friendship with experience, which holds the wisdom of life on Earth. Tending this friendship is the work of being human. This too is both personal and Universal. It's time to ask one more time: who are you and what is it you feel called to do with who you are? It's time to ask at another depth: are you holding off the voices of others long enough to hear your own? At the same time, are you moving beyond your own stubbornness to learn from others? And what is your hard work opening, regardless of what you are producing? What are you facing that is breaking you open? Hard as it may be, is there a constraint or limitation in your life that is intensifying one of your gifts? Sweet as it may be, is there a small alignment of life that has introduced you to your truest self? Where are you in your very personal practice of discerning right action? Whatever it is you face: are you living with what is before you, trying to change it, or working to live somewhere else? Though it can change daily, are you living in accord with what you've come to know is true?

This is at the heart of the work of being human: to reconcile our humanness by untangling our relationships with everything, though experience will keep entangling us in the net of life. We can only do this with a commitment to stay whole-hearted. I encourage you to accept that we are here to come apart and be put together repeatedly. I encourage you to celebrate your humanness and to accept where it leads. I encourage you to stay whole-hearted.

We will be inquiring next into our friendship with each other, which holds the wisdom of care. This is the work of love.

THE
WORK OF
LOVE

The first duty of love is to listen.

—PAUL TILLICH

I know there is no place to go with your grief other than to feel it and ride it like a raft until that rough sea brings you to a strange, familiar shore that is both where you have been and entirely new. I know nothing I can say will ease the pain beneath your breathing right now. We can only gain strength from sharing our experience, without second-guessing any of it, just putting what we've been through into the small fire between us that has kept us warm for years. I want to walk that pathless path together; through grief and death and faith and the mystery that lives beneath fairness and unfairness. It is beyond understanding and beyond all mapmaking. We can only climb our way like those before us into a clearing that begs for our acceptance if we are to know any peace. This mysterious path doesn't remove the grief or the pain, but somehow, like a knife dropped in the sea, our grief and pain lose their edge. Just know that you are both alone and not alone. Though I can't go with you to the cliff of all you feel inside, I am near.

THE HUMAN GARDEN

*We are put here for a little space
that we may learn how to bear
the beams of love.*

—William Blake

How I love people. I love how we root and bloom, how we twine around each other and reach for the light, how as far as we grow in the dark of the Earth is as far as we stand in the world. How being human, we are always charged with the vibrancy of a larger presence. How the complexity of our humanity mirrors this larger presence. In truth, we mirror everything living as we climb and stumble our way up the mountain to the cliff of yes. I recognize each person I come across because I am each on any given day. What matters is whether I shun those who bear my flaws or help them up; whether I turn away when this larger presence seems too strong or keep my birth-eyes open; whether I find a way to meet what is incomprehensible and somehow draw strength from it. What matters is if we can make it to the cliff of yes and shout our secrets to the sky till Heaven is the song we choose to sing on Earth.

This raises a central question: What is the proper use of our will? How useful is it to insist that we can will things to happen, if we are seeds growing into roots and shoots breaking ground? What if will is how we give our all to that growth? What if will is the sacred gritty act of holding nothing back?

Perhaps this is the work of love: to hold nothing back. Brother David Steindl-Rast reminds us that *I believe* means *I give my heart to this*. Perhaps, despite our lists of dos and don'ts, belief is less about the assumptions or conclusions we enshrine as principles and more about our devotion to engage and listen to life. Of course, we don't stay rooted in one place. And so, a paradox and challenge for every spirit born to Earth is how to inhabit a thoroughness of being wherever life takes us. This leads to a life of compassion, of being with other living things in a way that lets them grow. This too is the work of love.

Long ago, a disciple of Confucius, Zi Gong, asked, "Is there any one word that could guide a person throughout life?" The Master replied, "How about *shu* (reciprocity)? Never impose on others what you would not choose for yourself." This is another form of holding nothing back and giving your heart to another. This is one of the earliest voicings of the golden rule.

All of us are roots and shoots in the human garden. As far as we root in the earth is as far as we sprout in the world. Each of us destined to find our particular path to the light, so much depending on whether we choke each other or not along the way.

A Reflective Pause

JOURNAL QUESTIONS

○ If you are a plant, or flower, or tree in the human garden, describe yourself and describe your roots and shoots.

○ Whether affirming or troubling, describe one aspect of yourself that you see in another. How does it look in someone else? How do you feel encountering yourself this way?

Meeting Each Other

I led a conversation recently at a retreat center with about eighty people. After swimming in each other's presence for an hour or so, a sense of authenticity filled the space. A young woman asked, "Do you have anything for twenty-somethings?" She was very alive, and her eyes made me re-feel that young open place within me. I offered without much thought, but with all of my presence, "Listen to everything with your heart—*Everything*—and be still with it before acting on what you feel." At once, it felt like an instruction for me as well.

Then an elderly woman blurted out, "Do you have anything for sixty-somethings?" We all laughed. I turned to her and said slowly, "Listen to everything with your heart—*Everything*—and be still with it before acting on what you feel." We sighed together. This felt right. I had voiced what meeting each other had yielded. In this way, authentic conversation is like jazz: truly meeting each other without pre-arranging or knowing what you or I will say or hear.

Three Covenants

Our love needs to be bigger than our insanity.

—HENK BRANDT

There are three covenants that keep us engaged in the work of love. To begin with, when we see something true and beautiful in someone, it is *not* the work of love to change them or force their growth in our direction. It *is* the work of love to create conditions by which what is true and beautiful in all we behold can grow and blossom, bringing forth its deepest nature. At the same time, the work of love depends on giving others, especially young people, a sense of safety in the world, nurturing their confidence to lean into life and the unknown—not *away* from these eternal resources. Still, being human, we constantly slip from integrating our experience to being consumed by our experience. We move, almost daily, from having our fear, pain, and worry live in us to living within our fear, pain, and worry. So the third covenant of love is to keep each other company when we're drowning in our experience and awash in our feelings, until it all can right-size, until our experience and feelings can once again sustain us. These covenants exercise the muscle of compassion we call the heart.

Finding Our Face

I have a friend who, among other things, is a painter. Years ago, when starting out, she felt compelled to begin a painting of two women entering an embrace. When she arrived at their heads, she couldn't see their faces and so she had to stop. Life happened and experience began to paint her. Years later, she found the unfinished painting in her attic and realized, after becoming and shedding many selves, that this evolving painting was the story of her own soul and its double in the world.

All the intervening years were necessary for her to discover their features. Now, after many sufferings and many joys, she can finally see how the one is the face she shows no one and the other is the face she shows the world. Now she closes her eyes in the evening after work and surveys her long life for the expressions that have accompanied her. And struggling to understand how her life has unfolded, she is beginning to paint their faces and they are slowly finding their embrace. It is becoming clear to her that the mystery of learning how to embrace one's self is the same work of love that makes the mystery of embracing another possible.

We all need this quiet unfolding: the passion to paint what we dream, the honesty to only paint what we know, the courage to stop and live into what we don't know, the humility to return years later, and the courage to use the blood of our life as the colors needed to finish the embrace. This is the unfolding of the human flower. Until the face of our soul and the face we show the world is one, the same.

A Reflective Pause

JOURNAL QUESTION

- o Describe the face you show no one and the face you show the world. Without judging either, begin a conversation between the two.

The Closeness Opened by Kindness

The reward for love is closeness, a treasure that can't be bought or stolen or achieved. It is a law of the living: care leads to intimacy. Often we discover our dearest friends when stopping to help another or when someone is kind enough to carry us when we have fallen. There is no substitute for going through things together. There is no way to language what two whales share who swim around the world together or what binds two friends who climb through a forest of years in each other's steps.

Kindness itself is a way of life. There will always be those who wait for others to lift the heavy load, those who count on you or me to make the extra effort. Do not begrudge them. For though they suffer, they have not suffered enough. They cause themselves more harm than they know. When you lend a hand, you open a way for your heart to touch the heart of everything. This is a wealth that only grows. While those we help may leave or die or simply grow into their own beauty and be loved by others, the closeness uncovered by kindness turns to light in the body, until the closeness generated by kindness makes a lamp of the heart.

Falling Through

Lyn Hartley, an independent educator who lives in the wilds of the Yukon, tells the story of two skiers crossing a frozen lake at night. Sliding through the snow with flashlights, they came upon a moose fallen through the ice. The enormous creature was stuck shoulder high. It was clear the moose couldn't get out and they alone couldn't pull it out. The temperature was dropping. So they stayed the night and, though the moose resisted, they covered it with their tent, settling in to shine their small lights on its face and on the edges of broken ice, to keep the ice from freezing into shards that would cut the moose. In the morning, when the sun reappeared, they went for help. Together they roped the moose and slowly pulled it to the edge till it could find its own way out.

This is a powerful metaphor for how to listen to and be with those who have fallen through: stay close and keep them warm, resisting the urge to prematurely solve the situation. If nothing can be done, sit with them, and withstand the urge to abandon those who seem stuck. Offer your tent and stay till the way out presents itself, not forcing a rescue. How I need to hear this. For life is long enough that we will have our turn at falling through and being stuck, and at coming upon the fallen, not knowing what to do.

Before we meet like this, help me learn the skill of heart that lets love meet truth like small lights on ice. In the truth of each other, there is a way out.

A Reflective Pause

A MEDITATION

- Brother David Steindl-Rast reminds us that "I believe" means "I give my heart to this."

- Sit quietly and breathe steadily.

- Focus on something you believe in. It could be as simple as "I believe in light."

- Inhale deeply and say, "I believe in . . ." and name what you have chosen.

- Exhale deeply and say it again.

- Breathe fully and substitute for "I believe in" "I give my heart to . . ." and name what you have chosen.

- Inhale slowly and say this two more times.

- Consider how giving your heart changes what you're saying.

- Consider how you can give your heart more fully to what you believe.

- Sit quietly until your words and thoughts ripple back into silence.

TABLE QUESTIONS

> *To be asked over dinner or coffee with friends and loved ones. Try listening to everyone's response before discussing:*

○ In a form of conversational jazz, have one of you begin by completing the sentence "It isn't that simple . . ."

Rather than debating what is said, have each person continue the conversation by adding a sentence or two to the unfolding story.

Go around the circle till everyone has spoken three times.

Discuss what you collectively have said.

○ In your experience, what is the work of love?

After listening to everyone, voice a collage of sentiments, including one phrase or image from each person.

HOW WE INJURE OURSELVES

We are, when blessed, worn to the best
of what we don't break.

IT'S EASY TO learn unhealthy habits and adhere to them and hard to stay true to what is authentic. We're creatures of habit, but why are we pulled to that which is self-destructive? Often, it's simply because that's what we learn first, and the comfort of what is familiar is often stronger than our sense of what is good for us. Often, the unhealthy habit is linked to our sense of home or identity. When this happens, there's an added power to the behavior, because losing it feels at some level like losing who we are.

For example, while growing up and in an earlier marriage, I was always asked to carry everyone's emotions. This was all done nonverbally, and I accepted the role. Though I worked hard to change, when I stopped doing this for everyone, I felt disoriented and lacking. Likewise, if you've always been treated as helpless, as incapable of making the simplest decision, you will probably feel shaky in the sudden vacuum of other voices no longer telling you what to do. It's like leaning against a wall that is always pressing in on us. After a while, we learn that holding up that wall is normal. When that wall is removed, we have to relearn how to stand.

Our comfort with what we've learned runs deep. The fear of change has an ancient gravity all its own. It is archetypal. Consider the story of Moses. Though his people were enslaved and oppressed, though they cried out for relief and freedom, once Moses led them out of Egypt, many complained and wanted the comfort and familiarity of their bondage. What this old story tells us is that each of us has an impulse of soul that will lead us out of bondage and each of us has a strong change-resistant voice that, no matter the pain or abuse, will utter, "It's not so bad. It's home. It's how I know my way." How we engage these voices has much to do with how vital and authentic our lives can be.

We could call the impulse of soul our Moses voice, and the change-resistant voice of the familiar our Hamlet voice. For Hamlet is the archetype of the *yes, but* aspect in us that stubbornly, through indecision and rationalization, keeps us off the point we need to face. Repeatedly on the verge of doing what he knows he needs to do, Hamlet talks himself out of every action, dispersing his resolve again and again by too much deliberation.

The Hamlet in us appears in many different ways. For example, I have a very dear friend who struggles with an addiction. Over the years, after many cycles of addiction and recovery, we came to realize that whenever faced with the chance to stay true to what's healthy, he'd admit his need to do so, but confess to being weak and fragile and overwhelmed. He'd say, "I know this is true, but I just don't know if I can do it. You have to be patient with me."

We'd stall into a compassion for his limitations. But finally, I started to witness that, very soon afterward, when faced with opportunities to be unhealthy, he'd become incredibly strong and formidable and stubbornly resourceful in his will to return to the comfort of his bondage. One day, while we were eating sandwiches in the sun together, he sat up and realized the truth of his situation. He turned to me and said, "I'm strong as a bull, only weak when seduced into not facing my life." His Hamlet had been manipulating his Moses for years. Of course, this is part of any addiction; the persuasiveness of the insane voice to have us follow it as sane. My dear friend's struggle, which is our own, is to restore the impulse of soul and to enlist its inner strength in facing what is true. Clearly, we all suffer this opportunity repeatedly.

A Reflective Pause

JOURNAL QUESTIONS

○ We each have a bondage we struggle to be free of, and we each have a desert to cross. Give the history of your bondage and your desert. Where are you currently in relation to the two?

○ As an act of loving yourself, identify one way that you injure yourself. How can you stop?

Our relationship to change is never-ending and seldom simple. It seems we are challenged at every turn to discern true ways from false ways. This is part of the work of loving ourselves. And the crux of this discernment is the need to acknowledge that we have an impulse of soul that will follow what is true and a change-resistant voice that will adhere to what is familiar. To be clear, it's not the familiar that is troublesome, but our adherence to it. It's not having coffee every day on the deck while watching the birds that is troublesome, but not changing your schedule if a friend needs you at that time.

Admitting that we obey these voices and openly allowing the two to dialogue within us is an important practice of being in the world. Not trying to eliminate either, but withstanding the tensions of their energies till we can learn to live more fully beyond the habits we've assumed. Until the freshness of being alive in any given moment is what is familiar. Until being alive and awake itself is our home.

This isn't easy but necessary. How do we relate to our change-resistant voice, which says *yes, but* to everything? Much has to do with choosing to enter life rather than retreat from it. The renowned psychotherapist Erik Erikson suggests that we can respond to life in three basic ways: *creatively,* by leaning into the emerging situations that connect us to the life around us; *neurotically,* by retreating into isolations

that keep us from the unpredictable life around us; or more dangerously by reframing our retreating behaviors as necessary stances in a
harsh world.

Of course, we do all three in infinite combination. But when we can
enter life rather than retreat from it, we begin to engage the struggle
points of transformation. However, when we retreat more than we
need to, we thicken the walls of our habits. And though there is nothing
inherently wrong with isolating from the chaos of the world or reframing the violence of the world to gain a better foothold, when isolation
seals us off from life and reframing what we encounter becomes a way
to deny the truth of things, we are giving the key to our soul to the
Hamlet in us. When retreating far enough, we can falsely ennoble the
aspects of our isolation as traits to be admired. In this way, we take up
residence there, arrested near thresholds of growth.

By ennobling our isolation, we can reframe life-draining behaviors
as virtues to uphold. We can reframe mistrust as maturity in a harsh
world. We can reframe guilt as the self-effacing sacrifice to serve others.
We can reframe insecurity as self-deferring humility. We can reframe
indecision as adaptability. We can reframe stagnation as the discipline
of stillness. We can reframe isolation itself as independence. And we
can reframe despair as a stoic acceptance of reality. All the while, we
are losing touch with what true maturity, service, humility, adaptability,
stillness, independence, and acceptance hold for us.

Engaging the life of these voices and working with them is never easy,
which is another reason why we need honest friendship and the comfort of others. Thankfully, that tradition has gone on forever as well.
For centuries, the shamans of a tribe in Indonesia have poured lavender
and flax seed into a satin pouch, placing it as a blessing on tired eyes.
The weight of seed on tired eyes opens the face. Loving each other
often feels like this: leaving seeds on each other's eyes. Once our faces
open, what e.e. cummings imagined seems possible; that beneath how
we injure ourselves, "Yes is the only living thing."

A Reflective Pause

A MEDITATION

- ○ Sit with your palms up.

- ○ As you inhale, close your hands.

- ○ As you exhale, open your hands again, palms up.

- ○ Begin to focus on something you are saying "yes, but" to.

- ○ As you inhale, close your hands, and say, "but."

- ○ As you exhale, open your hands, palms up, and say, "yes."

- ○ Repeat this several times.

- ○ Sit still and in your heart, disconnect "yes" and "but."

- ○ Begin to focus only on "yes."

- ○ Breathe deeply and open and close your hands, saying, "yes."

- ○ Repeat this several times.

- ○ Focus on your issue, saying, "yes, yes."

TABLE QUESTIONS

To be asked over dinner or coffee with friends and loved ones. Try listening to everyone's response before discussing:

- ○ Tell the story of a situation you reframed and how that helped you. Tell the story of another situation you reframed and how that hurt you.

- ○ Describe an unhealthy habit you are formidable in upholding. Now describe a healthy habit you are tentative in upholding. How might you reverse these efforts?

A STEADFAST TEACHER

If we want to be held, we have to behold.

WELL INTO MY THIRTIES, I felt a natural yearning to be seen and heard. In time, this became urgent and draining. Over the years, I came to realize that being held is more important than being understood. When held, I don't care so much about being seen or heard, because being held *is* being seen and heard in a way that affirms our very existence, much the way that the warmth of the sun affirms a flower into blooming. And being as present as a flower opening to the sun is the soul's way of holding the mystery of life itself, which attended will reciprocate and hold us back in an embrace we call wonder or awe. This means that, when present enough to behold the Universe, we will be held by the mystery.

As a vulnerable human being, I still want to be seen and heard and understood for who I am. When bestowed without agenda, these are the gifts of love. I don't think we ever lose this need, but the absence of these affirmations no longer rules my life. It still hurts to be ignored, especially if I've shown myself completely. It still feels thwarting to be misunderstood, especially if I've spoken my heart as plainly as I know how. But the truth doesn't need to be explained to be true. And the elements don't withhold their innate power because we turn our backs to them. We are like tall leaning trees. We sway in our humanness every which way, while our spirit roots firmly in an ever-deepening connection to the Earth.

lonely

Without a felt sense of this connection to the web of life, the need to be seen and heard can rule us, overwhelm us, and even devastate us. Without this larger firsthand connection, I can become dependent and even addicted to external validation. Yet when I can find the courage to be fully present in any given moment, I just might feel the tug of all we are tied to. This tug of connection can restore my innate authority of being. To be sure, this felt lifeline between our very core and the Universe won't eliminate loneliness, but it will right-size it. This felt presence of everything larger than us won't eliminate pain, but it will absorb it.

I know I'm being held by the nature of things when I feel this ache way inside. When young, it appeared as a sadness I couldn't explain. I thought if I could just get rid of it, I might be happy. But after cancer, I began to realize that this deep ache is the tuning fork of my soul. It is how I know I am close to what matters. In actuality, this deep and nameless ache in the presence of beauty and suffering has been a steadfast teacher and friend. It breaks me open to truth when I am too busy or numb to take in beauty. And these breakings of heart are awe-filled events from which I don't recover but through which I am uncovered.

All this has led me over time to accept that the heart is a muscle that *wants* to be exercised. And though it feels like I will end each time my heart is broken, my heart only breaks into a larger version of itself. When I am present to this process, I am broken open. When I withhold my presence, I am just broken. I only know that after my heart is broken, I am still here. And each time, I breathe deeper. I stand taller. Each time I wake to an unexpected ability and urge to be kinder.

A Reflective Pause

A MEDITATION

- ○ Sit quietly and bring to mind a time when you felt you wouldn't survive your heart breaking.

○ Inhale deeply and try to remember the moment the breaking began to turn to an opening.

○ Exhale deeply and try to remember what that felt like.

○ Inhale fully and put your hands on your heart, trying to feel the strong place at center where your heart began to mend.

○ Exhale fully into the world, accepting the mystery that a broken heart, if given time, is a stronger heart.

JOURNAL QUESTIONS

○ Tell the story of an important time when you weren't seen or heard and what that took away from you. Now tell the story of an important time when you were clearly seen and heard for who you are and what that gave you.

TABLE QUESTIONS

To be asked over dinner or coffee with friends and loved ones. Try listening to everyone's response before discussing:

○ Who or what is a steadfast teacher for you, one you return to when you lose your way? How did you first come to realize this was such a teacher for you?

IN THE HUT WE CALL
THE SELF

I'VE BEEN LISTENING way inside, where the Universe rushes through me like wind through a hole in an old door in a hut near the edge of a cliff. I've been going there and listening, on the inner edge of everything. There, I've heard two irrevocable truths: the truth of life, the very fact of it, how it comes out of nowhere like a strong breeze to lift our faces, how it goes on its way; and the truth of how life like a storm can rough up our hearts, how we have no choice but to feel that wind move through us and around us. Trying to give words to this is difficult. But the first truth can be offered as *the truth of things as they are,* and the second as *the experience of being human.* These have become my teachers: trying to accept the nature of what is and trying not to deny its impact.

So when you ask, "What are we here for?" I'm stopped by this wind which rushes through the hole in my heart. From this far down, it's like asking the cliff itself, what is it here for. We might say: to hold up the world. The cliff might say: to *be* the world. I can only say that my heart and eyes and mind keep being worn open.

Let me tell you what life is like in the hut these days. Like many of us, I have known centeredness as a calm and the experience of difficult feelings as forms of agitation. Like many of us, I swing between these poles: needing to calm down when stirred up and wondering how long the calm will last before I'm stirred up again. Like many of us,

I've come to associate the lack of agitation (lack of pain, fear, confusion, or anger) with peace and the presence of such agitation as being pulled into the tangle of the world.

I'm learning, though, that the absence of agitation alone is not necessarily peace and that the presence of such difficult feelings does not mean we are necessarily off-center. Rather, the task of being fully alive challenges us to stay in the center *while* feeling the full range of life on Earth. This is quite a task, which I'm not sure how to do. Nonetheless, listening way inside to these two teachers—*the truth of things as they are* and *the experience of being human*—I find myself here.

This all descended on me recently when I found myself drawn, again, into relationship with a person who didn't mean what he said. The details don't matter. Just that this person was unreliable and won't accept that he broke his promise. For sure, I have not lived up to all the promises I have made. But this time I could feel my heart tear like a secret pocket in the same spot it had torn before. And for all my practice at not having expectations, at letting go, at surrender and acceptance—this disappointment ripped me.

Yet after flipping back and forth, I've been jarred into feeling *both* centered and hurt at once: accepting that the situation won't change and, at the same time, not shutting down what the disappointment feels like. I'm not trying to run from the agitation in the name of peace, but trying to relax my being until I'm spacious enough to be a container for both: the peace *and* the agitation.

This is new and, not surprisingly, this race between peace and agitation, whatever the cause, has reached its limits. For peace and agitation are stitched together and, tugged on, they unravel a thread of Oneness. It's enough to make me break down the ancient door in the hut of my self, so the wind of life can bluster through. But then, the whispers that arrive one by one through the ancient hole way inside, the whispers we know as truth, would be lost in the unfiltered fury of the wind.

A Reflective Pause

truth

A MEDITATION

- ○ Center yourself and think of a recent moment of peace.

- ○ Breathe slowly and let its feeling return.

- ○ Stay centered and think of a recent moment of agitation—of fear or confusion or pain.

- ○ Breathe slowly and let its feeling return.

- ○ Inhale deeply until your heart expands, and let both the peace and agitation mix there.

- ○ Sit this way for several minutes and practice spaciousness.

JOURNAL QUESTION

- ○ Where do you go to sit on the inner edge of everything and what do you hear there?

TABLE QUESTION

To be asked over dinner or coffee with friends and loved ones. Try listening to everyone's response before discussing:

- ○ Share the story of a promise that was broken, when someone didn't mean what they said, and how this experience has affected you.

FINDING BIRDSONG

WE ARE NEVER FAR from the need to let in beauty while we're suffering and to listen to loss and what it opens. These two ongoing tasks exercise the heart and make us resilient, when we can engage them.

We forever drift in and out of the miracle before us. As our eyes dilate and constrict in order to see, we are opened by love, wonder, and truth into the immediacy of all that is incomprehensible, only to wrestle with pain, loss, and obstacles that make us constrict. And during the wrestle, the miracle of life seems out of reach. Though once enduring what we're given, pain and loss open us further. This is how the human heart sees.

Modern culture tells us that we are entitled to a perfect, happy life. Yet if we insist on deifying a painless life free of loss, we will only be battered by the pain and loss we are given and miss the point of the journey. Much as we'd like, we can't be happy all the time, any more than we can dilate or inhale all the time. We need to dilate and constrict, and inhale and exhale, in order to live. And so, the heart, mind, and soul need to open and close to the entirety of the human experience in order to make sense of things as they move through. Difficult as they are, pain, loss, and obstacles are dynamic forces of life that make us open and close. It is up to us to make sense of our lifelong conversation with them.

To be clear, we don't have to invite pain and loss, for we can't avoid our share of them any more than we can avoid the full measure of weather. And we don't have to make gods of pain and loss either. It's the give-and-take between pain and wonder and the way the weather of experience shapes us that *is* life's journey, which though we can deny, we can never escape.

Consider how some days we wander into a wash of birdsong and are filled with the quiet music of the Universe. But no matter how we linger, the birdsong fades and we must enter our day. Other days, the birds seem to come out of nowhere, from behind buildings or under bridges, and their song covers us with an invisible mist that reminds us: life is so much more than the machinery of our tasks. But they swoop on, taking their sweet medicine with them. Either way, we are refreshed and left with the work of listening: to keep the song that comes out of nowhere alive in what we do, wherever life leads us.

Truth often appears to us like the song of these birds. We wander into a wash of it and, no matter how we linger, it fades. On other days, truth seems to come out of nowhere to remind us how rare it is to be here at all. Then off it goes with its refreshing medicine and we are left with the work of keeping the song of truth alive in the days that remain. This lifelong conversation with love, wonder, and truth in counterpoint with pain, loss, and obstacles is how we dilate and constrict our way into the essence of our aliveness.

A *Reflective Pause*

JOURNAL QUESTIONS

o Tell the story of a time when you were challenged to let in beauty while you were suffering or when you needed to listen to loss and what it opened. How has this experience exercised your heart? How are you different for this experience?

Raven Talk

Recently, I was on my way home after a week of recording teaching conversations about staying awake for Sounds True in Boulder, Colorado. It was a deep, expansive experience with kindred spirits. I was feeling grateful and at peace, like a smooth piece of driftwood floating in a larger sea. Then I bumped my head on the plane and got off with a headache that wouldn't go away. Then a sinus infection kicked in. I never had trouble with sinus, and so this kind of headache, cramping behind my eyes, was new to me. It all felt deep, too near my brain, oddly like the tumor that lived in my skull twenty-four years ago. I began to have trouble cleaving then from now. Everyone said that sinus infections take time to heal. But the infection and the bump constellated a strange sensation near the scar, a thickness in my head I hadn't felt since my cancer days. My view of things began to constrict. I woke that night with a jolt of fear that the cancer had returned, like a dragon waking after a very long sleep. "Not now!" I screamed in silence as Susan slept next to me, "Not Now!"

I was wrestling for the expansive view of life I had just been immersed in, wrestling with the body memory that was overtaking me. Losing my ability to keep the fear at arm's length, I sat up in bed telling myself, *That was then, this is now,* telling myself, *Don't fall into the rabbit hole.* But the old oyster in the shell of my survival trembled in reply, *Too late, too late.*

I was already drowning in what-ifs, and the fear began to circle like a raven gliding near my heart, waiting for an opening to tear its piece. I lived this way for several days, dilating and constricting, measuring the ache in my head, the rip in my past; not wanting to begin another journey of diagnosis, not wanting to be governed by the fear of doing nothing.

Finally, Susan accompanied me to our internist, who took my blood pressure, which was high. A severe headache could elevate my pressure. She poked her small thumbs under my eyes. She poked around my temples. She too thought it was a sinus infection but given my history, gave me a script for a CT scan of the brain, which I could schedule for peace of mind. More dilation and constriction.

Something deep in me knew I was healthy, but the fear kept my trust of this just out of reach. This went on for three weeks. The headache wasn't going away. By now I was turned inside out. Running into tests too soon only feeds the fear (give the thing a chance to heal), but avoiding these tests after three weeks is foolish (if there's a tumor, I can't ignore it). Knowing when to face things is a skill we're asked to develop constantly: in facing conflict, in facing loved ones, in facing those who have hurt us, in facing the truth of our past or the truth of our limitations. And no one can determine right timing but you.

I had the CT scan. While waiting for the results, it was difficult to find my footing. Every time I felt a return of perspective, some other pain would give the fear new strength. Like an unseeable python, it would wait and constrict me further. Fear if fed can do this. Then a wisdom tooth in my upper right jaw began to die and send its stubborn ache, which only sharpened the headache that wouldn't go away. I was certain the tumor was spreading.

Turns out the dying tooth was causing it all: the sinus infection, the deep relentless headache, the elevated pressure. After the root canal, the scan results arrived. My head is normal. I'm fine—no cancer. But though it's over, the damn fear won't stop. It keeps circling like a raven, and I'm stuck in its dark wing. I cry out to no one, "How can something a quarter of a century ago grip me so completely? Why can't I break the constriction of this fear and pain, even when the problem's solved?"

A depth within replies, "Because we needed something this jarring to loosen the wounds you've been carrying for twenty-four years." It's true. The tooth has given up its piece of hard wisdom. So now I'm up again in the night trying to shoo the dark bird of fear. I put my hands on my heart and exhale slowly, trying to draw the fear into my hands, to let it steam out of me without landing on anyone else.

After twenty minutes—or is it twenty lifetimes?—the bird seems farther away. I doze and keep dreaming the fear from my heart, through my breath, out my hands. And in between worlds, I see a walkway of brick covered with leaves that scatter in a sudden wind of light. I doze some more. Then stir to a lake gleaming in a sun I can't see. I'm watching through a sway of bowed trees. And there—the raven, harmlessly perched on a dead limb. I want to stay here, in between, but know I must wake. And the raven will follow because it wants the light too. The things that frighten us just want to be held.

By morning, my heart is beginning to uncramp. I hear the fall leaves rustle about their wisps of light. Beauty is beginning to be beautiful again. I start to well up. Pain and fear have had me by the neck, the way surf crashes to scrape us along the bottom. But standing as a speck beneath the open sky, fear has no place to intensify. The sun teases the clouds to show their white belly. I'm expanding again. Thank God. Thank the mystery. Thank the undeniable flow that no one sees. It is not about being scraped along or being brilliant like the sun. We are kept alive by both. The unmowed field is swaying beneath the blue. The sun throbs slightly. I throb slightly. The curl of light under the fallen log rises like a slow truth I've been looking for.

The Filament

My dentist said, "Take a look at this." The nerve of that dying tooth on the cotton swab was the size of a hair. I was astonished. How could something that tiny cause such pain and rearrange my entire consciousness? The image has stayed with me and seems a metaphor for the filament that connects all life. So often the filament goes unseen and unheard but, when tugged or cut, has the power to gather a life's worth of attention in an instant. When the nerve is touched, our entire consciousness can be rearranged. In truth, each of us is a tiny conduit connecting everything. Each living being, a hair-like filament in the fabric of existence.

As such, we are incredibly fragile and incredibly powerful. Our touch, nerve to nerve, has the power to change the course of a life. Thankfully and humbly, we can't intend that change or control what the change, being to being, will look like. When touched ourselves, we are forced to listen for our lives, though we often need each other to make sense of what we've heard.

Carl Jung thought of poets and artists as filaments who, against their will, find themselves used as lightning rods for the collective unconscious. In this regard, we are all poets and artists, waiting for a deeper form of listening to let one person's humanity reveal the whole of humanity, even briefly. It is often through an unexpected empathy that we become a conduit for the human struggle beyond our own awareness. I offer this story within a story as an example.

Shortly after the Virginia Tech massacre, in April 2007, my heart was gripped by one of the victims, Professor Liviu Librescu. Often when confronted with tragedy, our heart tries to hold on to one detail as a living symbol of all that is incomprehensible. For me, it was the image of Professor Librescu, a Holocaust survivor who was teaching a course in solid mechanics that day, and how he held the door of his classroom shut as the mad gunman, Seung-Hui Cho, tried to enter. While all but one of the students escaped, Cho shot and killed Professor Librescu through that door. I couldn't stop seeing the two of them on both sides of that door and how we all live on both sides of that door. The image wouldn't let go of me until I opened my heart to the deeper history of our human struggle pulsing in that moment. Thinking about Professor Librescu, though I never knew him, changed me and led me to writing my account of that terrible day, called "Suffering and Loving the World," which was published in my book of stories *As Far As the Heart Can See.*

Four years later, in 2011, Karen—who works at Virginia Tech, who lived through that awful day, who knew Professor Librescu, who cried uncontrollably with Mrs. Librescu after helping her set up her husband's memorial fund—Karen came across this telling of her story, their story, which somehow arced its way through me, and somehow, though we've never met, she writes that it's given her a measure of peace, that she no longer freezes at the sound of sirens. And her reaching out has given me some peace. I have no wisdom about such inexplicable tragedy. I was only trying to lessen the shard of pain that had landed in me.

That this ounce of comfort could transfer between us in no way speaks to any insight on my part, but to the capacity of the mystical filament of heart that, if listened to, will lead us beyond what we know into the depth of our common humanity, into that place where none of us are strangers. That what I was compelled to voice could be of use to those who lived through this is spiritual evidence that we are tethered together in the deepest corner of our souls. It's all a writer or an artist can hope for—to be a medic of consciousness. We are all bells that time rings—sometimes harshly, sometimes gently—and where we're struck strikes us all.

Often, when opened to our own experience, we find at the bottom the rich moist earth of everyone's experience. In this way, *feeling* is the constant listener who leads us, beyond our readiness, into the difficult and majestic ways we are called to be alive and called to voice each other's aliveness.

Lesson Plan

> *The lost bird remembers how to sing*
> *as it splashes in a puddle*
> *and forgets how to fly.*
>
> *This was the teacher's answer*
> *to his student's complaints*
> *about living on earth.*

All of our listening brings us home. This is the teacher's answer to his student's complaints. This is what the teacher-soul keeps saying to the student-self in each of us: to accept our place in the miracle before us, to listen to our experience, to our bodies, to our pain, to our wonder, to our place in the mystery, until we land and sing—this is what all birdsong calls us to remember.

Try as we will to fly away, all flight leads us to land where we began, different but the same. Try as we will to run from suffering, all our pain lands us back on earth in the puddle of our life where we can listen to our reflection. Try as we will to get out of here, life simply and harshly returns us to *the heart of here*, which, if listened to, opens us to the heart of everything. What the teacher says to the student who complains is that there is no lesson plan for living but to live. And all our dreams and plans and strategies are necessary detours to the brilliant reality of the life we already inhabit.

We've been describing many kinds of listening along the way: to what is said, to what is not said, to the ways we injure ourselves, to the music in the tangle of relationships, to the way time slows down when we give it our attention, to the silence opened up in nature, to the call of our soul and the Oneness waiting in our experience. Each is a capacity more than a skill that we must get to know and live with. Each is a quiet teacher that will withdraw if we frighten it with our noise and grandiosity.

With each way of listening, we are asked to invoke another aspect of courage. With each depth of listening, we are asked to keep a vow beyond what we already know, a vow beyond our awareness that reminds us that each moment is yet to be lived. And so, knowing others have wanted to move the world and were forced to accept how the world moved them; knowing others have suffered too much and that some grow dark while some weaken into bliss; knowing thousands have called out to God in their most private despair long before we were ever born; knowing the wisdom in silence and water has received them all; knowing the spark we call love has made hard men soft and determined women reconsider; knowing the withholding of love has sent flowers into exile no matter how bright the spring; knowing the long breath of one star consumes a hundred generations; knowing how little and how much one speck of dream accounts for; knowing how easy it is to let the material energies take over; knowing that when misunderstood we can swallow the rush of anything that will help; knowing how common the weight of having to make do; knowing how much is at stake, it is imperative to close our knowing, as a cliff diver closes his eyes, and live . . . as if no one has ever lived.

A Reflective Pause

A STANDING MEDITATION

○ Close your eyes, breathe slowly, and let all your knowings—your worries, your tasks, your yet to be realized dreams—rush by your mind.

○ Inhale and let your sense of personal history rush by your heart: what you've wanted, what you've lost, what has hurt you.

○ Exhale and sense where your breath thins into the larger air. Feel the edge of all you know.

○ Repeat this inhaling and exhaling until you feel safe at the edge of where you've been and where you've yet to go. This is the moment we are always in.

○ Inhale and open your eyes. Imagine yourself as a diver on a cliff.

○ Now exhale and dive into the unscripted day.

TABLE QUESTIONS

To be asked over dinner or coffee with friends and loved ones. Try listening to everyone's response before discussing:

○ Describe a time when the constriction of pain or fear diminished your sense of life and what was possible. How did this experience impact you? How did you see your way through this?

○ Speak of a time when your unexpected empathy made you aware of the larger human struggle. Given this experience, how does empathy add to your life? If you haven't experienced this, it is not a flaw but rather a story you have yet to meet. Given this, how might you better practice empathy in readiness for the stories that await you?

THE ENDLESS SEARCH

THE HINDU SAGE Ramana Maharshi said, "There is no greater mystery than this, that we keep seeking reality though in fact we are reality." Not accepting this paradox is the cause of much of our suffering, as we are forever chasing horizons, forever searching for some secret of life other than where we are. There is nothing wrong with seeking or searching with a destination in mind. Nothing wrong with working toward some goal or state of being in which we might inhabit our better selves. But we are so addicted to the intoxication of our will that we are led to believe that *not* getting what we want—*not* arriving where we aim, *not* achieving what we dream of—is a failure, from which many of us never recover.

The truth is that no matter how gifted or blessed we might be, no one ever gets all they want. This is not how life unfolds. Nothing in nature grows according to plan, but according to the constancy of the elements. As human beings, we are shaped by the constant elements known as time and experience. All our destinations and goals and aspirations—noble and sincere as they might be—are only starting points for our uncharted growth, the way vines and brush in a forest braid in unimaginable ways as they grow.

Still, the impulse to search is natural and human. We are born with a thirst for love and truth and meaning. But the deeper forms of search have no destination. At these deeper levels, we search more like fish who keep swimming because if they don't keep water moving through their gills, they will die. It doesn't matter where they go, just that they go. For creatures living in the deep, this endless search is a way of being. As spirits in bodies living on Earth, we swim through the rivers of time and experience, and the heart is our gill. If we don't keep moving through the days, if we don't keep taking in experience through the gill of our heart, we will die.

So we must look more closely at fish and the miracle of their gills. Though we've all learned about this in school, the fact of it is quite astonishing. Fish breathe oxygen though they have no direct access to air. Amazingly, they *extract* the oxygen from the water passing through their gills and discharge what's left. Completing the analogy, each of us needs to extract what will keep us alive from the experience that moves daily through our heart. Each of us must learn how to let the heart do its work of extracting only what is essential from what we go through and how to discharge the rest. This is the purpose of the endless search.

This headlong swim into the days with no specific destination helps us inhabit the life we are born to. Let's look at the life of a particular fish for one more parallel to our earthly journey. The mighty salmon actually *change* their physiology *twice* in their lifetime. Born in the headwaters as freshwater fish, they are drawn irrepressibly to the larger sea. Once launching into the ocean, they enter adulthood by changing their biology so they can live in salt water. As if this is not miracle enough, they eventually awaken into elderhood with a growing urge to return to the place of their birth to spawn. Entering the last stage of their journey, they *change* their biology *one more time—back* to being freshwater fish.

The way of the salmon translates to the spirit's journey. For us, the endless search—into the larger sea of life and back into the river of our days—transforms how we take in what matters over the course of our lives. When we can follow our inborn call into the larger sea of life beyond the confines of our personal concerns, we mature and the very life that carries us changes for entering the deep. If blessed to live into elderhood, we are drawn to return to the place of all birth—where self and other are the same.

There is the search that chases life and the search that reveals life.

Yet we often confuse the two. The search that reveals life is different than the search for gold, or an image of love, or an image of God. The storyteller Margo McLoughlin says, "I know my practice is slipping when I don't feel wonder or awe." This is a good way to discern if we've drifted from the search that reveals life-where-we-are to the search which assumes that what matters is always somewhere else.

When losing our sense of wonder and awe, we need great compassion, as no one stays in wonder and awe constantly. When these deep teachers remain absent too long, we must renew the deeper practice of searching without searching, of seeking with no destination. We must relax and open the gill of our heart. But how?

A Reflective Pause

JOURNAL QUESTIONS

○ Describe your impulse to search and where it's taken you. Now describe how the elements of time and experience have shaped you. Without judgment, note the path each has uncovered.

Three Ways to Search

We can begin again every day. All we have to do is wake to the countless opportunities to unlock our heart, as if we've never opened it before. To practice opening our mind and heart, the pianist and teacher Michael Jones offers three archetypal ways. First is the search for whole-mind thinking, which can re-establish our sense of the living Oneness we are a part of. This is often done through metaphor. Then there is the search for belonging, which can renew our bond to the living. This is often done through storytelling. Finally, there is the search for authenticity, which can reanimate our experience of beauty and truth. This is often done through poetry.

Whole-mind thinking is not only viewing our experience from the largest perspective possible but, more importantly, remembering when we can't that there *is* a larger view than what we're limited to in any given moment. But why insist on seeing things from beyond us? Because, as the teacher Prasad Kaipa says, "To see more expands and deepens our wisdom and to feel more expands and deepens our compassion." Together, they braid a lifeline that can withstand almost any storm.

Such lifelines are crucial because, being human, we live between the large and the small, between the whole and the detail; between the underlying grasp of everything that keeps us sane and the tiny splinter we can't find that keeps us from walking. And metaphor is the shifting image that correlates the two. Metaphors make the intangible briefly tangible through something analogous in the physical world. In that correlated moment, seeing the relationship—between the large and the small, between the whole and the detail, between everything and the damn splinter—opens our perspective enough to help us find our way.

When the Sufi poet Ghalib says, "For the raindrop, joy is entering the lake," we are opened to a conversation about the very relationship of a single soul to the ocean of life. As we search for our purpose while on Earth, this small but potent image opens us to a larger perspective that can affect the way we return to whatever the day is bringing us.

A Reflective Pause

JOURNAL QUESTION

This is a journal question that leads to a table question. Invite a trusted friend or loved one to do this with you:

○ As a way to introduce yourself to whole-mind thinking, I invite you to reflect and journal, when you can, by describing a time you experienced the larger fabric of life, whether you could make sense of it or not.

TABLE QUESTION

○ After a time, tell this story to your trusted friend or loved one,
inviting them to share a story of whole-mind thinking with you.

The search for belonging—in our own skin, with each other, in the
world, and even in the history of life—is probably our most persistent
and confusing urge, because belonging is a tangled gift. At the heart of
it, all belonging is dependent on the strength and health of our connections. And story is and has always been the connective tissue of humanity. As long as we ache to belong, we will ache for a story. Lingering
honestly in any moment will reveal a story.

Recently, while teaching in Prague, I wandered into the ancient Jewish Cemetery in the old Jewish Ghetto. As a Jew born to Russian immi-
grants, I stumbled back in time through crooked, broken gravestones,
carved with Hebrew letters covered with moss. The more I stood in
the November air, the more the story of these lives seeped up from the
ground. I returned several times during my stay, drawn to uncover a
sense of belonging I'd never known.

I kept returning to one worn, stubborn grave. With my hand on
that cold ancient stone, I said aloud to no one, "I was born a Jew." I've
spent my life trying to understand what this means. Is it an accident of
birth? Or a strength of acceptance discovered on the far side of suffering? There were others there, slowing in their walk—Czech, French,
German, Russian—each of us certain about something that can't be
named. I could feel it in the story rising from the ground.

The Old Jewish Cemetery in Prague

A Reflective Pause

JOURNAL QUESTION

This is a journal question that leads to a table question. Invite a trusted friend or loved one to do this with you:

o Again, I invite you to reflect and journal, when you can, by describing a time when you felt a strong sense of belonging and what qualities made you feel that you belonged. If you haven't felt such a moment, describe a time when you didn't feel accepted or welcome and what qualities made you feel unwelcome.

TABLE QUESTION

o After a time, discuss this with your trusted friend or loved one, inviting them to share a story of belonging or of feeling unwelcome.

The search for authenticity is as basic as lungs needing air. We need to feel authentic to be alive. There are a thousand openings to being real. No one can name them all or master them all. But we don't have to. We only have to find one, breathe deeply, and leap.

That leap of authenticity *is* poetry. Sometimes it's written. Sometimes it's stitched in silence. Sometimes it's in a stranger's hands trying to piece back together the one thing we never wanted to break. Authenticity is how we live with truth. And the poetry of authenticity can connect us to the Wholeness of humanity and the Universe at any time in any way.

In our workshop in Prague, we invited people to tell the story of a small kindness that helped them know their true self. As a way to invite people into a sense of their own authenticity and belonging, we asked them to just be quiet and still for thirty seconds, to let that act of kindness find them. Amaranta, a researcher from Holland, spoke tenderly of a moment five years earlier. She was reading alone in her home and night fell and the room grew very dark. She just kept reading and suddenly and quietly, her now ex-husband appeared with a lamp to help her see. This small moment, now that they are no longer together, touched her deeply. She saw it as a metaphor for all we can do for each other, how the smallest light will fill every corner of a dark room. I listened to her closely and thought—this is the gesture of all education. In truth, the lamp we carry from darkness to darkness is our heart.

A Reflective Pause

JOURNAL QUESTION

This is also a journal question that leads to a table question. Invite a trusted friend or loved one to do this with you:

○ This time, tell the story of a small kindness that helped you know your true self. As a way to begin, just be quiet and still for thirty seconds, to let that act of kindness find you.

TABLE QUESTIONS

o After a time, discuss this story with your trusted friend or loved one, inviting them to share their own story of such a small kindness.

o If the person who showed you this kindness is still alive, consider letting them know how their kindness made a difference.

Against All Odds

We start out eager to go somewhere, and in time we might. But along the way, if blessed, the search stops being about travel and starts being about the swim through experience that expands our understanding of life, animates our sense of belonging, and uncovers a sweet authenticity that makes it impossible to ignore the mysterious abundance that never stops forming and re-forming.

Ultimately, being the reality we seek doesn't stop us from searching. It simply brings us closer to the elemental sense of moving through life until we accept and willfully enter the process of being and becoming that nothing alive can escape. Surrendering to this inborn process when keenly authentic lets us glimpse and feel the threads that connect everything, the way sunlight breaking through the clouds will reveal a silkworm's threads spun between leaves.

This brings us to Indra's Net, which offers a compelling image by which to understand the universal web of connection. Indra is the Hindu god who symbolizes the natural forces that protect and nurture life, and it is said that above the palace of Indra you can see an infinite net. No one has seen it all, but at each knot in the net, there is a clear and radiant jewel. Each jewel mirrors the entire net and all the jewels that hold the net together. These irreducible jewels are the brilliant souls on Earth and when clear, each soul mirrors the other and the totality of life. Together, these jewel-like souls hold the infinite net of life together.

When authentic, we feel the tug of Indra's Net connecting everything to the jewel of our soul. I think wonder and awe are the tug and ache of being alive, the sensation of feeling our place as a jewel of soul in Indra's Net. And every time we move our heart through the river of experience, every time we extract what is essential, we are saying, admitting, declaring to another, "Look, I'm a jewel of soul in the net of all things." Every time we feel a tug of belonging below our bag of names, we are saying in wonder and awe, "Look into the truth of me and you will see all things reflected."

And when, against all odds, someone is authentic in return, we feel the tow and sway of time and the Universe. And that sway—like the wind that blows above all birds and the fire out of view at the center of the Earth—that sway is the sensation of Oneness that sages have always praised as sacred.

A Reflective Pause

A MEDITATION

- Sit quietly and stop your searching.

- Breathe deeply and feel the tug and ache of being alive.

- Drop your hands open on your lap. Feel them pulse.

- Inhale deeply and feel the strong gill of your heart. Feel it pulse.

- Exhale slowly and feel your place as a jewel of soul in Indra's Net.

- Close your eyes and feel the tug of Indra's Net, feel the tug of everything in the Universe.

- Inhale deeply and see the entirety of life reflected in the clear mirror of your soul.

- Don't worry if you can't see this reflection for very long or if you can't feel the tug of the Universe for very long. It's all still there.

- Open your eyes and breathe slowly and feel your place as a jewel of soul in the web of things.

TABLE QUESTIONS

To be asked over dinner or coffee with friends and loved ones. Try listening to everyone's response before discussing:

○ Tell the story of a search in which you worked hard toward some aspect of life and, without judgment, compare that experience with the story of a search in which some aspect of life was revealed to be exactly where you were.

○ Speak about the last two times you felt wonder or awe. What did those situations have in common? How might you look for more moments of wonder or awe?

○ After everyone shares, discuss the nature of wonder and awe that your common experience points to.

NOT GETTING WHAT WE WANT

WE ARE TAUGHT early on that to have an ambition and to work toward it is how we contribute to the world and move ahead. In and of itself, this is true. But along the way, we often incubate a self-centeredness that breeds like bacteria in the dark corners of our psyches and something else happens. We begin to associate getting what we want with success and not getting what we want with failure. We begin to see ourselves as little gods who create everything out of nothing and expect that we can *will* things to happen, that we have some right to control events. We are deemed skillful if we can steer people without their knowledge. Soon we wake with a sense of entitlement: that we have a right to have things go our way; a right to get what we want; a right to steer people and events toward our will.

Of course, life has other things to say about all this. Sooner or later, everyone will face not getting what they want. How we respond to this unavoidable moment determines how much peace or agitation we will have in our lives. This is the moment that opens all others, for our acceptance of things as they are and not as we would have them allows us to find our place in the stream of life. Free of our entitlements, we can discover that we are small fish in the stream and go about our business of finding the current.

This deeper chance to shed our willfulness doesn't preclude our sadness and disappointment that things aren't going the way we had imagined. But when we stay angry and resentful at how life unfolds beyond our will, we refuse the gifts of being a humble part in the inscrutable Whole. When we stay angry and resentful that—and you can fill in the blank—the stock market didn't reward our conscientious investing or the hurricane destroyed the truck we were going to inherit or the promotion we earned was given to someone else or the person we love so deeply doesn't care in the same way, we risk getting stuck.

It doesn't matter what you do or who you are—whether you are a world statesman or an auto mechanic or a Web designer or a struggling artist—the wonder and resilience of being aligned with the miracle of life waits on the other side of this inevitable disappointment of ego. It is not that we need to be broken to know joy, but that we need to be broken of our willfulness, which like a screen keeps the light and wind from filling our face.

When we can stop blaming others or nature or God for not getting what we want and be honest about what this inevitable rearrangement does to us, then humility and compassion are possible. The question waiting beneath all our entitlements and disappointments is: what do we truly need other than to wake and how can we share this treasure? Meeting things as they are is not unique to us or our times. It is an archetypal passage. Strangely, harshly, beautifully, life begins when the story we've made up to bridge the unknown falters.

Eventually, we are asked to undo the story we've been told about life—or the story we have told ourselves—so we might drop freshly into life. For under all our attempts to script our lives, life itself cannot be scripted. It's like trying to net the sea. Life will only use our nets up: tangle them, sink them, unravel them, wear them down, embed them in its bottom. Like the sea, the only way to know life is to enter it. How then do we listen below our willfulness?

A Reflective Pause

A MEDITATION

- ○ Sit quietly and center yourself.

- ○ Breathe slowly and think of all you have and all you don't have.

- ○ Breathe deeply and recite this poem:

> What we want and
> what we're given often
> serve two different Gods.
>
> How we respond
> to their meeting
> determines our
> path.

- ○ Breathe fully and let what you want and what you've been given meet in your heart.

- ○ Try to let go of where you've been and where you think you're going.

- ○ Breathe deeply and keep your heart open until it accepts all you have and all you don't have as pebbles in a larger sea.

- ○ Breathe slowly and meet what you want with what you have.

- ○ Sit quietly and center yourself.

JOURNAL QUESTION

- ○ Describe something important to you that began as a dream, that you turned into a goal, and then how that dream-turned-goal somehow shifted into an expectation and even an entitlement— something you felt you deserved and even felt you were owed.

Examine the range of feelings that this genesis released in you. What do you make of this turn of events? *betrayal*

TABLE QUESTIONS

To be asked over dinner or coffee with friends and loved ones. Try listening to everyone's response before discussing:

o Look at your life and begin to tell the story of what you have wanted or still want and the story of what you've been given. How do they differ? How are they the same? What has each taught you?

o After everyone has shared, discuss how what we want and what we're given differ.

We've seen that care is a pathless path that lives beneath fairness and unfairness. And the work of love involves holding nothing back and being with other living things in a way that lets them grow, that affirms their sense of safety in the world. All the while, we recognize ourselves in everyone we meet, both darkly and lightly. All the while, we need the love of others to mirror what we have and show us what we need. When touched at the core, we are forced to listen for our lives, though we often need each other to make sense of what we've heard. The work of love enables us to let in beauty while we're suffering. The biology of love has the heart, mind, and soul open and close to the entirety of the human experience in order to make sense of things as they move through. Slowly, the reward for being kind is that we discover our kinship to other living things. And the closeness uncovered by kindness turns to light in the body, until the closeness generated by kindness makes a lamp of the heart. We are returned to the mystical fact that there is no substitute for going through things together. And it is often through an unexpected empathy that we become a conduit for the human struggle until one person's humanity reveals the whole of humanity. In this way, kindness itself is a way of life.

All of this is the work of love, the most personal and crucial teacher we will ever meet. Take some time to describe your friendship with love and care. How does care speak to you? What do you hear? How is love asking you to grow?

These questions speak to your love of others: Are you leading with your care or measuring who deserves it? As you read this today, is the effort to care a burden or a lift? If a mix of both, what makes the burden bearable? How do you meet someone who is stuck? How do you want others to meet you when you are stuck? Do you affirm the life around you as much as you want to be affirmed?

These questions speak to your love of yourself: How different is the face you show the world from the face you show no one? Is your sense of what's familiar stronger than your sense of what's good for you? What is the feeling you associate with being most alive? What is the feeling you associate with being disconnected? What is each trying to tell you? What does the wind of love say through the hole in your heart? Where does all the love you've been given live in you? Can you draw on its strength?

From here, we will explore how the work of being present lands us in the mystery of the moment. We will explore how care fits all things together and how love helps us endure the many ways we're asked to be here.

THE STILLING OF OUR PAIN

IN A PROFOUND moment after pain, I fall below all the particular things I want and strive for and the many things I fear and turn away from. In this moment I realize briefly that we all run from death. The things we run after or from may change in how they occupy us, but our mastery of what gets in the way never gets us closer to the Source. For all of this, it seems that love and suffering, if we don't resist them, wear away the differences that thicken our skin till we realize with a tenderness, again and again, that we are at heart the same.

Being human, we keep getting lost in the running until some great kindness or pain opens us like a flower that needs nothing but light and rain to grow. Even after being transformed by such moments, we are pulled back into the complexity that living with others on Earth brings. In our modern hive, it feels at times that we are a colony of light-keepers buzzing about so fast that the flames we carry keep snuffing out.

When our light flickers, we try to manage life and stall. In stalling, we lose our grasp and feel of the Whole. Then we begin to split and isolate. By living in our feelings singly—in fear, sadness, anger, happiness, worry, confusion, or doubt alone—we suffer their acuteness. Yet this splitting and isolating is not a flaw but a part of living. The danger is that when we get stuck in a moment of splitting, our isolation can grow into a way of life. Then we suffer even more.

When we can still our pain enough to experience our feelings in their connectedness, their depth and oneness ground us and make us resilient. Together, our feelings are a powerful resource. When we slow, the light we carry spreads. When I honor this, I regain my grasp and feel of the Whole, which gives me the strength to stop running. When I am quiet enough to listen to my pain, I can remember and experience how everything is joined, and regain a sweet resilience from every point of joining.

We Will Be Quieted

For all the emphasis we rightly put on stillness, there is nothing wrong with motion. We simply need to inhabit a balance of nature's gifts. Living in a world of motion, we are constantly asked to quiet ourselves in order to glimpse and feel the truth of things, the way we wait for water to go still so we can see the bottom. This is particularly hard when in pain.

If we resist stillness, we will be quieted. I met a man who as a boy pulled a pot of boiling water off the stove. It gave him third-degree burns on his stomach. In order to heal, he had to be still for months, which was very hard for a boy. But through the stilling of his pain, the inner world appeared to him more and more each day. It slowly spoke to him and led him to his life as a painter. He would have preferred not to have been burned so badly, but acknowledges that being forced to be still opened him to his deeper self.

Stillness calls us into joy as well. Near the end of his very long life, the great poet Stanley Kunitz recalled spending summers as a child on the family farm in Quinapoxet, Massachusetts. One of his chores, which he delighted in, was to go into the fields at dusk with the shepherd dogs to bring in the cows. The stillness at dusk stayed with him his whole life. This strikes me as a beautiful image for how, when quiet enough and attentive enough, we can walk with the shepherds of our intuition into that timeless land between day and night; coaxing, circling, guiding the incarnations of beauty and truth to come with us for a while. For it's not about inventing or creating what's never been. But living a life of welcome and care till what's essential relaxes in our company.

A Reflective Pause

JOURNAL QUESTIONS

○ Describe a time when the acuteness of one feeling—fear, sadness, anger, happiness, worry, confusion, or doubt—took over your being. What did this feel like? What did this do to you?

○ Now describe a time when you were able to hold yourself open to more than one feeling at the same time. What did this feel like? What did this do to you?

○ Have you ever run from death? What did this look like in your life? What has such an experience taught you?

○ Describe a circumstance or experience that stopped you against your will and what that sudden pause felt like and what it opened you to.

Carried Along

Like everyone, I have struggled with being still and quieting myself my entire life. Yet, after all this way, I feel like a leaf that has somehow fallen in the middle of a stream, only to be carried along.

Time and again, I am humbled—broken and opened at once—by the mysterious fact that life is all things at all times. For every death there is somewhere a birth. For every clarity there is somewhere a confusion. For every pain there is somewhere a joy. And being simple human beings, we can't possibly comprehend or hold it all. But briefly, when still, we can feel it. Like a shell being hollowed by the sea, we are slowly cleansed. Hard as this is, it is worth everything.

The light today stops me. It is both merciless and merciful in its beauty: stilling my pain, softening the break, and illuminating what has been opened. We can resist this fierce blessing, but seldom escape the teaching of the break and the teaching of the light.

In this unexpected moment after pain, I realize that, when things fall apart, they make a lot of noise. When things come together, they do so quietly and slowly. And so, we often miss them. Our culture is obsessed with how things fall apart. The news reports only the noise of things breaking down. The weather is even called *Storm Watch*. Yet things are constantly coming together, though we have forgotten how to hear them.

It seems that much of our work is helping each other stay awake to the one common world, individually and in community. What makes this a compassionate journey is the inescapable fact that we all run from the sleepiness of our own world to the wakefulness of our common world; until weighed down by the noise of our society, we long for the silence of our personal inlet to eternity. Back and forth we go. In each case, we are humbled to think that what matters is elusive, when it's the stilling of our pain and the stilling of our urge to run from our pain that lets the human winter give way to spring.

A Reflective Pause

A MEDITATION

- Sit quietly and let a pain you are feeling present itself.

- Inhale deeply and let your breathing diffuse the acuteness of this pain.

- Exhale deeply and know you are larger than this particular pain.

- Close your eyes and inhale slowly, letting your slow breathing still the surface of your lake of feeling.

- Once still, let your inner eyes look through your pain to the bottom of all your feelings.

- Inhale fully from that bottom. It is the current of the one common world.

TABLE QUESTIONS

To be asked over dinner or coffee with friends and loved ones. Try listening to everyone's response before discussing:

o Share an instance when you heard the loudness of something falling apart.

o Share an instance when you heard the subtlety of something coming together.

o If the stilling of our pain is a fierce blessing we resist, offer what this means to you.

THE MYSTERY OF THE MOMENT

THE MYSTERY OF the moment is that it opens all moments. I know this in a felt way because of the brief and total feelings of Oneness I have fallen into during my life. This can be affirmed but never verified. It is something to be experienced, not proved. Life presents itself constantly through the miracle of the smallest part containing the whole while the Infinite Whole is always greater than the sum of its parts. It is we who fall in and out of our awareness and experience of Oneness. In the same way that the eye dilates and constricts, our sense of being opens and closes. It is the way the soul breathes on Earth. These openings and closings are not to be judged or censured, any more than we would censure exhaling over inhaling. We need both to live.

Most of the practices extolled by the spiritual traditions are aimed at restoring our openness of being, so we might fall into the mystery of the moment. Repeatedly, we chance to experience the eternal perspective animated by entering any moment completely enough that it reveals the vibrant pulse of all life. Even when blessed to experience this, we often don't know what to do with this blessing. Do we quit our job? Sometimes. Do we stop denying the love we feel? Hopefully. Do we deny the unpredictable fragility of life that is never far from us? Often. Mostly though we are simply asked to be awake, to stay awake, to live more compassionately, to be more aware.

Once we are exposed to the power of being in the moment, it is easy to want to live there. But what does this really mean? I can only speak from my own experience. The life-force waiting in the moment helped me survive cancer. It was only in the moment that I was free of fear, because fear lives in the future and calls us to it. Between the fear of trying to anticipate where cancer was leading me and the exhausted peace of collapsing in the moment, I came to understand that I couldn't *think* my way out of cancer. But from the eternal perspective opened to me in each moment, I could *inhabit* the inner resources to meet the journey as it was unfolding. What has stayed with me all these years is that I experience the moment with my heart and the future with my mind.

It's common to get distracted by working to stay in the moment above all else, but these blessings of complete immersion will happen. We don't have to work at them. I'm learning that when present in the moment, I view life more deeply, I meet life through an awakened sensibility, and I make more peaceful decisions. From the experience of Oneness that the moment opens, I am engaged with my heart and consider life choices from that felt, eternal perspective. When tripping along the gravel of circumstance, not able to enter any moment, I am engaged with my mind, trying to stay alert, trying to negotiate the obstacles of life without falling.

From the press of isolated experience, the mind feeling out of control tries to control everything. From the felt knowledge of the web of life, the heart tries to participate in the rush of life of which it is a part. Like all of us, I struggle with both: trying to control what happens and trying to participate in what happens. Today I feel clear enough to share these reflections. But if this makes sense to you, please remind me when you find me next week stirring my coffee nervously, staring off into the future, biting my lip.

A Reflective Pause

A MEDITATION

- ○ Center yourself and feel the moment you are quietly entering.

- ○ Breathe slowly and let yourself feel the tug of the future calling.

- ○ Breathe deeply and return to the moment you are in.

- ○ Sit quietly and let yourself feel the sway from the present to the future and back.

- ○ Breathe slowly and feel this moment ripple from you like water in all directions.

- ○ Breathe deeply and, as all water is connected, no matter where you enter it, feel this moment open you to all moments.

JOURNAL QUESTIONS

- ○ Describe a recent struggle you are in between the present and the future. What does your heart have to say about the present you are in? What does your mind have to say about the future you are anticipating? Let them begin a conversation.

TABLE QUESTIONS

To be asked over dinner or coffee with friends and loved ones. Try listening to everyone's response before discussing:

- ○ Describe a moment you fell into that opened a sense of all moments.

- ○ Describe your own rhythm of falling in and out of your awareness of the Oneness of things. What seems to pull you out of this awareness and what seems to return you to it?

A CLOSER GEOGRAPHY

The point in life is to know what's enough—
With the happiness held in one inch-square heart
you can fill the whole space between Heaven and Earth.

—GENSEI

If we had power over the ends of the Earth, it would not
give us that fulfillment of existence which a quiet devoted
relationship to nearby life can give us.

—MARTIN BUBER

IMAGINE THE FIRST clap of thunder and how the sky heard it by letting it move through its blueness to reach the Earth. Imagine the first rain and how differently the mountains heard it with their stone and the beaches heard it through their sand. Imagine how the sea listened to the rain by receiving it. Imagine the first birds driven to sing when hearing light. Imagine the first howl of the first wolf and how the moon heard that so far away. Imagine the first dream of the first weary traveler sleeping in a cave and how that cave absorbed the dream.

From our first waking moments, the life of experience calls us, willingly or not, into an apprenticeship of learning how to listen by receiving what comes our way, by letting things move through. From our first taste of experience, singing and crying empty us and open us so the one essential world can fill us and refine us.

One lesson of quantum physics is that if we go inside enough, nothing is solid or separate but fluid and unified, not particle but wave. This applies to the psycho-spiritual unit we call the self. Go inside and listen enough and the identity we call the self doesn't fall apart but reveals the waves of life that hold everything together. We are all unified by these essential waves of spirit and nature that are the lifeblood of all things. Knowing this provides a worldview of unity, but feeling this enables a kinship to life that can buoy us in our days.

Making Sense

We are sense-making beings. The way plants turn light into sugar, human beings turn experience into meaning. This is an inner sensibility that no other creature on Earth is blessed or burdened with, as far as we know. Since everything we encounter is alive and dynamic, we are constantly asked to let life speak to us, by letting it in, by letting it shape us. We do this by making sense of things. When strengthened by our mind, we rely on the *understanding* we can weave from our experience. When strengthened by our heart, we rely on *sensing* the experience itself. Of course, both are valuable. Making sense with the mind assumes that experience is heading somewhere. Whereas inhabiting sense with the heart presumes that living fully is the reward that doesn't lead anywhere. It simply reveals where we are.

Ultimately, making sense depends on keeping the notion of sense as a verb, not a noun; as a *process of sensing* that brings us into closer harmony with the ever-changing whole of life. When we make sense a product or a weighty thing we can stand on, it's often falsely comforting and over time confining. When we can lend our being completely to what is alive, no matter how small or elusive, then making sense is a relationship we tend: a dance between our heart and the world that keeps us vibrant.

These deep practices are hard to learn and hard to maintain. When we get ahead of our being, we tend to force premature frames and conclusions on what we see. When we can simply and deeply give attention to what is before us, pretty soon we listen like the sky to the first thunder and some detail will touch us, open us, and invite us to engage it. Then, the sense begins to work its way into us and the meaning appears more as a feeling than a conclusion. Somehow, everything far away and small, when brought near, is another world, an entire world. Yet when entered, we discover it is the same essential world to which we belong.

A Reflective Pause

JOURNAL QUESTION

○ If you believe all things are connected, what part of you is so connected and what does that kinship feel like?

Swimming Lessons

I used to jog, nothing dramatic, three or four times a week, maybe three miles a run. I loved it, more as a moving meditation in the light than as exercise, though the exertion felt good. But one day, my right knee dropped out from under me, like a tire blowout, and I went down. I had torn the meniscus. I had the arthroscopic surgery, two neat little holes. The scars are barely visible. Though it healed cleanly, it hurts to run, like gears with no oil.

So I decided to try swimming, which I also love. Again, though the exertion feels good, it's being in the water that, if not pushed, can be mystical. I feel, at certain moments, like a note that is close to finding its place in a symphony. These moments draw me more completely into the water. After a few swims, I started quite suddenly to use my whole body; remembering, at some atavistic level, that my arms and legs are not separate from the rest of me. Suddenly when I stroked, I was lifting my entire side.

When I reached the end of the pool, I laughed, and the real swimmer in the next lane eyed me like a fish without missing a stroke. But I had remembered, again, to use *all of me*. It was like when I danced only with my arms, forgetting my legs. This is the secret door to everything: to let *all-of-who-we-are* engage each act and thought. Again, I had tripped into it. And laughing at the edge of the pool, I realized that in my twenties, I played basketball, and it was chasing the ball in the air that so mystified me. But a torn ligament in my left ankle forced me to start again. In my thirties, I played racquetball, loving the dance of effort off the walls. But cancer threw me on another shore. Then in my forties, it was jogging, the eventual lightness of my own footfalls going nowhere, just following the light. Now it's swimming.

As I look back, the movement from one immersion and exertion to another was not about endurance and resilience. From inside, it felt more like drifting from one connection to another, once I'd used up my capacity to connect there. Or it used me up. I share this as testimony to the need to exercise, not just physically, but the need to exercise the act of *beginning again*. The need to sense and discover the openings that immersion brings until some limitation forces us, not to start over, as our fear of failure would have it, but to add to our experiences of the numinous life-force hidden in the kinetic relationships that only immersion and devotion can release.

So when I reached the end of the pool, I laughed: at the simplicity of truth and how hard it is to remember, at how its tap on our shoulder humbles us. Standing there in the water, I was reminded that humility brings us close, the way an open hand of sugar near the ground will make a horse bow and nibble.

As We Wake

Only when falling on my back did I stop and see the sky.

I was visiting a dear friend in New Hampshire. We were in a gallery in Dover when I came upon a triptych, a compelling etching by J. Ann Eldridge, entitled *My Religion Has Something to Do with Compost*. It spoke to me immediately. For aren't we all ground over time to what matters, unrecognizable and richer for it? It seems very little actually happens the first time around. Until we are worn to the smallest part of beauty, the smallest part of truth.

Isn't this the way? In time, the mountain trying to reach the sky crumbles softly to join the sea. In time, we outlive our ambitions, happy to land as the grain of sand a small fish mouths. Eventually, when moved to be still way inside, I somehow open like an iris no one sees and a tear falls within, nowhere to be found, though it sends being through my blood into my arms, into my hands, into my very fingers. Then, I am compelled to barely touch anything coming alive: the closed eye of a dog sleeping or the bluebird egg waiting to hatch. Then, I am refreshed by snow quieting the gash in the earth and the snow-like silence coating the wound in my heart.

As we wake, it becomes clear that the Earth bows toward the sun and the day begins. In just this way, listening is a humility that begins each time we fall toward the light. And falling, I think we're turned by experience back into what matters. When overwhelmed, I try to remember this and that the gift and safety of our very large heart appears when we tend to something small—feeding a finch, watching a doe, combing a dog. I try to remember that our inborn gift appears when we are completely present to the moment we are in. When I can stay in these moments, the rest, which can't be imagined, seems to take care of itself. I do what I can when I can. I try to open my heart and quiet my mind. Then somehow I am able to feel the gift in others. Then I am revisited with a sense that things will be all right. I am only one person. You are only one person. If we try to feel what we feel, but not carry everything, we can make it through.

A Reflective Pause

A MEDITATION

This is a silent, meditative walk. Bring a journal:

- In Hindu, an Upaguru is the teacher that is next to you at any moment. This is not limited to a person.

- Set aside thirty minutes to an hour and walk in silence. It can be an urban or rural setting that you enter.

- As you walk, slow your pace and your breathing.

o Breathe deeply and follow what you are drawn to. It might be a branch, a tree, a smell, an expanse of water, a birdsong, a broken window, or a dirty brick.

o Welcome whatever draws your full attention. It is your Upaguru.

o Settle near it and listen, deeply listen.

o Sit quietly beside this small teacher of the moment and begin by writing down its details—what it looks like, smells like, how it moves.

o Sit quietly and imagine and journal its history.

o Inhale deeply, and in silence, without words or thoughts, ask it for its wisdom.

o Breathe before it in silence for several minutes.

o Now begin to journal your dialogue with this small teacher. Write down what you sense it has to say to you.

o After a time, close your journal and bow as you leave.

o Wait three days and read what you have recorded.

TABLE QUESTIONS

To be asked over dinner or coffee with friends and loved ones. Try listening to everyone's response before discussing:

o The Universe reveals its felt meaning through details that touch us unexpectedly. Recount being touched by such a detail and the sense it opened in you.

o Tell the story of your immersion into some topic, process, or relationship.

o How are you addressing the need to exercise the act of beginning again?

TO ENDURE AND ENDEAR

I HAVE BEEN THINKING about this for a long time; trying to understand how we are asked by merely waking to endure the hardships of living and how we are asked, in the midst of that struggle and often through the openings that struggle creates, to endear ourselves into the fabric of life.

Recently, I find myself in another medical journey that makes all this very real. I need to know how to endure and endear at yet another level. During the winter, there was a nasty stomach flu going around. I caught it for twenty-four hours and was violently sick. These things are particularly hard for me, given the damage the chemo did to my esophagus twenty years ago. The flu passed and I went on.

Over the four months that followed, my stomach was never quite right. I kept having more attacks that would grip and burn just below the breastbone. These attacks would last for two to three hours. Afterwards I was exhausted. I couldn't eat normally and couldn't figure out any pattern. I began to lose weight. Of course, I began to fear some kind of cancer growing within me.

It is now the end of June and I have just been through a gauntlet of tests and procedures to discover there is no cancer. You can imagine my relief. But my stomach is not emptying properly and no one knows why. This is called idiopathic gastroparesis. I have just begun a course of medicine for a month, and we shall see. Every case is unique. Some people recover. For others, the stomach never regains the ability to empty properly and it becomes a chronic condition. I have become afraid to eat, for fear of an attack.

Today I wake with the realization that I must uncover what it is I need to digest and let pass. Today I wonder what kind of practice this is and what it has to do with our need to endure and endear. I am being asked to learn this physically but know already that I can't unless I learn this in deeper ways. For instance, I'm overwhelmed and afraid I've been thrust into another debilitating phase of life. What if this never corrects? How can I live this way, eating cottage cheese in the morning and grapes for lunch and feeling full from that? How can I make peace with the relentless, incidental fact that some dark microbe wasn't washed loose from the lining of my stomach in winter, and that it's now festered in my gut to change my life, perhaps permanently? I have to digest these things and let them pass. This is the biology of acceptance.

And this is the human context of our conversation. Not my particular journey, but the human journey. Nothing is abstract unless we abstract it. Every point of question and learning, every unanswerable point of living, is inseparable from its very real and daily context. Gravity is not a concept. It is erosion and avalanche. Pain is not discomfort, but my gut dragging me about the house in the middle of the night. And love is not some airy light waiting over the horizon. It is my wife holding my head until the pain passes. So as we ask what it means to endure and endear, I invite you to think of where these things live in you and in your very human and personal life.

A Reflective Pause

JOURNAL QUESTION

○ Give your own history of how you've learned to endure and endear.

The Biology of Acceptance

While pain and fear will descend at times like a cloud to blind us from all that will help, while we will try at times to leave our bodies, our circumstances, even our life, it is the underlying acceptance of what we are given that enables us to move through it. We can't move through fear until we accept that we are afraid. We can't unlace confusion until we accept that we are confused. We can't fully live until we accept that we will die.

How we accept things and let them pass is the still point from which our lives unfold. Like inhaling and exhaling, enduring and endearing are never far from each other. They are dependent on each other. Together they keep us alive. We could say this is the work of love: to inhabit these capacities that together enable our survival and carry us into our peak moments of living. Together they braid the mind and heart and pull us deeper and deeper into the nature of living. Outwardly, our job is to endure. Inwardly, to endear. And living long enough, the line between the two is worn faceless and we grow a certain beauty by loving everything in the way.

The words themselves are revealing. *Endure* means *to carry through, to continue in existence, to suffer patiently without yielding. Endear* means *to make beloved*. And the prefix *en-* means *to go into, to cause to be*. So how does going into our existence, into our suffering, make who we are and where we are dear? How do we take in what we encounter and turn it into something beloved?

Stepping into Life

Enduring and endearing has something to do with not letting our suffering become everything, even though this is the nature of pain. For every time we step out of bed or out the door or open our mouth or reach for someone or some thing, we face a choice between love and fear. It is a recurring choice-point. Which way we go is the eternal story of free will. Standing in love or fear, we become Abel or Cain. From this precipice, whole societies manifest, as Charles Dickens said, into the best of times or the worst of times. Though, in truth, every age is both. Every life has both.

There is a lineage of love as well as a lineage of fear. Each has its traditions and ancestors, and how we step into life through this choice is the realm of meaningful education. Yet no matter how we study or analyze or hone our skills, the greatest teachers have always been love and suffering. Like it or not, there is no escaping the lessons of either. You could say that history is the endless story of our attempts, through love and suffering, to keep stepping into life.

It is a mystery why we sometimes love and sometimes fear. The difference can be so life-changing that readying ourselves for these moments bears a devotion all its own. Once in the beautiful maelstrom of our days, we have to somehow find the courage to choose between brokenness and openness. Yet no matter which way we stumble, another opportunity always waits and our next teacher seems to appear when we pick ourselves up and step, once again, toward love rather than fear, toward unity rather than singularity. And failing, as we all do, an even greater opportunity appears when we dare to step *through* our fear toward love, and *through* our brokenness toward Wholeness. The way that heat allows ice to thaw and irrigate the earth, our capacity to endure and endear is an act of integrity that allows love to thaw the differences that freeze between us.

A Reflective Pause

JOURNAL QUESTIONS

- ○ Which is currently stronger in you: love or fear? E daí? What is your next step into life?

Ingesting the Medicine

This morning I took the first dose of medicine. I drew 3.125 milliliters of a liquid compound of erythromycin into a needleless syringe and pushed it into my mouth. It was the consistency of pale honey. I had to wait an hour to eat. I just had an English muffin. So far, so good. What dose of what pale honey do we need to keep stepping into life?

The Buddhists speak of *upekkhā* and *mudita*, two compounds of being that help us endure and endear. Upekkhā is the practice of equanimity, which can give us a place of calm from which to encounter the storm. Many traditions speak of equanimity and peace as the endpoints of long journeys that will keep us from having to experience the storm. From my experience, I don't think this is possible. Life is both storm and calm, and the challenge of living is how to use the calm to endure the storm, not bypass it. It is important to note that the only true place of calm in a storm is the very center. So the only thing to do, once in the storm, is to make our way to the center of it, hard as that might seem.

The American Buddhist monk Bhikkhu Bodhi says that "Upekkhā is freedom from all points of self-reference." And the Greek term for *tranquility* is *ataraxia,* a lucid state characterized by freedom from worry or any other preoccupation. To put these words in a human context, let me share my latest moment of beauty and pain.

It was a sweet slow day in June that an oriole came to our feeder. It only comes once a year. And just at that moment, as my heart widened to see the beautiful bird, my stomach gripped me in a contraction of pain. And there I was—expanding and contracting at the same time, in my own moment of choosing between everything and nothing. It was my next appearance of the exquisite risk: the risk to be here, to stay here, to not shut down.

For the pain was real and so was the oriole in the sun. It was an added pain to think I had to choose between them. The oriole remained beautiful as it ate in the sun, and I was beautiful as I leaned over in my pain. And so I endured and endeared to keep feeling both. That moment taught me that, as real as my pain is in any given moment, when I can accept that life is larger than that pain, then I can feel the flow of life beyond my own circumstance—beyond my own self-reference. Then, without denying my circumstance, I can let in that larger field of lifeforce which will help me endure.

This leads to the practice of mudita, or appreciative joy. When I can appreciate the larger flow of life, it softens my circumstance and absorbs some of my pain. In this way, to endear expands our spirit. By enduring our way to the calm at center and endearing our way to an expansiveness of spirit, we can return to this elusive state of inner tranquility. And however brief the peace, the underlying calm of life will free us from our worry and preoccupation, and free us from the weight of our self-reference. Again, not to pull us out of our lives, but to move us more deeply into them.

Strangely, only by letting in a perspective outside of our worry can we comfort and negotiate our worry. Only from a view beyond our self-reference can we find a path for this wakeful, sleepy thing inside we call the self. Only from the still breath in the center of the struggle can we move through the struggle. This is hard and unteachable. Only livable.

Somehow, in the face of adversity and suffering, we are asked to appreciate life and endear ourselves to it. Not by replacing adversity with joy and not by turning from the difficulties and injustices of living, but by facing them with truth and gratitude for being here anyway. Even after cancer, and in the midst of this journey now, I don't know how to do this but know I must. We must.

It was during my time in Prague last year that I discovered Vaclav Havel's understanding of hope:

> Hope is definitely not the same thing as optimism. It is not the conviction that something will turn out well, but the certainty that something makes sense, regardless of how it turns out.

It is this orientation of spirit that lets us mix a compound of suffering and joy that in time might resemble honey. I often thought, along the way, that wisdom was the end of knowing. But after falling down so many times, I've come to realize that while knowing truth leads to wisdom, experiencing truth leads to joy. And while wisdom is helpful, joy is essential. While I can certainly live better with wisdom, even it becomes a burden to carry without joy. It's time for my next dose of medicine.

A Reflective Pause

TABLE QUESTIONS

To be asked over dinner or coffee with friends and loved ones. Try listening to everyone's response before discussing:

o Tell the story of a moment in which a particular pain and a particular beauty were competing for your attention.

o In your own biology of acceptance, what do you need to digest and let pass?

o Describe the next dose of medicine that life is asking you to take.

o After everyone has shared, discuss what these medicines have in common.

WANDERING AUTHENTICALLY

It may be that when we no longer know what to do,
we have come to our real work;
and that when we no longer know which way to go,
we have begun our real journey.
The mind that is not baffled is not employed.
The impeded stream is the one that sings.

—WENDELL BERRY

WHEN JARRED INTO feeling how precious life is and how swiftly time moves through us, we are overcome with an urgency not to waste another second. Now we feel the need to speed up and rush, grabbing what we can in fear that the fire of being alive will bring down the house. What we do next is a turning point in our lives. While such urgency is understandable, it is only by slowing down that time drops its movement. Only when opening everything—our urgency, our worry, our fear, our regret—are we welcomed into the timeless pool of being.

After all we go through, we are asked to lead a life of honest expression, which always starts with listening as a way to remember what matters, to name what matters, and to voice what matters. These are the practices that keep us authentic.

A Reflective Pause

JOURNAL QUESTION

○ Open yourself to this moment and listen. Try to remember one thing about living that matters, try to name it, and try to give voice to it. Then journal how this experience makes you feel.

Want and Dream

I have wanted so many things, reaching so few. From here, it's clear that I have been blessed *not* to get everything I've wanted. For my want hasn't always been good for me, or anyone near. Often, the things I want are compensating for something I'm not ready to face. In this way, my want often twists the dream, which in turn twists me. It's made me think of dreams differently: not as individual aspirations, but more as transpersonal conduits of grace; filaments of soul that help us find each other and illumine the world. Now I think of dream as a state of being and not a place to arrive at. Now I think that dreams skip from heart to heart like glowing neurons arcing across synapses in the Universal body. We get so caught up in whether the dream comes true or falls away, when its purpose is to charge the circuit of life between us. When we can feel a dream moving through—and drop its name, even more, drop its game—it expands us with a moment of aliveness that enlightens us, lightens us from within. So, really, any dream will do. It is the dreaming that's essential; not its imagined real estate, but the places it lights along the way.

The First and Second Path

As all the Heavens were a Bell
And Being, but an Ear . . .

—Emily Dickinson

In later life, the great Argentinean writer Jorge Luis Borges said, "I fear I have been reading the books of astronomers but never really looking at the stars." I don't view this as the confession of a life wrongly lived but a poignant reminder of the inevitable cycle of staying true in an ever-changing world. The constant challenge is to lift our eyes from our treasured knowledge and *realign our being with what rings true.* Not once or twice but endlessly.

For as the sun makes the forest grow over any path, no matter how often it is cleared, what is immediate and true keeps growing over what we have learned. Our obsession with getting somewhere makes us forget that the first path of living follows direct experience while the second path follows the conclusions we draw from our experience. Meaning well, we often drift from what is true and forget that our allegiance is to the first path. Yet falling off from what is real is not a breach of character but a natural experience of weather over time. The essence of wandering authentically is to return our feet to the earth, to follow the sun, and to look breathlessly again to the stars.

A Reflective Pause

JOURNAL QUESTIONS

○ Discuss a time when you fell off from what is real for you. How did you become aware of this? How did you return to the river of the authentic? What would you say to a friend or loved one who has drifted away from a sense of what is true?

Taking in a Hundred Rivers

Cease and desist [until] you are like an ocean taking in a
hundred rivers. When you get there, there is no grasping
or rejection.

—DOGEN

I often hear two responses to the mystery of life. One is a declaration of how awful a world this is and how overwhelming the burden of what needs to be righted. The other is a declaration of how enlightenment and perfection are possible if we only work hard enough. The mood of these responses is either one of despair and apathy (What difference can I make?) or one of pushing for a romantic ideal (Imagine a world where children never cry). These responses lead to either a life of isolation and dark endurance or one of missionary zeal to reshape the world into some form of Heaven.

Though I've spent time lost in each, I find both responses insufficient. In declaring only how awful a world this is, we avoid our journey on Earth by retreating from life through resignation (It's all too much to bear; though sometimes it is). In declaring that perfection is what we're after, we avoid our journey on Earth by hiding in the future (My hope is in tomorrow; though sometimes that is true). Devoted to either extreme, we are seduced to leave and bypass the work of being here.

Historically, the Western view is that life can be improved and, therefore, it is our responsibility to control and shape our behavior and the behavior of others in order to make the world a better place. The older Eastern view is that life cannot be improved upon, only experienced. Life was complete before you or I arrived and will be complete when we pass.

Herein lies a central paradox of being human. While we can't eliminate hunger, we can feed each other. While we can't eliminate pain, we can hold each other. While we can't improve upon the nature of reality, we can make things better for each other while we're here.

In light of this, falling to either the pessimistic or romantic side of this paradox is a distraction from being here and helping each other while we can. In truth, I have more sympathy for those clouded with despair. For this romance with the ideal in the face of true suffering can be dangerous, leaving others in jeopardy while the state of things as they are is being denied.

One side of our challenge is to feel the pain in being human and not escape down the rabbit hole into despair, but to stay here and hold each other up in the mystery. The other side of our challenge is to not escape the other way, using the difficulties of being here as a fulcrum to reach for a perfect world always out of view. Dreaming in this way is its own addictive sedative.

This is why I am moved by the courage and love of a bodhisattva. In Mahayana Buddhism, a bodhisattva is a person well on their way toward enlightenment who chooses to use their wisdom to help other human beings liberate themselves. On the threshold of an enlightened life, such a wisdom-being refuses to cross over, committing to wait till all beings can come and join. Though this too is a dream of Heaven, what moves me is the implicit truth that a bodhisattva knows that all will never come. And so, in essence, he or she embraces an awakened life on Earth. Not shaping or purifying others, but wandering authentically among the living.

In Time We Might Sing

Over time and through the sweet experiments and harsh failures of the many lives within my life, I am getting there. And when I finally exhaust my smaller self, I will sit where it falls and smile to have been worn to the deeper, simpler self waiting underneath. Then I will be as congruent as a tiger so far from home its next step is home. I will sit where the old hunger falls and listen to the ancient wind voice its truth through the cracks in the one remaining wall that stands between us. My dream is that in time we might sing what we privately suffer and wonder.

When we touch like this, a deep knowing glows that can be passed but not easily understood. To touch like this requires that we listen to each other, especially beyond what we readily understand or agree with.

During my first year of college, forty years ago, I visited my uncle

Irwin and aunt Hellaine in Brookline, Massachusetts, bouncing my way there on a Greyhound bus from upstate New York. At the time, I was overwhelmed with mystical feelings, waking to the larger elements of life and just beginning to sense the spiritual sea we all swim in. This in itself was a threshold of listening that would open me to my life. Uncertain of what was happening, I had great difficulty in explaining these feelings to others. I had no company at the time and felt a bit crazy, except in my expanding sense of solitude.

The way I was received in Brookline led to a very important moment for me as a young man being flooded with what would be my life's work. As a young poet spinning with a heightened sensitivity, I felt all the colors of life and they tumbled me, as if I was falling inside a kaleidoscope with no way out. I felt very alone. I'm not sure how much of my intuitive ramblings my aunt and uncle understood or agreed with. But they listened, not just to my words over dinner but they opened their listening long enough for all of me to show itself; the way the sun listens to the earth after a storm until all the smaller creatures come out. The way I was received helped me accept what I was feeling, even though I had no language for it. Their kind listening allowed me to hear myself. It gave me confidence to stand firm in the unknown, something that would become a lifelong skill.

That first night, my uncle took me out. We stopped for a while in a tavern and sat at a long wooden bar. I talked incessantly. And he didn't look at his watch once. He gave me his full attention. I can't know what was running through his mind. No doubt, he saw himself holding me as a newborn. No doubt he was marveling, as we all do, at how such small creatures, as we are, grow into these walking questions that feel and think and wonder and ramble. I loved sitting next to him that early evening in Boston. It felt safe, and I felt heard at a time when I wasn't sure myself what I was hearing. My uncle taught me that night that to listen even when we don't understand, especially when we don't understand, is a gift. I think this is how we water what is in each other's heart, with warm welcome and listening. It is the way we practice vulnerability.

Perhaps all we have explored here, through all these pages, comes down to this necessary invocation for us to water what is in each other's heart. Perhaps the essence of wisdom is in the deep reception of each other and the space such listening opens. It is not lost on me that I have led you through a two-hundred-and-fifty-page conversation about listening. Some would say we might have done better to sit somewhere in silence. But we have always had to speak about what is unspeakable, to call into the open that which can't be seen, to drink meaning together from the very air. So in deep ways, by reading this far, we have stood together firmly in the unknown and have sipped from the well out of which all books arise. Like lost seekers whose honest meeting makes the oasis visible, I hope you feel refreshed.

A Reflective Pause

TABLE QUESTIONS

To be asked over dinner or coffee with friends and loved ones. Try listening to everyone's response before discussing:

○ Speak of a time when not getting what you wanted turned out better for you.

○ Tell the story of a dream that didn't come true but which offered you a moment of unexpected aliveness along the way. Which was the dream: what you had hoped for or what showed itself along the way?

○ Having come this far, how do you understand the work of being here? What does it mean to you to embrace an awakened life?

A MEDITATION

This last reflective pause is to be entered with a trusted friend or loved one:

○ Sit facing each other with two stones in a bowl and two cups of water between you.

○ Breathe slowly and think about the work of being here.

○ Breathe deeply and give thanks for the presence of the person before you.

○ Inhale slowly and take in the love of the other person.

○ Exhale slowly, letting your love flow toward the other person.

○ Sit quietly and receive each other in silence.

○ Now enact this invocation to water what is in each other's hearts.

○ Lift a stone and hold it in your open hand over the bowl, while your loved one pours a cup of water over the stone, saying, "I water what is in your heart."

○ Switch places and repeat the invocation, saying, "I water what is in your heart."

○ Vow to listen to each other in all the ways you can.

NO STRANGERS IN THE HEART

*I tell you, the more I think, the more I feel that there is
nothing more truly artistic than to love people.*

—VAN GOGH

I HAVE BEEN WRITING for forty-five years—poems, stories, journals,
dreams, essays—and all of it can be reduced to this phrase: *no strangers
in the heart.* Like a bird who keeps waking in a new place only to sing
the same song at the sight of light, all that I have written, regardless of
where I find myself, ends up praising the mysterious fact that *there are no
strangers in the heart.* Whenever we dare or are forced to lift each other
up or ease each other down, we have the glorious chance to find what
we've lost in each other.

When I can get past the thing that breaks me open, whatever it
might be, I always find the safe, illumined place we all come from.
Sometimes it opens without breaking, through the sudden appearance
of truth or beauty. Sometimes it is relaxed open by wonder and awe.
Sometimes it is thawed open by the constancy of love like sun on ice
in March. It is this common patch of eternity that we carry within all-
we-go-through that can restore us in a second. For the eternity carried
inside every ordinary moment is healing, if we can only drink from it.

I had a dream the other day in which my job was to sweep the temple
floor at dawn. I couldn't find the temple and wasn't sure where to begin
when an old man came up to me. He looked like one of those small
ancient monkeys with thousand-year-old eyes. He took my broom and

examined the handle. He gave it back and said, "You're holding it too tightly." Then he hopped like a monkey and continued, "The secret is that the temple is anywhere you wake." He left and I started sweeping where I stood and a path appeared which I felt compelled to take. Then I woke.

Now I wonder if waking and loving and sweeping go on forever. Now I wonder: is listening with our heart a form of sweeping away all the noise and distraction that life keeps whipping up? I remain convinced that, when we can listen deeply—beyond our need of being heard, beyond the rustle of our own concerns—*there are no strangers in the heart.* When we can truly listen, we slowly, through the sweep of love, become each other.

After all the searching and suffering, are we here to love the rain out of every cloud and to listen every seed into a tree? Is our task while alive to stir the angel that sleeps within until it uses our hands as a soul at work on Earth? It seems at times that life can move and mount without our knowing like a deep current that eventually breaks surface as a wave. So being here involves more than just reacting to the things that come at us. It requires that we initiate a love affair with all that calls to us, seen and unseen; that we run with open arms into questions and moments of living as urgently as we do burning buildings to retrieve who and what we love.

After a lifetime of study and conversation, after falling below concepts and well-thought-out principles, it's becoming clear that the end of all flight is to land. And when we land, we do not *lose* our access to Heaven. We *enter* it. For when the walls break down, the light, which has been waiting, simply enters. And so, during the days that remain, we are asked by our suffering to look for ways to accept the flow of life rather than control it.

My whole life I've been seeking the truth, inching closer, marveling at what is revealed, bit by bit. Circling it. Reflecting on it. Speaking with others about it. Happy to swim in it. But who would have thought that disappearing *into* it, the way sugar dissolves in water, is what deep being feels like. And yet, miracle of miracles, I'm still here, still me. And more than looking at things, more than listening to things, more than relating to things, more than having compassion for all things, as holy as this progression is—can it be that, ultimately, the reward for facing things is *becoming* things? Not at the expense of being who we are, but as the spiritual consequence of living at the center. From inside, there is less and less to say. From inside, there is less and less to know.

I didn't know until I asked a thousand times that the work of being involves keeping what is true before us, and the gift in receiving is that, by taking things in whole-heartedly, we wake to a reality that keeps unfolding. But not knowing how to listen to all that is not said, I found myself lost in the presence of sages with no way to understand their wisdom. It wasn't till I could truly enter silence that I first felt God blinking. It made me put everything down, even my want to understand, and I was opened to the one living sense. This is the reward for deep listening, a conversation with the elements that lifts our sorry head when the world feels too much.

I didn't know until I broke a thousand things that the work of being human is to go back into the fire because this is how we learn to restore confidence. When I can untangle the net and outwait the clouds, I can hear the call of my soul and know where we are. When you and I can listen there, the feelings of a lifetime, harsh and sweet, begin to form a honeycomb. The nectar there can keep us alive.

I didn't know until I gave a thousand things away that the work of love is a steadfast teacher. And not getting what we want, we might get past the ways we injure ourselves and enter a closer geography in which the days are spent fitting things together. Then deep in the human garden, in the hut we call the self, we are left with the endless search to still our pain until the mystery of the moment opens us to reverence. To endure and endear, we must wander authentically until there are no strangers in the heart.

My heart pounds as I reach the end of this long conversation. During it, I thought we'd be together forever. It always feels like that. This is the truth and braid of our journey. We meet in the clearing and climb the mountain side by side, and somewhere along the way we have to part and take different trails, promising to meet on the summit, but never truly knowing if we will. We are close to that place now, where we must go our ways for a while. So let me say, there is no greater joy than to meet like this and ask, "What is it like to be you, to be alive, to eat the wind, to be eaten by the day?" I wish you the chorus of an open sky and sure footing. Each time we give of ourselves, we add a precious hour to our time on Earth.

AFTERWORD

T RAVELING AROUND THE COUNTRY, I'm blessed to meet so many people. We gather and sit in large circles and small, for days sometime, exploring the gifts and challenges of what it means to be alive. I always leave renewed and humbled by the wisdom I find and how listening is a constant resource that connects us to each other and life.

One thing I've learned is that everyone has a great listener within, worn open by time. It's our commitment to listening that keeps us from being isolated and embittered by the storms of experience.

As you have seen, this book is the trail of my journey with listening through the years. I hope it has introduced you to your own great listener, so you can live closer to your gifts and hear your own wisdom as it trickles like rain into the ground of your days. When we can listen to our own authority of being, a drop at a time, we realign with the majesty of life itself. The strength of this realignment is life-giving.

I encourage you to return to the reflective exercises in this book, as a way to befriend your great listener. These invitations to mediate, journal, and be in conversation with others will help you personalize what is Universal.

Thank you for being part of the journey. If we meet along the way, tell me a story of what you've heard. I'll sit with you and listen.

—MN, October 1, 2013

GRATITUDES

T HERE HAVE BEEN MANY kind and deep listeners in my life, beginning with my grandmother, who listened her way from one continent to another, from one century to another. And early on, the trees of upstate New York listened the wind into my limbs. Then the ocean kept counseling me to return to the deep. And my dogs, Saba and Mira, who listened an urban boy beyond his comfort zone into the wonders of nature.

For this book and much more, I am grateful to my agent, Brooke Warner, for her whole-hearted company. And to my editor, Leslie Meredith, for her clarity and openness and the way she's fertilized the soil of this book. And to my foreign agent, Loretta Barrett, for the way she's seeded my work around the world.

Gratitude to my dear friends for how we take turns listening to each other and where we're being led. Especially Eileen, Bob, Michelle, Rich, Jill, Dave, Pat, Karen, Paul, Pam, George, Paula, Skip, Don, TC, David, Ellen, Eleanor, Linda, and Sally and Joel. And to Parker, who listens for the common heart among us. And to Wayne, who listens for the resting place in all things. And to my father, for the long walk home.

Gratitude to Paul Bowler, who listens like the sun. And to Robert Mason, who listens like a bird in glide. And to my wife, Susan, for always hearing where I am strong when I am lost and feeling weak.

NOTES

Epigraphs and poems without attribution are by the author.

v   *We will not perish:* From Abraham Joshua Heschel, *Man Is Not Alone* (New York: Farrar, Straus & Giroux, 1951), p. 26.

To My Reader

xi   *Olasope Oyelaran:* Dr. Oyelaran was the director of the College of Arts and Sciences in the School of International Studies at Western Michigan University. Born in Nigeria and educated in the United States, Dr. Oyelaran has been instrumental in higher education in Nigeria for many years.

The Work of Being

1   *The Universe is a continuous web:* From Stanley Kunitz with Genine Lentine, *The Wild Braid: A Poet Reflects on a Century in the Garden* (New York: Norton, 2005), p. 3. We are indebted to Genine Lentine for allowing us the privilege of quietly witnessing these last glimpses of conversation between a great poet and the mystery he kept allegiance to. It's like sitting in the back of a shrine listening to the ancient wind voice its prayer through cracks in the altar wall.

Beyond Our Awareness

10   *I don't know Who:* From Dag Hammarskjöld's *Markings* (New York: Knopf, Inc., 1964), his book of diary reflections.

Keeping What Is True Before Us

16 *Faith is not an insurance:* Abraham Joshua Heschel, *The Earth Is the Lord's: The Inner World of the Jew in Eastern Europe* (1949; Woodstock, VT: Jewish Lights Publishing, 2001).

18 *U Thant:* During U Thant's first term as secretary-general of the United Nations, he was widely credited for his role in defusing the Cuban Missile Crisis and for ending the civil war in the Congo. He was also a firm opponent of apartheid in South Africa. His once good relationship with the US government deteriorated rapidly when he publicly criticized American conduct of the Vietnam War. His secret attempts at direct peace talks between Washington and Hanoi were eventually rejected by the Johnson administration.

U Thant died of lung cancer in New York in 1974. At this time, Burma was ruled by a military government which refused him any honors. On the day of U Thant's funeral, tens of thousands of people lined the streets of Rangoon. His coffin was snatched by a group of students before its scheduled burial in an ordinary Rangoon cemetery. The student demonstrators buried him on the former grounds of the Rangoon University Student Union (RUSU).

For a week, the student demonstrators built a temporary mausoleum for U Thant and gave anti-government speeches. In the early morning hours of December 11, Burmese troops stormed the campus, killed some of the students, removed U Thant's coffin, and reburied it at the foot of the Shwedagon Pagoda, where it lies today. In reaction to the storming of the Rangoon University campus and the forcible removal of U Thant's coffin, riots broke out in the streets of Rangoon. Martial law was declared.

19 *By being what we are:* Heschel, *The Earth Is the Lord's*, p. 108.

20 *I do not know:* Sir Isaac Newton, in Banesh Hoffman, *Albert Einstein: Creator and Rebel* (New York: Penguin, 1972), p. 257.

The Gift in Receiving

22 *Can you hold the door:* Lao Tzu, *Tao Te Ching*, trans. Witter Bynner (New York: Columbia University Press, 1944), no. 10.

22 *to keep the gift of life flowing:* For more about this sense of giving and receiving, please see "The Boy and the Drum" in my book *Finding Inner Courage* (San Francisco: Conari Press, 2011), pp. 32–35 (originally published as *Facing the Lion, Being the Lion*, San Francisco: Red Wheel/Conari, 2007), and *Living the Generous Life: Reflections on Giving and Receiving*, ed.

Wayne Muller and Megan Scribner (Fetzer Institute, 2005), available as a teaching resource at www.LearningtoGive.org/materials/folktales.

A Reality That Keeps Unfolding

28 *The one moon reflects itself:* Yoka Daishi (c. 713 CE) was a Chinese Zen master, a disciple of Hui-nêng. This quote is from "Cheng-tao Ke" (Song of Enlightenment), in D. T. Suzuki, *Manual of Zen Buddhism* (London: Rider, 1950), p. 97.

28 *"Thirteen Ways of Looking at a Blackbird":* The poem appeared in Wallace Stevens's first book of poems, *Harmonium,* published in 1923. In his *Letters,* Stevens said of the poem, "This . . . is not meant to be a collection of epigrams or of ideas, but of sensations."

29 *"breathing in and breathing out":* In *Prayers of the Cosmos: Meditations on the Aramaic Words of Jesus,* trans. Neil Douglas-Klotz (San Francisco: Harper-SanFrancisco, 1990).

31 *"There's a deeper speech":* From a Fetzer Institute dialogue on story as practice with Rabbi Lew, Angeles Arrien, Allan Chinen, Jack Kornfield, and Frances Vaughan in Sausalito, CA (November 30, 2004). Rabbi Lew is one of the leaders of the burgeoning Jewish Meditation movement. Please see his book, *One God Clapping: The Spiritual Path of a Zen Rabbi* (Woodstock, VT: Jewish Lights Publishing, 2001).

31 *a minyan of Jewish men:* The story of the Jewish men singing is from the same conversation with Rabbi Lew.

32 *William Edmonson (1874–1951):* From an exhibition of African-American Portraits, *Let Your Motto Be Resistance,* at the International Center of Photography, New York City, 2007.

How Do We Listen to All That Is Not Said?

36 *There are no others:* Ramana Maharshi, in *The 2008 Shift Report* (Petaluma, CA: Institute of Noetic Sciences, 2008), p. 71.

36 *Narrative Rounds:* I visited Columbia medical school on May 7, 2008, at the invitation of Dr. Rita Charon, the vibrant midwife of this series and of a newly imagined master's program in narrative medicine at Columbia, through which stories and expression, and therefore deep listening, are considered potent forms of medicine with tools and skills as precise as heart monitors, lasers, and MRIs (please visit www.narrativemedicine.org).

38 *a street in Kazimierz, Cracow:* A photograph by Roman Vishniac, 1937, from the Vishniac Collection in the International Center for Photography, New York City, accession no. 219.1974.

Being Lost

41   *The moment we awaken:* Helen Luke, "The Introduction," in *Dark Wood to White Rose: The Journey of Transformation in Dante's Divine Comedy* (New York: Parabola Books, 1989).

42   *Maimonides:* Maimonides (1135–1204) was a Jewish rabbi, physician, and philosopher in Spain and Egypt. He was by far the most influential figure in medieval Jewish philosophy and the center of Sephardic thinking. His works were written in both Arabic and Hebrew. Among his most important works are *The Commentary on the Mishna* and *The Guide for the Perplexed,* which was written in the twelfth century in the form of a letter to his student Rabbi Joseph. The main purpose of *The Guide* is to explore the heart of Jewish mysticism.

In the Presence of Sages

51   *There are four types:* The *Pirkei Avot* contains several of the most frequently quoted rabbinic sayings, including Hillel's famous set of questions cited here: "If I am not for myself, who will be? If I am only for myself, what am I? If not now, when?" (1:14). In simple Hebrew, Hillel's questions read: *Im ein ani li, mi li? U'ch'she'ani l'atzmi moh ani? V'im lo achshav eimatai?* Hillel the Elder lived from the end of the first century BCE to the beginning of the first century CE. He is considered the greatest sage of the Second Temple period.

52   *There are some: Protagoras,* trans. R. E. Allen, pp. 342e–343b.

52   *Diogenes points out:* Diogenes Laertius 1.27ff., in R. Martin, "Seven Sages," in *Encyclopedia of Classical Philosophy,* ed. D. Zeyl, (1997), p. 487; Parke & Wormell, pp. 387–388.

Entering Silence

61   *We make a space:* Martin Heidegger.

God Blinking

65   *When wiggling through:* This appears as the poem "Living Through Things," in my book *Surviving Has Made Me Crazy* (Fort Lee, NJ: CavanKerry Press, 2007), p. 16.

65   *The Sufi Master Ibn al-'Arabī:* Please see the work of the Sufi scholar William Chittick, who opens the mind of Ibn al-'Arabī with great clarity.

A Conversation with the Elements

68   *If you don't become the ocean:* Leonard Cohen, in *The Sun* (Chapel Hill, NC), no. 376 (April 2007), p. 48.

69   *Have you searched:* Robert Service, "The Call of the Wild," in *The Spell of the Yukon and Other Verses* (New York: Barse & Co., 1916).

71   *Candace Pert:* is the neuroscientist who discovered the opiate receptor, the cellular bonding site for endorphins in the brain. Her groundbreaking book is *Molecules of Emotion: Why You Feel the Way You Feel* (New York: Simon & Schuster, 1999).

71   *Nature never did betray:* William Wordsworth, in *The Sun,* no. 370 (October 2006), p. 48.

72   *"We have two glorious tasks":* Michael Jones, from a dialogue on transformational leadership at the Fetzer Institute, September 28, 2007. Please see Michael's compelling album, *Seascapes.*

72   *The name Walla Walla: Walla Walla* and *koos* are words from the Sahaptian language of the Columbia Plateau tribes of the Pacific Northwest. *Walla Walla,* written *Wolla Wollah* by Lewis and Clark, derives from a Nez Perce and Cayuse word, *walatsa,* meaning *running,* a probable reference to *the running waters.* Another example of a repeated name is *Peu-Peu-Mox-Mox,* a revered chief of the Walla Walla tribe who was murdered in 1855 while being held as an unarmed prisoner of white volunteers. My thanks to Megan and Kevin Scribner, Walla Walla natives who shared this history.

One Living Sense

75   *the mind-heart:* For more on the mind-heart as the seat of contemplation, please see the chapter "The Eyes of the Deep" in my book *The Exquisite Risk* (New York: Harmony Books, 2005), pp. 172–178.

75, 76   *"For some reason," "Deafness does not mean":* These citations come from an essay on hearing, written by an anonymous intimate on behalf of Evelyn Glennie, which can be found on her website, www.evelyn.co.uk/hearing.htm.

77   *It is the attainment:* Hazrat Inayat Khan, *The Music of Life: The Inner Nature and Effects of Sound* (New Lebanon, NY: Omega Publications, 1983), pp. 83, 88, 95, 323. Hazrat Inayat Khan (1882–1927) was an exemplar of Universal Sufism and founder of the Sufi Order in the West in 1914 in London. His universal message of divine unity (Tawhid) focused on themes of love, harmony, and beauty. He taught that blind adherence to any book rendered any religion void of spirit.

80   *"Sooner or later"*: Teilhard de Chardin, *The Phenomenon of Man* (New York: HarperCollins, 1975). This classic work was published posthumously in 1955.

81   *"It is your business"*: In Agnes de Mille, *Martha: The Life and Work of Martha Graham* (New York: Random House), p. 264. De Mille tells the following story: "The greatest thing [Martha] ever said to me was in 1943 after the opening of *Oklahoma!*, when I suddenly had unexpected, flamboyant success for a work I thought was only fairly good, after years of neglect for work I thought was fine. I was bewildered and worried that my entire scale of values was untrustworthy. I talked to Martha. I remember the conversation well. It was in a Schrafft's restaurant over a soda. I confessed that I had a burning desire to be excellent, but no faith that I could be.

"Martha said to me, very quietly, 'There is a vitality, a life force, an energy, a quickening that is translated through you into action, and because there is only one of you in all of time, this expression is unique. And if you block it, it will never exist through any other medium and it will be lost. The world will not have it. It is not your business to determine how good it is nor how valuable nor how it compares with other expressions. It is your business to keep it yours clearly and directly, to keep the channel open. You do not even have to believe in yourself or your work. You have to keep yourself open and aware to the urges that motivate you. Keep the channel open. . . . No artist is pleased. [There is] no satisfaction whatever at any time. There is only a queer divine dissatisfaction, a blessed unrest that keeps us marching and makes us more alive than the others.'"

81   *During a recital in Berlin: Bartlett's Book of Anecdotes*, as quoted in *The Sun* (Chapel Hill, NC), no. 385 (January 2008), p. 48.

Deep Listening

83   *"Your gut is where"*: Puanani Burgess is a poet, cultural translator, and developer of community-based organizations. She has extensive experience in community, family, and values-based economic development, mediation, and conflict transformation through storytelling. Her stories and remarks come from a dialogue on transformational leadership held at the Fetzer Institute, May 1–4, 2008.

84   *You can run around*: Nancy Evans Bush, from a meeting at the Fetzer Institute on Exploratory Research on Near-Death Experiences, June 24–26, 2007. Nancy Evans Bush is the former president of the International Association for Near-Death Studies, an educator and pastoral counselor who has written extensively on the transformative effects of near-death experiences.

87   *musicians and composers began*: Michael Jones, from a dialogue at the Fetzer Institute, September 28, 2007.

THE WORK OF BEING HUMAN

How We Learn

97 *Pema Chödrön tells this story:* From the chapter "Groundlessness," in Pema Chödrön, *The Places That Scare You* (Boston: Shambhala, 2001), pp. 133–139.

97 *prajñāpāramitā (the perfection of wisdom):* Prajñāpāramitā is also known as the Goddess of Transcendental Wisdom.

Restoring Confidence

104 *The deepest words:* Antonio Machado, trans. Robert Bly, in *The Enlightened Heart,* ed. Stephen Mitchell (New York: Harper & Row, 1989), p. 129.

105 *beyond our current understanding:* After waking from my journey through cancer, I explored the paradox of suffering in an essay called "A Terrible Knowledge," which can be found in my collected essays, *Unlearning Back to God.*

Honeycombs and Thinking-Strings

108 *"My body needs strength":* "Sun Man and Grandfather Mantis," adapted 108 *Sun Stories, Tales from Around the World to Illuminate the Days and Nights of Our Lives,* ed. Carolyn McVickar Edwards (New York: HarperCollins, 1995).

Going Back into the Fire

113 *Lesia was severely burned:* I am grateful to these remarkable human beings, Lesia Cartelli and Don, whom I met at the 2006 Burn Survivors World Burn Congress in Sacramento, CA, where they shared their stories. I have not been able to learn Don's last name but hope he might stumble on this telling of his journey. Lesia is founder and director of Angel Faces, an innovative healing retreat for adolescent girls with facial disfigurements, www.angelfacesretreat.org. The Phoenix Society, www. phoenix-society.org, is a caring organization offering resources and support to burn survivors and their loved ones across the country. Director Amy Acton says, "[Starting in 1977], this Society has continued to grow and evolve as a community of individuals who are committed to Founder Alan Breslau's original vision of ensuring that every burn survivor, their loved ones, and caregivers have the necessary support on their road to recovery." Alan Breslau was extensively burned in the crash of a commercial airliner in 1963. If you or a loved one have been touched by the

trauma of fire, the annual World Burn Congress (about 900 strong) is a great place to find solace and company (www.phoenix-society.org/programs/worldburncongress/).

118 *the active power:* Erich Fromm (1900–1980) was a preeminent psychoanalyst and humanistic philosopher whose seminal books include *Escape from Freedom* (1941) and *The Art of Loving* (1956).

What Happens When You Really Listen

121 *"To see a world":* William Blake, "Auguries of Innocence," in *The Portable William Blake,* ed. Alfred Kazin (New York: Penguin, 1977).

> To see a world in a grain of sand,
> And a heaven in a wild flower,
> Hold infinity in the palm of your hand,
> And eternity in an hour.

123 *"What Happens When You Really Listen":* This is a tale from South India collected in Hyderabad in the Telugu language in 1988. In *Folktales from India: A Selection of Oral Tales from Twenty-Two Languages,* ed. A. K. Ramanujan (New York: Pantheon Fairy Tale and Folklore Library, 1991), p. 55.

123 *the Ramayana:* is one of the two great Indian epics, the other being the *Mahabharata.* The *Ramayana* (Sanskrit for *Rama's Journey*) tells about life in India around 1000 BCE and offers models in dharma (our universal being which upholds the natural order of things). The hero, Rama, lived his whole life by the rules of dharma. Sita is Rama's wife, who is abducted by Ravana, the ten-headed king of Lanka. Hanuman is the deity-leader of a monkey tribe allied with Rama against Ravana. Hanuman has many magical powers because his father was the god of the wind.

The original *Ramayana* was a 24,000-couplet poem attributed to the Sanskrit poet Valmiki. Oral versions of Rama's story circulated for centuries, and the epic was probably first written down sometime around the start of the Common Era. It has since been told, retold, translated, and trans-created throughout South and Southeast Asia, and the *Ramayana* continues to be performed in dance, drama, puppet shows, songs, and movies all across Asia. (From a very rich reference site *MythHome,* www.mythome.org/RamaSummary.html.)

125 *impeccable mimes:* An earlier account of this encounter appears as the poem "On One Corner," in my book *Surviving Has Made Me Crazy* (Fort Lee, NJ: CavanKerry Press, 2007), p. 54.

Being Articulate

129 *Inhabiting Wonder:* This is the title poem of my book *Inhabiting Wonder* (Bread for the Journey, 2004), p. 60.

The Call of the Soul

136 *"Just because someone has invented":* Russell Means, *Words of Power: Voices from Indian America,* ed. Norbert S. Hill, Jr. (Oneida) (Golden, CO: Fulcrum Publishing, 1994), p. 51.

Seasons of Listening

139 *If your mind isn't clouded:* Wumen, *The Gateless Gate,* in *Zen Flesh, Zen Bones,* comp. and trans. Paul Reps and Nyogen Senzaki (Boston: Shambhala, 1994). Wumen Huikai (1183–1260) was a Song period Zen master renowned for gathering the forty-eight-koan collection *The Gateless Gate.* His commentaries on the koans are legendary. Wumen, also known in Japan as Mumon, was born in Hangzhou, China. He wandered for many years from temple to temple, wore old robes, grew his hair and beard long, and worked in the temple fields. He was nicknamed Huikai (the Lay Monk). At age sixty-four, he founded the Gokoku-ninno temple near West Lake, where he hoped to retire quietly, but word had spread of his wisdom, and seekers constantly came looking for instruction.

140 *In Chinese lore . . . all this knowledge:* This is a prose version of a poem of mine, "The Heavenly Pivot," that is the prologue to a collection of poems in manuscript called *The Fifth Season.*

141 *his first public performance:* On March 26, 1778, at the age of seven, Beethoven gave his first public performance in Cologne, Germany.

142 *his first musical work:* Before the age of twelve, Beethoven published his first musical work: Nine Variations, in C Minor, for Piano, on a March by Ernst Christoph Dressler (WoO 63).

142 *the gifted child left home:* In 1792 in Vienna, the young Beethoven took lessons with Haydn, then with Albrechtsberger and Salieri. He astonished the city with his virtuosity and his improvisations on piano. In 1793 Beethoven composed his Opus 1, Three Trios for Piano. The following year he made his first public performance in Vienna in which each musician was to play his own work. Then followed a tour—Prague, Dresden, Leipzig, and Berlin—before he left for a concert in Budapest.

145 *nearly a hundred unprecedented compositions:* Please see the outstanding biography *Beethoven* by Maynard Solomon (New York: Schirmer Books, 1977). Of the heroic decade following the Heiligenstadt Testament

(1802–1813), Solomon writes: "The end of the crisis in late 1802 ushered in a long period of relative equilibrium and the highest order of creativity. . . . Beethoven attained an awesome level of productivity during these years. His works included an opera, an oratorio, a mass, six symphonies, four concertos, five string quartets, three trios, three string sonatas, and six piano sonatas, plus incidental music for a number of stage works, four sets of piano variations, and several symphonic overtures. Every year saw the completion of a cluster of masterpieces, each of a highly individual character" (p. 126).

146 *listening to it in the middle:* Beethoven's sonata for piano *The Tempest* (Sonata no. 17 in D Minor, op. 31, no. 2), Vladimir Ashkenazy, *Beethoven: The Piano Sonatas* (London: Decca Records, 1995), disc 6. My thanks to Anders for opening me to Beethoven so deeply.

146 *The Ninth Symphony premiered:* I have drawn on the account of the Ninth Symphony premiere found in Wikipedia, http://en.wikipedia.org/wiki/Symphony_No._9_(Beethoven) and details of Beethoven's life from http://www.lvbeethoven.com/Bio/BiographyLudwig.html.

Outwaiting the Clouds

150 *The role of spiritual practice:* "Who Hears This Sound?" an interview with Adyashanti by Luc Saunders and Sy Safransky in *The Sun* (Chapel Hill, NC), no. 384 (December 2007).

Untangling the Net

160 *In his early work in Mexico:* In a conversation with John Paul about concepts that don't quite translate into English, at the Fetzer Institute, March 22, 2006. Please see *The Moral Imagination* and *The Journey Toward Reconciliation,* both by John Paul Lederach.

160 *Enredo, to be all tangled up:* John Paul Lederach, "The Poetic Unfolding of the Human Spirit," in *Exploring the Global Dream Series* (Fetzer Institute, 2010), pp. 14–15.

Playing Hands with God

166 *I can't go on:* Samuel Beckett, *The Traveler's Journal,* ed. Lim and Sam Shapiro (Bali: Half Angel Press, 2007), p. 63.

166 *"How then shall we live":* Please see Wayne Muller, *How Then Shall We Live: Four Simple Questions That Reveal the Beauty and Meaning of Our Lives* (New York: Bantam Books, 1997).

167 *It is the task of the conscious mind:* Carl Jung, *Answer to Job* (Princeton, NJ: Princeton University Press, 2002), pp. 97–98.

Knowing Where We Are

172 *To Live Out the Gift:* This poem originally appeared in my first book of poems, *God, the Maker of the Bed, and the Painter* (1988), p. 17.

THE WORK OF LOVE

179 *The first duty of love:* Paul Tillich, *Dynamics of Faith* (New York: Harper and Brothers, 1957), p. 14.

The Human Garden

184 *I give my heart to this:* Brother David Steindl-Rast, from a dialogue on science and spirituality at the Fetzer Institute, November 22, 2007.

184 *"Is there any one word":* The Analects of Confucius, trans. David Hinton (Washington, DC: Counterpoint, 1998), no. 15, p. 24.

185 *Our love needs to be bigger:* Henk Brandt is a dear friend who is a poet, philosopher, and therapist. Please see his book of poems, *Songs of Sophia.*

187 *two skiers crossing a frozen lake:* Lyn Hartley, from a dialogue at the Fetzer Institute, September 28, 2007.

How We Injure Ourselves

193 *Yes is the only living thing:* e.e. cummings, *100 Selected Poems* (New York: Grove Press, 1959), p. 114.

Finding Birdsong

208 *With each way of listening:* This paragraph appeared in an earlier form as the poem "A Vow Beyond Awareness," in my book *Surviving Has Made Me Crazy* (Fort Lee, NJ: CavanKerry Press, 2007), p. 70.

The Endless Search

211 *the heart is our gill:* An earlier treatment of this analogy is found in "The Necessary Art," in my book of poetry *Inhabiting Wonder* (Bread for the Journey, 2004), p. 8.

212 *three archetypal ways:* Michael Jones developed these notions into the frame of an immersion workshop he and I and Judy Brown guided at the Twelfth Annual International Leadership Association Conference, held in Prague, November 11–14, 2009.

213 *To see more expands:* One of the most gifted teachers about wisdom and compassion at work today is Prasad Kaipa. A physicist by training, a Hindu by birth, Prasad has devoted twenty years to bringing the wisdom traditions to bear on the art of business. He is the executive director of the Center for Leadership, Innovation and Change at the Indian School of Business, Hyderabad, India.

213 *"For the raindrop":* Mirza Ghalib in *Nine Gates: Entering the Mind of Poetry,* Jane Hirshfield (New York: HarperCollins, 1997), p. 5. Ghalib (1797–1869) is the famous Sufi poet who lived in India during British colonial rule. His uplifting poetry is all the more remarkable given his living witness to the brutality of the British in defeating the Indian Revolt of 1857.

214 *ancient Jewish Cemetery:* In Prague, *Starý Zidovský Hbitov* was founded in 1478. It holds over 12,000 gravestones in a courtyard where 100,000 people have been buried.

217 *Indra's Net:* This paragraph is drawn from a larger discussion in my book *Finding Inner Courage* (San Francisco: Conari Press, 2011), originally published as *Facing the Lion, Being the Lion* (San Francisco: Red Wheel/Conari, 2007), p. 81.

Not Getting What We Want

222 *What we want and:* This is from my poem "Chant," in *The Way Under the Way,* a book of my poems in progress.

The Stilling of Our Pain

227 *Stanley Kunitz recalled spending summers:* Stanley Kunitz with Genine Lentine, *The Wild Braid: A Poet Reflects on a Century in the Garden* (New York: Norton, 2005), p. 19.

A Closer Geography

234 *The point in life:* Gensei, "Poem Without a Category," in *Grass Hill: Poems 234 Prose by the Japanese Monk Gensei,* trans. Burton Watson (New York: Columbia University Press, 1983). Gensei (1623–1668) was a Japanese Buddhist monk of the Nichiren sect known for his fondness of animals.

234 *If we had power:* Martin Buber, *I and Thou,* trans. Walter Kaufmann (New York: Touchstone Editions, 1996). Martin Buber (1878–1965) is the preeminent Jewish philosopher of the twentieth century, best known for his philosophy of dialogue, centered on the I-Thou relationship whereby the presence of God and the Divine only appear in the space animated between two living, authentic centers. His classic *I and Thou* was first published in 1923.

To Endure and Endear

244 *"Upekkhā is freedom"*: The American Buddhist monk Bhikkhu Bodhi, in *Toward a Threshold of Understanding,* cited on www.accesstoinsight.org, ©1998–2010.

245 *Hope is definitely not:* Vaclav Havel, *Disturbing the Peace: A Conversation with Karel Huizdala* (1986; New York: Vintage, 1991), ch. 5.

Wandering Authentically

247 *It may be that:* This is Wendell Berry's poem "The Real Work," in *The Collected Poems of Wendell Berry, 1957–1982* (San Francisco: North Point Press, 1987).

249 *As all the Heavens:* Emily Dickinson, "I felt a Funeral in my Brain," in *The Poems of Emily Dickinson: Variorum Edition* (Cambridge, MA: Harvard University Press, 1983).

249 *"I fear I have been reading":* Jorge Luis Borges, "Lecture 1: The Riddle of Poetry," in *This Craft of Verse: The Norton Lectures,* ed. Calin-Andrei Mihailescu (Cambridge, MA: Harvard University Press, 1967), audio CD 1.

250 *Cease and desist: Rational Zen: The Mind of Dogen Zenji,* ed. and trans. Thomas Cleary (Boston: Shambhala, 1993), p. 60. The Zen Buddhist monk Dogen (1200–1253) is the Kyoto-born teacher who founded the Sōtō school of Zen in Japan.

250 *While we can't eliminate hunger:* Please see my poem "Accepting This" in my book of poems *Suite for the Living* (2004), p. 24.

No Strangers in the Heart

255 *I tell you, the more I think:* Vincent van Gogh, in *The Sun* (Chapel Hill, NC), no. 337 (January 2004), p. 48.

PERMISSIONS

ABOUT THE AUTHOR

MARK NEPO is a poet and philosopher who has taught in the fields of poetry and spirituality for over thirty-five years. A *New York Times* #1 bestselling author, he has published thirteen books and recorded eight audio projects. His recent work includes the audio learning courses *Staying Awake* and *Holding Nothing Back* (CD box sets, Sounds True, Spring 2012), a new book of teaching stories, *As Far As the Heart Can See* (HCI Books, audio book by Simon & Schuster, 2011), *Finding Inner Courage* (Conari, 2011, originally published as *Facing the Lion, Being the Lion,* 2007), and audio books of *The Book of Awakening* and *Finding Inner Courage* (CD box sets, Simon & Schuster, 2011). His most recent book of poetry is *Surviving Has Made Me Crazy* (CavanKerry Press, 2007). As a cancer survivor, Mark devotes his writing and teaching to the journey of inner transformation and the life of relationship.

Mark has appeared with Oprah Winfrey on her *Super Soul Sunday* program on OWN TV, and has been interviewed twice by Oprah as part of her SiriusXM Radio show, *Soul Series.* He has also been interviewed by Robin Roberts on *Good Morning America* about his *New York Times* bestseller *The Book of Awakening.* As well, *The Exquisite Risk* (Harmony Books) was cited by *Spirituality & Health* magazine as one of the Best Spiritual Books of 2005, calling it "one of the best books we've ever read on what it takes to live an authentic life." Mark's collected essays appear in *Unlearning Back to God: Essays on Inwardness* (Khaniqahi Nimatullahi Publications, 2006). He is also the editor of *Deepening the American Dream: Reflections on the Inner Life and Spirit of Democracy* (Jossey-Bass, 2005). Other books of poetry include *Suite for the Living* (2004), *Inhabiting Wonder* (2004), *Acre of Light* (1994, also available as an audiotape from Parabola under the title *Inside the Miracle,* 1996), *Fire Without Witness* (1988), and *God, the Maker of the Bed, and the Painter* (1988).

Mark's work has been translated into twenty languages, including French, Portuguese, Japanese, and Danish. In leading spiritual retreats, in working with healing and medical communities, and in his teaching as a poet, Mark's work is widely accessible and used by many. He continues to offer readings, lectures, and retreats. Please visit Mark at www.MarkNepo .com, http://threeintentions.com, and www.simonspeakers.com/MarkNepo.

INTERVIEWS WITH MARK NEPO

T HESE EXCERPTS COME FROM interviews I did in fall 2012. Many thanks to the perceptive interviewers for the deep conversations each opened. The section "How Can We Listen?" is from an interview by Prem Anjali that appeared in *Integral Yoga Magazine*. The section "Staying in Conversation" is from an interview by Mark Matousek that appeared in his *Huffington Post* column. And the third section, "Knowing Our Aliveness," is from an interview by the Simon & Schuster team. I'm always amazed at what is uncovered when we look into what matters together.

—MN

How Can We Listen?

Prem Anjali: Your new book is titled *Seven Thousand Ways to Listen: Staying Close to What Is Sacred*. How can we listen?

Mark: Let me make your question more specific: "How do we develop our practice of listening for what is real? How do we develop a way to listen and follow our aliveness?" I have a chapter on the call of the soul. There's been a lot written about the soul's calling. But we have both capacities: the soul's calling and the call of the soul. The soul's calling is how we become in the world. What is the work we are called to? What is it that we can contribute while we're here? The call of the soul is to stay as close to aliveness as possible. That call doesn't care what we accomplish, achieve, or what it looks like. It wants us to stay in aliveness. Anything can become a prison, if it gets between us and our aliveness.

Even my writing, which is a sacred place, which is my place of practice, can become an obstacle, if I focus only on production. When I was younger, I worried about writer's block, about finishing projects I started. Now, at this point, thankfully, I'm in that space of aliveness and I may write something down or not. The words are really the trail of the aliveness. As a young poet I was devoted and wanted to be the best I could be and thought that, maybe over a lifetime, I could write a few great poems. In my mid-thirties when I went through cancer and almost died, I realized life was demanding I discover true poems that would help me live. Now I'm sixty-two, now I want to be the poem. That changes everything.

Prem Anjali: What are some of the different ways of listening?

Mark: All the different aspects of wakefulness we've been talking about require different kinds of listening that no one can tell anyone else how to do. We each have to discover them and practice them. Practice is a good use of effort but it's practice—it's practice for living, it's not living. There's a great parable about practice and meditation. It's a story of a Master and an apprentice. The Master reflects the teacher that is our very being, and the student represents the problem solver in us. The Master tells the student, "Go and sit by the river until you've learned all river has to teach you." The apprentice is very committed and studious. He spends an hour trying to find the perfect place to sit by the river. First he spreads his blanket close to the river, but soon discovers it's too close and noisy. Next he goes up on the bank and settles there, but realizes that it's too far from the river. So he settles midway, sits on the blanket, and for three days he meditates on the river.

On the third day, in middle of day, all of a sudden a monkey comes along, leaping into the river, splashing, jumping up and down and hooting. This cracks the apprentice. He begins to weep and in his confusion returns to his Master and tells him what happened. The Master replies, "Ah, the monkey listened, you just heard." So, the end of all practice, maps, and plans—valuable as they are—is to get wet, to jump into the river of life. The end of all practice is to live. We forget that.

There's nothing wrong with practice, nothing wrong with wanting things, nothing wrong with movement or stillness, but as human beings, our closeness to aliveness is constantly shifting and we need to stay true to what will bring us alive this moment, without demonizing or falsifying the tool that worked in the last moment. We all do this. It's one of the infections of judgment—that in order to validate whatever appears true now, we feel a need to judge and falsify what happened a minute ago. When a butterfly emerges from a cocoon, the cocoon isn't false; it just served its purpose. Whether it's a former self, a marriage, a friendship that no longer works, or a dream or map that has turned into a cocoon and reached the end of its usefulness, they've served their purpose.

We're called to wander authentically in life. There's a teaching about this from the sea. In large bodies of water, there are microzooplankton. Biologists have discovered that these microscopic organisms migrate daily in order to eat. They move from the bottom to the surface and back to the depths of the water. Biologists call this daily migration "a persistent drift." The metaphor is that this is also part of our journey, part of the practice of wakefulness. We're called every day to migrate from the depth to the surface and back to the depth, in a persistent drift so we can get nourishment. The role microzooplankton play in the ocean and deep lakes is to serve as cleansing agents for the body of water. For us, the inner work we do daily, if honest and authentic, not only moves us along our spiritual path, but the wakefulness we contribute becomes a cleansing agent for the living universe.

Staying in Conversation

Mark Matousek: In *Seven Thousand Ways to Listen*, you write about "staying in conversation with all that is beyond our awareness." How does listening help us stay close to the sacred?

Mark: I think that paradox is a great teacher. But the paradox here is that we have this amazing capacity in our minds and hearts to learn and gain insights and then to build a kind of personal storehouse of knowledge. The underside is that those insights harden and fill the spaces in our hearts and minds. They become assumptions, conclusions, and judgments. When we learn to listen, we can meet life completely anew, every day, but that is hard practice. Let's go back to relationships: My wife and I have been married eighteen years, and I know her well enough that I can finish her sentences—but listening means I don't. Listening means that I say, "Who are you now?"

I know how she thought about this or that, or about me or us, or about life or death. But if I ask, "Who are you now? How do you see this now?" I have to be willing to put all the information in my storehouse away and truly respond from where my heart is this instant. I think this is what meditation practice is all about—trying to put everything down and simply breathe and return to what it means to be alive now—and then move from there. The real challenge is to remember to see clearly when everything's flying around us and we're wrapped up in our wounds and traumas.

Mark Matousek: Intimacy only happens when we learn to listen?

Mark: In the moment. The moment is the doorway—the ever-present threshold to staying in conversation with everything that's larger than us. When I can be fully present and lean into whatever moment is before me, whether it's blissful or difficult, that is a doorway to oneness—it's the sweet ache of being alive. I think happiness is overrated, but joy is the key to the thousands of possible moods we can feel. And when we can rest in that joy, then peace is the moment of openness that holds all feeling. As a kid, I would have this depth of feeling that somebody labeled sadness—and I was told that I should get rid of this sadness, but I've never been able to. Then I realized that it's a much deeper feeling—it's the sweet ache of being here and it's one of my oldest friends. It's how I feel the pull of the universe and where I'm connected. So, how do we listen to where we're connected? . . . because that opens up our compassion for everything.

Mark Matousek: You talk about the "unending pull to center" being our greatest teacher, which I thought was just a beautiful phrase. Could you tell me what you mean by that?

Mark: Sure. In the way that I experience life, the physical world is really just the tip of the iceberg of reality. Whether it's trees or stones or water or animals or stars—everything has an ineffable interior quality. Indigenous Polynesian cultures use the word *mana* to refer to the luminous glow of spirit that's in everything, and Jung appropriated and defined *mana* in a psycho-spiritual way as the unconscious influence of one being on another—like the sun giving off warmth and light where things grow toward it. When we can be fully present, we grow toward each other. I feel that at the center of all life and traditions there is a common well of being that informs all of our lives and how we interact and live out in the world. For example, in the Bodhisattva tradition, being informs everything from the inside out and it helps us be here together in the world.

Knowing Our Aliveness

Simon & Schuster: What inspired you to write this book?

Mark: As nature erodes the earth into magnificent forms, life through endless experience opens us further and further to the essence of what matters. Each time I've been opened further, the way I experience life and receive things has changed. I needed to write this book to understand how we are opened and deepened and widened by life, for this entire process is how we are given the chance to stay close to our aliveness.

Simon & Schuster: What was the experience of losing your hearing and, through this, what did you come to realize about the importance of listening?

Mark: I have significant hearing loss, but I'm not deaf. This happened slowly over many years. I found out only recently that my hearing loss is due to how the chemo I had over twenty years ago damaged the cilia in my ears. This has taught me many things. One thing I learned, paradoxically, is that there is much to be heard in silence. When we are forced to stop the noise around us and in us, we begin to hear everything that is not us, and this is the beginning of humility and the renewal of our soul's energy; as only by listening to all that is larger than us can we discover and feel our place in the Universe.

Simon & Schuster: What steps can we all take to become better listeners?

Mark: In the same way that we have to clean wax from our ears and dirt from our eyes, we're all asked to clean out our conclusions and judgments, which block our heart from meeting the world. This doesn't mean we stop learning but that we stop solidifying our temporary knowledge into walls that separate us. We are also asked to lean into life and not away from experience. When we can help each other do this, we begin to open a conversation with life that keeps awakening our deeper nature.

Simon & Schuster: In what ways has a commitment to listening changed or improved your life?

Mark: I'm more easily touched by everything I meet. In a world where the great technologies enable us to record, replay, cut and paste, zoom in, and delete, listening is the crucial commitment to keep the heart touchable. Staying vulnerable in this way reminds us that life is ultimately unique and unrepeatable, that we are all connected at a deep and vibrant level. Listening reminds me how precious it is to be here at all. And so, listening is the first step to peace, both inner peace and the compassion that connects people. Keeping a commitment to listening has led me to my own growth, beyond any imagined dreams I may have had throughout the years.

Simon & Schuster: Why is it important to meditate, or take a moment to pause and reflect, throughout the day, and how can this teach us to act more mindfully?

Mark: Meditation, in all its forms and traditions, is an invitation to listen, to open, to quietly enlist the courage to be touched and formed by life. Just opening quietly for moments every day can create a path by which life can reach us, the way rain carves a little stream in the earth by which the smallest flowers are watered. We each need avenues by which we can be watered and grow. Whether you find it through mediation or sighing over tea or just turning all your devices off for five minutes, listening is an ancient lifeline by which we are awakened time and again. Once reawakened, we more easily find our way to each other, and so help each other live.

Simon & Schuster: What do you hope readers will take with them from *Seven Thousand Ways to Listen?*

Mark: The practice of listening is one of the most mysterious, luminous, and challenging art forms on Earth. Each of us is by turns a novice and a Master, until the next difficulty or joy undoes us. It is my profound hope that readers will discover their own gifts and wisdom by befriending their own abilities to listen. This is both very personal and Universal. I hope the journey of this book will enable readers to discover and enliven their own personal practice of staying close to the aliveness we are each born with, and so inhabit the durable and precious gift of life.